THE GLOBAL FINANCIAL CRISIS

The Global Financial Crisis
Triggers, Responses and Aftermath

TONY CIRO
Australian Catholic University, Australia

Routledge
Taylor & Francis Group

LONDON AND NEW YORK

First published 2012 by Ashgate Publishing

2 Park Square, Milton Park, Abingdon, Oxon OX14 4RN
711 Third Avenue, New York, NY 10017, USA

Routledge is an imprint of the Taylor & Francis Group, an informa business

First issued in paperback 2016

British Library Cataloguing in Publication Data
Ciro, Tony.
   The global financial crisis : triggers, responses and aftermath.
   1. Global Financial Crisis, 2008-2009. 2. Financial
   crises--Case studies. 3. Bank failures. 4. International
   finance. 5. Economic stabilization. 6. United States--
   Economic policy--2001-2009. 7. United States--Economic
   policy--2009- 8. Structural adjustment (Economic policy)--
   European Union countries. 9. Financial institutions--Law
   and legislation. 10. International economic relations.
   I. Title
   330.9'0511-dc22

Library of Congress Cataloging-in-Publication Data
Ciro, Tony.
   The global financial crisis : triggers, responses and aftermath / by Tony Ciro.
      p. cm.
   Includes bibliographical references and index.
   ISBN 978-1-4094-1139-0 (hbk)
   1. Global Financial Crisis, 2008-2009. 2. Capital market--Law and
   legislation. 3. Financial services industry--Law and legislation.
   I. Title.
   K1114.C57 2012
   330.9'0511--dc23

                                                          2011045192

ISBN 978-1-4094-1139-0 (hbk)
ISBN 978-1-138-26843-2 (pbk)

Contents

Contents

Preface

Writing a book is always challenging, especially when the topic is a constantly moving target such as the global financial crisis. The inspiration for writing the book involved the idea of providing commentary on and analysis of one of the most catastrophic global economic events to confront the international economy in the modern era. Not since the 1930s Great Depression has the world witnessed so much panic, volatility and uncertainty in international financial and currency markets.

In what is now described as the "Great Recession," the millions of workers who lost their jobs as a result of the financial crisis demonstrate the human face of the modern-day tragedy. The demise of Lehman Brothers was the single greatest catalyst for the global crisis that would eventually undermine confidence and trust, even with seasoned and sophisticated investors.

Despite staging a recovery following unprecedented government and central bank intervention, the international economy remains fragile and hostage to a "wall of worry." Headwinds in the form of the European sovereign debt crisis, burgeoning US government debt and global imbalances remain and continue to pose substantial challenges to the international recovery effort.

The Chinese proverb, "may you live in interesting times" is often described as a curse. Whilst intended as a curse, it may well be symptomatic of the current turmoil confronting the world's financial markets. Indeed, global events in the last decade have demonstrated great upheaval, economically, socially and environmentally. The current financial crisis has been no different. Financial markets had become dislocated, dysfunctional and disruptive. The global economy now needs a period of relative calm to prevail and a return to stable economic conditions. Indeed, financial markets all over the world need to experience less interesting times.

Publishing with Ashgate requires the manuscript to be peer-reviewed by experts in the field. I am grateful for the anonymous comments made by the reviewers that have been incorporated in the manuscript. I also want to thank Alison Kirk from Ashgate who was thoroughly professional and provided helpful comments and assistance along the way. I also want to thank my assistant De-anne English-McAdams who provided valuable assistance with the preparation of the Bibliography and Table of Contents. Last but not least, I want to thank my family, who have always provided me with encouragement and support.

Tony Ciro
Melbourne
Australia

List of Acts and Cases

Bank Holding Company Act 1956 (US)
Banking Act 1933 (US)
Banking Act 1935 (US)
Bank Products Legal Certainty Act 2000 (US)

China Currency Manipulation Act 2008 (US)
Commodity and Futures Trading Act 1974 (US)
Commodity Exchange Act 1936 (US)
Commodity Futures Modernization Act 2000 (US)
Corporations Act 2001 (Cth)
Cuomo v Clearing House Association Case No 08-453, 129 S.Ct. 2710 (2009)

Dodd–Frank Wall Street Reform and Consumer Protection Act 2010 (Pub.L. 111–203, H.R. 4173) (US)

Economy Protection Bill 2008
Emergency Economic Stabilization Act 2008 (P.L. 110-343; H.R.1424).

Federal Deposit Insurance Reform Act 2005 (US)
Federal Reserve Act 1913 (12 U.S.C. ch. 3)
Financial Services Act 1986 (UK)
Financial Services Act 2010 (UK)
Financial Services and Markets Act 2000 (UK)
Fraud Enforcement and Recovery Act 2009 (P.L. 111-21) (US)
Futures Trading Act 1921 (US)

Gambling Act 2005 (UK)
Gaming Act 1710 (UK)
Gaming Act 1835 (UK)
Gaming Act 1845 (UK)
Gaming Act 1845 (UK)
Gaming Act 1892 (UK)
Gaming and Betting Act 1912 (NSW)
Grain Futures Act 1922 (US)
Grizewood v Blane 138 ER 578, (UK)

Hill v Wallace 259 US 44 (1922), US Supreme Court, Washington, DC

List of Abbreviations

ABX	Asset-backed Securities Index
AIG	American International Group
AMEX	American Stock Exchange
BIS	Bank for International Settlements
BRIC	Brazil, Russia, India and China
CBO	Congressional Budget Office
CBOE	Chicago Board Options Exchange
CBOT	Chicago Board of Trade
CDO	Collateralized Debt Obligation
CDS	Credit Default Swap
CEA	*Commodity Exchange Act 1936* (US)
CFMA	*Commodity Futures Modernization Act 2000* (US)
CFTA	*Commodity and Futures Trading Act 1974* (US)
CFTC	Commodity Futures Trading Commission
CME	Chicago Mercantile Exchange
CPI	Consumer Price Index
DCOs	Derivatives Clearing Organizations
EC	European Commission
ECB	European Central Bank
ECOFIN	European Competition and Finance Council
EEA	European Economic Area
EU	European Union
FDIC	Federal Deposit Insurance Corporation
FHA	Federal Housing Administration
FOMC	Federal Open Market Committee
FRBNY	Federal Reserve Bank of New York
FSA	Financial Services Authority
FSCS	Financial Services Compensation Scheme
FSF	Financial Stability Forum
FSOC	Financial Stability Oversight Council
G8	Group of 8 Leaders Summit

G20	Group of 20 Finance Ministers
G30	Group of Thirty
GAPP	General Accepted Accounting Principles
GDP	Gross Domestic Product
GFC	Global Financial Crisis
ICFS	International Council for Financial Stability
ILO	International Labour Organization
IMF	International Monetary Fund
IOSCO	International Organisation of Securities Commissions
LTCM	Long-term Capital Management
MOU	Memorandum of Understanding
NASDAQ	NASDAQ Composite Index
NYSE	New York Stock Exchange
OCC	Office of Comptroller of the Currency
OCR	Official Cash RATE
OFHEO	Office of Federal Housing Enterprise Oversight
OFR	Office of Financial Research
OFSO	Office of Financial Stability and Oversight
OPEC	Organization of Petroleum Exporting Countries
OTC	Over-The-Counter
PDCF	Primary Dealer Credit Facility
RBA	Reserve Bank of Australia
RBI	Reserve Bank of India
RBNZ	Reserve Bank of New Zealand
RMBS	Residential Mortgage-Backed Security
SEA	Securities and Exchange Act of 1934 (US)
SEC	Securities and Exchange Commission
SMDI	Standard Maximum Deposit Insurance
S&P	Standard and Poor's
SMDI	Standard Maximum Deposit Insurance
TARP	Troubled Assets Relief Program
US Fed	United States Federal Reserve
VAT	Value Added Tax

About the Author

Professor Tony Ciro is the Deputy Head of School of Business (Melbourne) in the Faculty of Business at Australian Catholic University. He is a current member of the Victorian Bar and a member of CPA Australia. Professor Ciro is a graduate of both Oxford University and Monash University and holds a PhD from Monash University, a BCL from Oxford University, a Bachelor of Laws (Honours) from Monash University and a Bachelor of Economics (Accounting & Finance) (Honours) from Monash University. His research has been published widely in leading Australian and international refereed journals, and has extensive research expertise in taxation law, the global economy, financial derivatives markets, business law, corporation law and general commercial law.

Introduction
Timeline of the Crisis

Commentators have described the Global Financial Crisis (GFC) of the early 21st century as the greatest financial and economic crisis the world has seen since the Great Depression of the 1930s. Certainly, the GFC took many by surprise as governments, investors and experienced and sophisticated market participants were largely caught unawares by the speed and ferocity of the economic decline. Equally disturbing were the significant consequences that the GFC unleashed on the world's most developed economies.

The timeline for the GFC covered by this book stretches over the years from 2007 to early/mid-2011. This book deals with the events that led to the bursting of the US housing bubble and the associated demise of Lehman Brothers. The book also examines the disruption and dislocation in international credit and financial markets during 2008 and 2009, and goes on to examine the fallout and policy responses relating to the financial crisis from 2009 and to late 2011.

The GFC timeline is complicated, however, by the emergence in 2011 of a "new" financial crisis – the so-called "sovereign debt," or "euro debt" crisis. As this book goes to press, the debt crisis has not yet become a fully fledged global financial crisis; and although the book makes reference in several places to the "ongoing' nature of the debt crisis – particularly in relation to Greece, Ireland, Spain, Portugal and Italy – that is associated with the GFC, it is too soon to judge how it will unfold and whether in fact it will develop into a new global financial crisis.

At the height of the crisis, in 2008–2009, industrial production fell rapidly and unemployment rose dramatically. Banks led the assault on foreclosures in many towns and cities, especially in the United States. Businesses closed their doors and banks stopped lending. The GFC did not discriminate in its destructive nature, shattering consumer and investor confidence, undermining market sentiment and unnerving the very fabric of economic security.[1] The GFC led to significant and protracted decline in industrial production in both developed and emerging economies.

However, in the period immediately preceding the GFC, world economic growth was expanding at a brisk rate of over 4% p.a. The fast-developing nations, which included the BRIC nations (Brazil, Russia, India and China) had been growing at a much faster rate of between 8% and –12% p.a.

---

1 Nouriel Roubini and Stephen Mihm described the current financial crisis as a "hurricane" and a global pandemic because of its destructive and volatile nature. See Roubini, N. and Mihm, S. *Crisis Economics: A Crash Course in the Future of Finance* (New York: The Penguin Press, 2010), pp. 100–103, 115–34.

The fast pace of growth during 2005–2007 led to record commodity prices as global demand outstripped supply. By early 2008 crude oil prices had exceeded $US150 a barrel and there were some who forecast that oil would soon reach and rise beyond $US200 a barrel. Similarly, benchmark and spot prices for other commodities, including gold, silver, iron ore, alumina, zinc, platinum and nickel, were all pushing higher with no end in sight for bullish investors and speculators.[2]

The story was the same with soft commodities in the form of wheat, cotton, orange juice, coffee and cocoa beans, sugar and pork bellies. Even canola oil was on an aggressive uptrend as more growers were giving up their land for food production and replacing it with the more lucrative production of crude oil substitutes. All of this occurred within a time frame and against a backdrop of booming global economic conditions. For many, the global boom seemed to be a permanent feature of a new golden age with technological advances driving economic growth and replacing the previous boom–bust cycles with a new dynamic economic nirvana.

The economic prosperity was heralded by governments the world over as a new global order delivering unimaginable wealth to the industrialized nations of the First World. The poor in emerging economies, particularly in the BRIC nations, would also share the economic benefits of the global boom. Supporters of the new golden age claimed the economic prosperity would be sustainable and long-lasting. The powerful and dynamic phenomenon that is globalization would transform the lives of millions, delivering economic dividends in the form of full employment, rises in income and improved living standards for all.

Some were also suggesting that there would be a permanent realignment of a new world order. With previous economic booms, the developed nations of the world took centre stage and were the main beneficiaries of economic prosperity. However, this time it was claimed that the global boom cycle would be different.[3] Through the process of globalization the benefits of the new golden era of prosperity would be shared with the less fortunate. Millions of workers in China, India, Eastern Europe, South East Asia and South America would be transformed from poverty to become the new middle class consumers of finished goods.

With industrialization and urbanization of the world's most populist nations, China and India, there would be a rebalancing of economic power and leadership. China would be decoupled from the United States but also interlinked with it in the complex and dynamic process which is globalization. China would also be the new engine of global industrial production that would stimulate global growth and

---

2 The explosion of debt and speculation in the United States over the past 30 years had been described as a major catalyst for the crisis. See Foster, J.B. and Magdoff, F. The Great Financial Crisis: Causes and Consequences, *Monthly Review Press*, 2009, pp. 39–62.

3 In the lead-up to the Global Financial Crisis, the economic prosperity and global boom was described in the catchcry "stronger for longer." This was often used to justify the realization that the current consumer and investment boom would be somewhat different to the previous economic booms.

deliver economic dividends to its people in the form of higher living standards, lower unemployment and higher levels of income. In turn, the Western economies would also benefit by importing cheap manufactured goods that would help keep inflation down in otherwise high-cost Western nations.

As China developed and Westernized, growing and urbanizing its economy, it also exported deflation to Western economies. This, in turn, masked serious risks and asset bubbles that were emerging in developed nations. With export-led deflation, interest rates in the United States, the United Kingdom, Ireland, Australia, Spain and Portugal were kept artificially low for a considerable period of time.

For a while, all of this seemed to be working as planned. Sure there were challenges ahead, including environmental concerns, diminishing spare capacity and high commodity prices, to name a few, but on balance everything appeared to be manageable. World economic growth was steaming ahead, inflation had been kept in check, stock markets the world over were booming, investor and consumer confidence was at an all-time high and geopolitical tensions had eased somewhat.

Just as the world appeared to be moving along nicely, sub-prime mortgage woes began to emerge from a number of towns and cities in the United States. Not many fully appreciated the buildup in speculative risk that had been occurring in the United States. Nor was it clear what would soon emerge, after all there had been mortgage defaults and foreclosures before without serious or systemic ramifications. The US economy was also considered to be strong, robust and sufficiently advanced to be able to absorb any of the likely defaults. What began in 2007 as some sort of isolated and containable event would soon come to trigger the biggest economic and financial catastrophe the world has seen since the 1930s Great Depression.[4]

The crisis sparked debate and controversy and raised a number of important questions: What caused the crisis? Was there more than one underlying cause? Why did the crisis occur in the first place? Could the crisis have been averted? How has the crisis differed from other economic crises? Why was the crisis not readily foreseeable? What have been the main consequences flowing from the crisis? These questions, along with others, will be the topics for discussion in the following chapters of the book.

How sub-prime mortgage defaults could trigger the global downfall was surprising to say the least. More disturbing was the speed and scale of the decline. The initial response from governments appeared to be ineffective in dealing with the fallout from the crisis. World governments, central banks and regulators were simply caught unawares, asleep at the wheel. Panic would soon replace the inept actions of governments and central banks as the crisis deepened.[5] At its height,

---

4   The book by the Nobel Laureate in Economics, Paul Krugman, *The Return of Depression Economics and the Crisis of 2008* (New York: W.W. Norton, 2009), provides similar points of comparison between the 1930s Great Depression and the current crisis.

5   According to Krugman, the wrong lessons had been learnt from previous crises affecting Latin America. Ibid., pp. 52–5.

the economic and financial foundations of the world's largest economies were teetering on the abyss. Market regulators, central bankers and Treasury officials were overwhelmed with the staggering tsunami that was to engulf the entire global economy.[6]

At the time Lehman Brothers went into bankruptcy, in September 2008, the world was staring over a precipice, at a point of no return. Indeed, the Chairman of the US Federal Reserve, Ben Bernanke, was quoted as saying "by Monday we will have no economy." The previous US Federal Reserve Chairman, Alan Greenspan, was quoted as saying in late 2008 that in his opinion the US economy was the worst he had seen.[7]

The collapse of Lehman Brothers created a catastrophic series of events, which gained a momentum all of its own.[8] Prior to the Lehman catastrophe considerable debate raged as to the merits of bailing out large financial institutions with taxpayer money. At stake was the potential for systemic, unforeseen and unknown interlinkages between a Lehman collapse and other parts of the financial and real economy, both in the United States and internationally. There was also the inherent problem of moral hazard with the very real prospect of rewarding, instead of sanctioning, market failure.

Moral hazard and "too big to fail" concerns came to dominate the intellectual discourse among policymakers and regulators, including the US Federal Reserve and the US government.[9] The arguments in favour of a Lehman bailout were

6   In testimony provided before the Senate Committee of Government Oversight and Reform, the former US Federal Reserve Chairman described the global financial crisis as a "once-in-a-century credit tsunami." Greenspan went on to say "this crisis has turned out to be much broader than anything I could have imagined." Greenspan 2008 (Testimony of Dr Alan Greenspan to the Senate Committee of Government Oversight and Reform, 23 October 2008. Washington, DC: US House of Representatives), p.1.

7   "Oh, by far," Greenspan said, when asked if the situation was the worst he had seen in his career. "There's no question that this is in the process of outstripping anything I've seen and it still is not resolved and still has a way to go and, indeed, it will continue to be a corrosive force until the price of homes in the United States stabilizes. That will induce a series of events around the globe which will stabilize the system." See Stein, S. 2008 (Alan Greenspan: This is the worst economy I've ever seen. Huffpost Politics. Available at: <http://www.huffingtonpost.com/2008/09/14/greenspan-this-is-the-wor_n_126274.html>).

8   US Treasury Secretary Henry Paulson later wrote a book about his experiences in the days, weeks and months in the lead-up to Lehman's collapse. According to Paulson, the reaction of the market to the collapse of Bear Stearns, AIG and Lehman was nothing short of panic, chaos and in locked down mode. See Paulson 2010a (Paulson, H.M. 2010a. *On the Brink: Inside the Race to Stop the Collapse of the Global Financial System*. New York: Business Plus, Hachette Book Group), pp. 246–8.

9   See A.R. Sorkin's account of the raging debate and the tug of war between US federal regulators, including the US Federal Reserve, the US Treasury Secretary, the Securities and Exchange Commission, and representatives from Lehman Brothers and AIG: Sorkin, A.R. *Too Big To Fail* (London: Viking Penguin, 2009), pp. 216–21.

persuasive. Equally compelling was the notion of moral hazard and letting losses lie where they fall. Ultimately, history will show that Lehman Brothers did in fact go into bankruptcy with no bailout protection provided to its stakeholders. There is continuing controversy regarding the fate of Lehman Brothers. Senior management figures remain convinced that Lehman was salvageable and was a victim of the prevailing market sentiment at the time of its demise. Senior policymakers and regulators in the United States have been less sympathetic to this contention and have laid blame directly at the inherent riskiness of Lehman's business model.

Whatever the true nature of the allegations surrounding Lehman's financial health and wellbeing, the demise of the company wrought havoc in financial markets all over the world. The collapse of Lehman Brothers in late 2008 could not have come at a worse time for investor and market confidence.

As financial markets seized up, stock markets collapsed and credit markets froze, concerns were mounting that the world was in the midst of another Great Depression.[10] At the beginning of 2009, the crisis that began in financial markets soon swamped the real economy. Industrial production in most countries fell, with developed nations leading the dramatic declines. Even the formerly dominant BRIC economies could not withstand the economic tsunami that was engulfing the world. Investors and markets soon came to the realization that there was no safe harbour. The so-called "decoupled" economies of China, India, Russia, Canada, Brazil and Australia were all adversely affected.

The crisis which had its genesis in the US sub-prime mortgage market spilled over to wreak havoc in the real economy. Industrial production declined substantially as banks withdrew their lending and credit markets froze. GDP in almost all developed countries also began to decline which, in turn, led to a rapid acceleration in the level of unemployment. Workers were laid off at an alarming rate and the "bubble" economies – the United States, Ireland, Spain, the United Kingdom and Portugal – suffered the most, since they were the main beneficiaries of escalating house prices in the boom period.

Structure of the Book

There has been conjecture as to whether asset bubbles caused, or at the very least triggered, the current crisis.[11] The residential housing bubble in the United States was at the centre of the sub-prime mortgage crisis that later spread to the

---

10   According to Paulson, President George Bush asked whether the current crisis was the worst since the Great Depression, to which the US Federal Reserve Chairman, Ben S. Bernanke, replied in the affirmative and added that the current crisis could even become much worse. Ibid. (n. 8), pp. 255–6.

11   The prominent economist and Nobel Laureate for Economics, Joseph Stiglitz, draws an analogy of the causes of the current crisis with the crime of murder, and posits the question: The anatomy of a murder: Who killed America's economy? See Friedman, J.

mainstream housing market, which, in turn, later spread to financial markets. As Chapter 1 explains, bubbles have been around for centuries. An asset bubble, whether it is an overvalued stock market, an overheated housing market, or unsustainable commodity prices, will eventually be deflated. However, the crucial issue with a deflating bubble is whether the economy will be exposed to a soft or a hard landing.

History has demonstrated that with the demise of an asset bubble an economic recession is not always inevitable. There have been asset bubbles in the past which have been allowed to deflate and have not led to an economic recession. Some bubbles can be isolated, one-off events which have little or no systemic consequences. However, history has also demonstrated that some bubbles that do deflate can lead to significant economic contractions. Whether a soft or a hard landing will occur is often difficult to predict. The recent crisis proves that even when economic conditions appear to be favourable, events can occur which lead to rapid and unpredictable changes in fortune.

As Chapter 2 demonstrates, the precise causes of the recent crisis are still subject to debate. The causes may be described less as causes and more appropriately as triggers. It is often difficult to determine whether there are direct and clear causal factors in an economic crisis. Sometimes, prevailing economic conditions can exacerbate an already weak or slowing economy. Hence, deterioration in the overall economic climate can heighten existing problems or alternatively, make of something a problem where one did not originally exist.

The analogy here is the famed evolutionary conundrum – the chicken and egg analogy and the origins of life. Scientists have mulled over this issue for years. Why would it be any different for economists? What caused the recent crisis may well be less of an issue, however important the question may be. This is because one singular event viewed in isolation may not lead to any noticeable adverse change. However, when taken in its totality, along with the prevailing economic environment, the cause or causes can develop a life of their own. A cause or a trigger can at times be problematic but not necessarily lead to major economic damage. This is because certain triggers can be fairly isolated non-events and not capable of producing long-term systemic consequences.

The focus of much of the current debate has been on asset bubbles and the dangers that they pose to the real economy. The housing bubble in recent times has been the source of much of the current analysis. This is especially the case in the United States, the United Kingdom, Ireland, Spain and Portugal, where house prices rose quite dramatically in the lead-up to the global crisis. As the crisis took hold, these countries, which enjoyed the stimulus provided by the housing and construction boom, witnessed severe economic contractions when houses prices began to decline.

What Caused the Financial Crisis? (Philadelphia: University of Pennsylvania Press, 2011), pp. 139–49.

However, in other countries house prices have not declined but, rather, have remained relatively robust. An example of this phenomenon is Australia, where not only have house prices not declined but instead reportedly rose a hefty 20% or more in capital cities across Australia in 2009–2010.[12] One major explanation for Australian house prices bucking the world trend was the fact that Australia avoided a recession in 2009, whilst much of the Western world recorded substantial declines in industrial production and GDP. With a relatively robust economy, house prices in Australia did not suffer the same fate as the rest of the world. Despite this, a number of commentators have argued that a housing bubble has formed in Australia and house prices will decline over time.[13]

Whatever may be the case for asset price bubbles, regulators have become increasingly uneasy and are now more likely to aggressively target speculative and excessively risky activity. The problem for regulators is: how do they go about deflating asset bubbles that have already formed without engineering a slowdown in the wider economy? The weapon of choice for central bankers is monetary policy. Through the use of restrictive monetary policy, monetary regulators can try to deflate asset bubbles before they lead to unforeseen consequences for the real economy. As is discussed in Chapter 5, the main problem with using interest rates to control asset prices lies with the very fact that monetary policy is a blunt instrument, which can have adverse ramifications for other parts of the economy.[14]

Other commentators have suggested that alternative and less draconian policy measures should be used to control asset prices. Instead of using restrictive monetary policy, which has as its central control of consumer prices, asset prices and speculation could be controlled through prudential regulation. The use of supervisory oversight by monetary regulators as well as other financial market regulators could provide effective management and containment of speculators

---

12   The Real Estate Institute of Victoria (REIV) reported a 26.8% rise in Melbourne house prices between 2009 and 2010. See <http://www.reiv.com.au/home/inside.asp?ID =1048&nav1=652&nav2=165>.

13   One of the most avid critics of the Australian property market is Professor Steve Keen, who has argued that a debt bubble has emerged in the Australian residential property market and hence, over time, house prices in Australia will need to fall to restore equilibrium. See <http://www.debtdeflation.com/blogs/>.

14   According to Ben Bernanke in a speech delivered in January 2010, "Economists have pointed out the practical problems with using monetary policy to pop asset price bubbles, and many of these were illustrated by the recent episode. Although the house price bubble appears obvious in retrospect – all bubbles appear obvious in retrospect – in its earlier stages, economists differed considerably about whether the increase in house prices was sustainable; or, if it was a bubble, whether the bubble was national or confined to a few local markets. Monetary policy is also a blunt tool, and interest rate increases in 2003 or 2004 sufficient to constrain the bubble could have seriously weakened the economy at just the time when the recovery from the previous recession was becoming established." See Bernanke 2010b (Monetary policy and the housing bubble. Speech at the Annual Meeting of the American Economic Association, Atlanta, Georgia, 3 January 2010).

without subjecting the broader economy to the ill effects of restrictive monetary policy. The current Chairman of the US Federal Reserve, Ben Bernanke, favours robust prudential or supervisory regulation to deal with asset bubbles rather than restrictive monetary policy.[15] However, Bernanke did keep open the option of using monetary policy to deflate asset bubbles if prudential regulation proved to be ineffective.[16]

As Chapter 3 illustrates, the recent crisis has been a truly global phenomenon. The speed, ferocity and systemic nature of the crisis proved that the world had become even more interlinked than was previously thought. Globalized financial markets created the almost perfect transformation of a largely US domestic crisis into a full-blown international tsunami of biblical proportions. The transmission of a domestic problem to the international stage has occurred in the past.

Economic history tells us that adverse events that plague small nations can undermine confidence and security in much larger economies. This has been illustrated in recent times with the sovereign debt crisis involving Greece, which has led to a run on the euro and has spread risk to other countries. Does this mean that investors are irrational? Or does it mean that investors have become extremely risk-averse in times of heightened uncertainty? These issues are explored in detail in Chapter 4. Investor behaviour and the markets' response to the crisis provide important clues as to why the crisis became so pervasive and destructive to the global economy. Almost overnight financial markets ceased to function in a rational and orderly manner. To borrow a phrase from the former US Federal Reserve Chairman, the demise of Lehman Brothers contributed greatly to the "irrational exuberance" of financial markets.

There remains considerable conjecture as to the appropriate role of regulators in a market-driven economy. This debate continues to rage and is the focus for discussion in Chapter 5. There is widespread belief that enhanced regulation would be of significant benefit to financial market participants as well as to the broader community. Prior to the European debt crisis, attention was focused on the relatively weakened state of financial and banking regulation that existed in the United States. The collapse and subsequent bailouts of mortgage originators

---

15 Bernanke stated: "That conclusion suggests that the best response to the housing bubble would have been regulatory, not monetary. Stronger regulation and supervision aimed at problems with underwriting practices and lenders' risk management would have been a more effective and surgical approach to constraining the housing bubble than a general increase in interest rates. Moreover, regulators, supervisors, and the private sector could have more effectively addressed building risk concentrations and inadequate risk-management practices without necessarily having had to make a judgment about the sustainability of house price increases." Ibid.

16 Bernanke stated: "However, if adequate reforms are not made, or if they are made but prove insufficient to prevent dangerous buildups of financial risks, we must remain open to using monetary policy as a supplementary tool for addressing those risks – proceeding cautiously and always keeping in mind the inherent difficulties of that approach." Ibid.

Freddie Mac and Fannie Mae, investment bank Bear Stearns, and AIG, all pointed to market failure and ineffective regulation.[17]

Not since the Great Depression had there been a colossal failure of confidence and trust by investors, financial market participants, banks, credit providers and equity and credit markets. For the first time since the 1930s the collapse in confidence represented a synchronized and systemic failure in all things financial and economic. Why did financial markets fail so spectacularly? Why did credit markets seize up in 2008? What were the causes of the unprecedented market volatility? Why had fear gripped equity markets the world over? What could regulators have done to prevent, or at least, minimize the downside risks? Could enhanced regulation and supervisory oversight over banks and financial markets have prevented much of the crisis? These questions along with others will be explored in Chapter 5.

In Chapter 6 rescue packages, including taxpayer-sponsored bailout measures, which were deployed by various governments, central banks and other regulatory authorities, will be examined. The bailouts have been costly and were not without controversy. At the height of the crisis, it was estimated that the financial damage to the US economy would run into the hundreds of billions of dollars. The overall world economy would be $US3 trillion worse off. In 2008 the US government announced a $US700 billion bailout package designed to prevent any further bank failures. George W. Bush, in one of his last acts as President of the United States, signed the *Emergency Economic Stabilization Act* of 2008, commonly called the Troubled Assets Relief Program (TARP), into law.[18]

In addition to the TARP program in the United States, the European Union in 2010 enacted a similar program to help stabilize the Greek economy and provide support to the plunging euro. After initially resisting moves to support the Greek economy, European finance ministers were forced to act when international currency markets began to react adversely and devalue the euro. Sensing that a run on the euro could unnerve already volatile equity and currency markets, and put at risk a fragile recovery, the Council of the European Union Member States and the International Monetary Fund agreed to a €750 billion financial stability package.

In a press release issued by the Council of the European Union, the EU concluded that "The Council and the Member States have decided today on a

---

17 Kroszner and Shiller argue, as a major lesson to be learnt from the current crisis, for reforms to be made to United States financial markets which should be designed to make the markets more robust. See Kroszner, R.S. and Shiller, R.J. *Reforming US Financial Markets: Reflections Before and Beyond Dodd-Frank* (Cambridge, MA: The MIT Press, 2009), pp. 51–81.

18 Although there had been considerable disagreement concerning the merits of taxpayer-funded bailouts, the Bill was passed by the US Senate on 1 October 2008 and the House of Representatives passed the final version of the Bill on 3 October 2008. See the *Emergency Economic Stabilization Act 2008* (Pub.L. 110–343); H.R.1424.

comprehensive package of measures to preserve financial stability in Europe, including the European Financial Stability mechanism…."[19]

The ambitious financial stability package was justified on the basis of investors' perceptions that underlying structural weaknesses existed in some key member states, including Portugal, Italy, Ireland, Spain and Greece. The Council of the European Union was of the view that continued uncertainty and volatility in financial and currency markets would undermining confidence in the euro, which in turn could lead to systemic risk in the European Union: "In the wake of the crisis in Greece, the situation in financial markets is fragile and there was a risk of contagion, which we needed to address. We have therefore taken the final steps of the support package for Greece, the establishment of a European stabilization mechanism and a strong commitment to accelerated fiscal consolidation, where warranted."[20]

As is discussed in Chapter 7, the controversy stirred by the bailout packages was fuelled in part by the public's negative perception of Wall Street executives. There was little sympathy on Main Street with taxpayer funds being used to bail out banks, mortgage originators and investment firms. This was especially the case when a number of small- to medium-sized enterprises were experiencing extreme difficulties in accessing lines of credit which were crucial in day-to-day operations. The banks, in turn, had their own difficulties in funding their retail lending books because following the collapse of Lehman Brothers, bank access to international wholesale debt and credit markets had been restricted.

The financial crisis later caused damage to the real economy when much of the international economy was forced into recession. This was made evident by significant declines in industrial production and GDP, along with the simultaneous dramatic increase in unemployment all over the world. Fearing another Great Depression, governments responded with aggressive stimulus packages, which were designed to overcome the gap in private sector expenditures.

However, the large increases in stimulus brought forward a new crisis, namely one involving fiscal deficits and sovereign risk. As is discussed in Chapter 7, the recent sovereign risk debt crisis was most acute in Europe, particularly for Greece, Portugal and Ireland. Other European countries, including Italy and Spain, continue to cause consternation amongst investors and bondholders.

As the mood shifted away from the ill effects of private household debt and commercial borrowings, sovereign debt became the new issue for investors to focus upon. And focus they did. Financial markets and currency speculators had become obsessed with the overall stability of the euro. All of a sudden the euro, which had earlier become the beacon of stability and a possible candidate for the world's reserve currency, was placed under the proverbial spotlight. It was argued

---

19 European Union Council. 2010. (Extraordinary Council Meeting on Economic and Financial Affairs. Press release 108 (9596/10), 9/10 May 2010. Brussels: Council of the European Union), p. 6.

20 Ibid.

that the euro had structural weaknesses, since whilst the European Central Bank had control of monetary policy, the European Parliament did not have centralized fiscal powers or fiscal responsibilities. Instead, fiscal policy was the responsibility of the individual member states of the European Union (EU).

Now a new and related crisis, namely sovereign debt risk, had threatened to derail the fragile global recovery. As the EU rolled out its own bailout package for struggling European member states, the Bank for International Settlements (BIS) proposed new capital and liquidity requirements for banks. The Basel III capital liquidity ratios will require banks to keep more of their assets "liquid." One of the effects of the enhanced liquidity requirements is to effectively recapitalize weak banks so that they either raise capital from their investors, or through taxpayers, or are forced to close.

Chapter 8 evaluates the various policy options that have been developed to overcome the adverse effects of the global financial crisis. Some have argued that the crisis has revealed structural weaknesses in regulatory and supervisory frameworks which are outdated and lack the ability to properly regulate modern financial and banking systems. The global regulatory architecture may need to be overhauled, some institutions having become out of date or ineffective. There may be some truth in this assertion, given that some of the key regulatory agencies that are currently in place have been there since the 1930s.

A point worth exploring is whether institutional structures that have largely been in place since the Great Depression are still the most appropriate to regulate modern, interlinked and globalized financial markets. Indeed, there has been debate as to whether a future financial crisis can be averted through the creation of new, global, "super-regulators," which would be responsible for overseeing regulation and bank lending. On the other hand, some have argued that the current crisis proves that financial markets, left to their own devices, are prone to failure and hence require more enhanced regulation and supervisory oversight.

Whether the way forward as articulated in Chapter 8 will be the most appropriate strategy remains to be seen. Ultimately, any strategic or structural improvement will be dependent upon the objectives of the regulatory reform process. If the objective is to avoid any future financial crisis, expectations may be set too high and may be ultimately unachievable. Crises, whether caused by financial meltdowns or triggered by other factors, have been around for a considerable period of time and have become a consistent part of the world's economic history.

Chapter 1
Previous Crises

Introduction

The global financial crisis that struck during the first decade of the 21st century was not the first economic crisis that the world has ever encountered, nor will it be the last. For whatever reason economic crises continue to occur and have often been mistaken for the boom–bust economic cycle. The current crisis has been described as the worst financial and economic crisis the world has encountered since the Great Depression of the 1930s. The GFC has, like other economic and financial crises, caused real economic damage.

The aftermath of the GFC has been substantial by any measure. World GDP and industrial production for both developed and developing countries have fallen considerably. It was not uncommon for industrial production figures to record falls of over 20% on an annualized basis.[1] Similar declines were recorded in the United States, the epicentre of the crisis. Global GDP growth rates were also adversely impacted. While much of the world recorded positive growth rates in the lead-up to the crisis, negative GDP recorded at the end of 2008 and during 2009 easily eclipsed positive growth rates recorded in the previous quarters. The crisis led to a significant and prolonged decline in industrial production and GDP output, which was described by the International Monetary Fund as the "Great Recession."

The world had suffered considerably through the Great Depression of the 1930s, as well as during and after World War II. The recession that took hold after the war affected many nations and resulted in a significant and widespread downturn. However, during the 1950s and 1960s most countries, particularly developed economies, enjoyed a global economic boom. It was not until the 1970s OPEC oil crisis that the world entered into a period of economic downturn with rising inflation. The OPEC oil crisis preceded the Vietnam War and the two combined to produce a significant malaise for the world's largest economy, the United States.

The malaise continued for much of the 1970s and early 1980s, until a new economic boom took hold, only to falter with the equity market crash of 1987. This stock market collapse was the most severe and pronounced equity market decline since the great crash of 1929. In a single day equity indices fell over 50%, with some individual companies almost having their entire market value wiped

---

1 See European Union Commission 2010c. Europe in Figures – Eurostat Yearbook 2010. Available at: <http://epp.eurostat.ec.europa.eu/portal/page/portal/product_details/publication?p_product_code=KS-CD-10-220>.

out. The 1987 crash, commonly called "Black Monday," sparked fears that the world would be heading into another depression. Policymakers were acutely aware of the potential for the stock market crash to develop into a much larger contagion. However their ability to respond quickly was hampered by persistent high inflation.

The dot-com bubble of the late 1990s burst in 2000. In the lead-up to the new millennium, speculators, investment banks and pension funds had poured billions of dollars into new technological ventures. The NASDAQ Composite Index was viewed as the new engine and driver for US dominance and superiority in technology and wealth creation. Technological startups were no longer valued on fundamental terms. It was argued that with the creation of a new economy, all of the old rules relating to fundamental or inherent value were no longer relevant. Hence, conventional wisdom and valuation methods based upon profitability or discounted cash flows were not applied and instead, non-conventional valuations premised upon turnover or revenue were used. All of this proved to be illusory when the dot-com bubble burst in 2000.

The terrorist attacks on 11 September 2001 also sparked widespread fear in financial markets. Following steep declines in equity markets on Wall Street and other international indices, and fearing a significant downturn in the real economy, the US Federal Reserve aggressively cut interest rates. The move to increase private sector liquidity was designed to stave off any economic downturn and restore confidence to a now insecure US consumer. The US Federal Reserve also adopted a range of measures designed to increase liquidity in the US economy.

Some commentators have argued that the US Federal Reserve's action to help restore confidence in the US economy following the terrorist strikes contributed to the great crash of 2008–2009.[2] It has been suggested that a prolonged period of low interest rates led to the creation of a dangerous and unsustainable housing bubble in the United States. We know now that the spectacular unravelling of the housing bubble during 2007–2008, which had its genesis in sub-prime mortgage lending, had devastating consequences for the entire global economy.

The 1930s Great Depression

The Great Depression was appropriately named. The significant repercussions from the economic decline which followed were felt all over the world. Industrial production and GDP fell dramatically as factories, shipyards, retail stores, mining, construction and manufacturing all effectively collapsed. Recorded unemployment

---

2   See, for example, Paul Krugman's comments on Alan Greenspan's Chairmanship of the Federal Reserve, where he states that Greenspan had the unique record of having presided over two asset price bubbles during his tenure at the US Federal Reserve. P. Krugman. *The Future of Depression Economics and the Crisis of 2008* (New York: W.W. Norton, 2009), pp. 144–8.

rose mercilessly to over 30% in key economies. The US and Europe, the great engines of economic growth, stopped growing and went into reverse at an alarming rate. The high levels of unemployment, the slump in industrial and factory output, the loss of income and wealth, the bankruptcies and foreclosures and widespread economic despair were evident everywhere. The catchcry now was that capitalism was dead and could not recover from the prolonged crisis. Social despair and crisis followed and alternatives to capitalism were born and embraced.

Popular belief laid the blame for the Great Depression with the Great Crash of Wall Street in 1929. It has been suggested that the collapse on Wall Street on Black Tuesday "caused" the Great Depression because the stock market crash led to significant investor losses and large financial collapses. The Great Crash of 1929 no doubt had a considerable negative impact on the US financial system and overall economy. And, yes, the Crash on Wall Street led to an almost complete, simultaneous panic on other international bourses and exchanges. What was not entirely clear, and was the subject of much ideological debate, was whether the Great Depression had other causes or triggers as well.

Two central theories emerged which attempted to explain the causes of the Great Depression. One explanation that was put forward was the demand-driven thesis, largely attributed to the prominent economist John Maynard Keynes.[3] The demand-driven hypothesis suggested that declining consumer and investment demand were key triggers, which led to significant decline in industrial output and economic growth. Since the US economy during the 1920s was largely driven by manufacturing and construction, declining consumer demand would have a substantial adverse effect on industrial output. Consumer and investment demand had fallen because of rising unemployment. Hence, as consumer and investment demand fell, so did industrial output. As output and economic growth slowed, unemployment rose and a feedback loop was created. Unaddressed and left to market forces, the feedback loop would be self-perpetuating, causing further declines in consumer demand, production, employment and wealth.

The Keynesian supporters further argued that the key to addressing the Great Depression crisis was to stimulate consumer demand. By increasing consumer expenditure and creating the conditions for consumers to spend their income on output, economic growth would improve. As economic growth and industrial production increased, so too would employment. In the demand-driven world, the economic boom–bust cycle would require governments to intervene to smooth out the highs and lows to ensure economic stability.

The Keynesian theorists placed great emphasis on the Wall Street crash for generating the initial decline in US economic output. Black Tuesday, as it had been described, caused much panic and contributed to heavy financial losses for investors. The panic that began on Wall Street soon spread quickly through

---

3   See J.M. Keynes. *The General Theory of Employment, Interest and Money* (Cambridge, UK: Palgrave Macmillan, 1936).

financial, credit, and commodity markets. The US government did not react
initially to the Crash on Wall Street. Nor did policymakers attempt to address the
uncertainty and market volatility on the New York Stock Exchange.

The delay from government and policymakers was later compounded by
anti-speculation measures that were adopted by the US Federal Reserve. The
famous monetarist and supply-side economist Milton Friedman stressed the
importance of the policy failure and restrictive monetary policy stance of the US
Federal Reserve during the Great Depression.[4] The current Chairman of the US
Federal Reserve, Ben Bernanke, writing in 1983, also commented on the apparent
failures of governments to deal adequately with the Great Depression between
1930 and 1933.[5] According to Bernanke, the Wall Street Crash in 1929 was
simultaneously associated with large bank failures in the US financial sector.[6] The
simultaneous occurrence of these events led to another adverse condition, namely
the deterioration in the macroeconomic environment in the US economy.

All of these compounding developments led to an alternative theory that was
put forward to explain the causes of the Great Depression, commonly called
monetary, or supply-side, economics. The monetarists believed that the significant
decline in the money supply in the United States in the late 1920s and early 1930s
contributed to the Depression crisis in the United States as well as elsewhere. The
decline in the money supply was a direct consequence of the large bank failures
in the US between 1930 and 1933. As banks went under, so did depositors, who
lost all of their bank deposits, and bank shareholders, whose capital was worthless.
This led, in turn, to a feedback loop, with lower liquidity and bank lending, which
exacerbated the economic downturn at the height of the Great Depression. The
failure of thousands of financial institutions and banks in the US during the 1930s
was a unique feature of the Great Depression. According to Bernanke, the number
of commercial banks that were left operating by 1933 was only about half of those
operating in 1929.[7] The banks that had survived the collapse continued to suffer
heavy losses, with some barely remaining financially viable.[8]

The causes for the bank collapses in the US in the 1930s were not entirely clear.
Some banks were marginally viable and so, with the macroeconomic environment
deteriorating, it was inevitable they would collapse. Bank collapses had begun
to occur with a number of smaller rural banks in the 1920s as the agricultural

---

4   See Friedman, M. and Schwartz, A. *A Monetary History of the United States, 1867–
1960* (Princeton, NJ: Princeton University Press, 1963).

5   See Bernanke, B.S. Nonmonetary effects of the financial crisis in the propagation
of the Great Depression. *American Economic Review*, Vol. 73, June 1983. This paper
was reproduced later in Bernanke, B.S. *Essays on the Great Depression* (Princeton, NJ:
Princeton University Press, 2000), Chapter 2.

6   Bernanke, B.S. *Essays on the Great Depression* (Princeton, NJ: Princeton University
Press, 2000), Chapter 2, p. 41.

7   Ibid., p. 44.

8   Ibid.

sector started to contract sharply.[9] With the deterioration in the macroeconomic environment in the US, depositors with major commercial banks panicked and began to withdraw their deposits at an alarming rate, causing a run on the banks. According to Bernanke, the banking crisis in the early 1930s differed from previous banking crises both in "magnitude and in the degree of danger posed by the phenomenon of runs."[10]

Bernanke provides a detailed chronology of the banking crisis that occurred between 1921 and 1936.[11] The banking crisis in the interwar years had its origins in Eastern Europe and the Baltic states in the 1920s. Banks began to fail in Sweden, The Netherlands, Denmark and Norway.[12] This was quickly followed by other bank failures in Austria, Spain, Poland, Japan and Germany between 1923 and 1930. The first large reported bank failure in the United States was the Bank of the United States in December 1930.[13] Further bank runs were recorded for Italy, Argentina, Poland, Hungary and Germany.

Most damaging for the United States was a series of runs on regional banks, which culminated in over 1,800 banks failing across the Midwest and West Coast of the United States.[14] The panic runs by depositors continued in the United States with a series of bank failures in Chicago in 1932, as well as other bank collapses along the East Coast of the United States.[15] The damaging runs on banks and other financial institutions created an environment of insecurity and fear that continued to undermine the health and wellbeing of the US and global financial system.

The second key feature of the Great Depression was the high bankruptcy rates among farmers, small- to medium-sized businesses, and households.[16] Households had large debts, driven largely by sizeable residential mortgages that were used to purchase the family home. Households had also become indebted with the growth of the consumer instalment debt that was another important feature of the financial and banking crisis of the 1930s.[17] The rise of small business debt was also occurring during the lead-up to the Great Depression. The increase in leverage for households, farmers and small- to medium-sized businesses introduced a new dimension and level of vulnerability to the strength of the US and European economies.

---

9   Upham, C.B. and Lamke, E. *Closed and Distressed Banks: A Study in Public Administration* (Washington, DC: The Brookings Institution, 1934), p. 247.

10   Ibid., (n. 6), p. 45.

11   Ibid., (n. 6), pp. 90–93.

12   Ibid., (n. 6), p. 90.

13   Ibid., (n. 6), p. 91.

14   Ibid., (n. 6), p. 92.

15   Ibid., (n. 6), p. 93.

16   Keynes, Ibid. (n. 6), pp. 46–7.

17   Bernanke reports that urban real estate mortgages in the United States rose from $11 billion in 1920 to $27 billion in 1929. Ibid., (n. 6), p. 47.

With the deterioration in the macroeconomic environment that had begun in the US and Germany, consumers and businesses that had fuelled the debt-driven boom in the 1920s were now vulnerable to any large-scale economic downturn. With unemployment rising and economic growth and industrial production dramatically falling, consumers could not spend their way out of the crisis. Instead, consumption and business investment fell, which, as Keynes pointed out in his landmark thesis, was a key ingredient in prolonging the Great Depression.[18]

A third key element of the Great Depression was the simultaneous weakening of the US economy. The Wall Street Crash of 1929, along with the household and business debt crisis and the banking crisis, which caused numerous bank runs, all came to a head with falling economic activity. The banking crisis exacerbated an already weakened macroeconomic environment and, according to Friedman and Schwartz, led to a "change in the character of the contraction."[19] What began as a manageable downturn in 1929 and early 1930 soon evolved into a much larger and more dangerous downward spiral.

The US had previously experienced recessions with the consequent rise of unemployment and contraction in economic activity. However, with the Great Depression the economic downturn that began in 1929 was soon coupled with a crisis in the US financial system, mass bankruptcies, failing banks and spiraling deflation. There is little doubt that taken as a whole, the conditions were ripe for a perfect storm wherein economic activity would decline substantially, leading to more bank collapses, bankruptcies, higher unemployment and further deflation. With a stressed financial system, deteriorating industrial production and rising unemployment, it would be difficult for the US or Europe to emerge from the crisis without clear stimulus policies and direct government intervention.

The problem with government policy and direction at the time was the continued belief by policymakers that the market would self-correct without any government intervention. This laissez-faire approach had its genesis in the belief that freely operating markets would deliver the most optimal outcome for society. Supporters of the free-market principle argued that government intervention would lead to price and wealth distortions and inefficient and sub-optimal allocation of resources. Hence, during 1929–1933, US policymakers and the US government did little to stem the tide of the crisis. According to Keynes, the indifference and inaction by government, along with the self-perpetuating belief in classical economics, were misleading and disastrous.

As unemployment rose to unprecedented heights and poverty and civil unrest began to mount, the US government decided to act. Under the leadership of President Franklin Delano Roosevelt the US Congress passed the New Deal. Under the New Deal a variety of work programs were approved, some of which

---

18   See J.M. Keynes. *The General Theory of Employment, Interest and Money* (Cambridge, UK: Palgrave Macmillan, 1936).

19   See Friedman and Schwartz: Ibid., (n. 4), p. 311. See also B.S. Bernanke: Ibid., (n. 6), p. 47.

were designed to create employment on national infrastructure projects. Between 1933 and 1936 the New Deal also saw a number of new regulatory bodies created which were designed to enhance regulation of securities markets, banking and telecommunications, labour relations, housing and welfare. Some of the New Deal initiatives continue to exist today, including the Federal Deposit Insurance Corporation (FDIC), the Securities Exchange Commission (SEC),[20] the *Social Security Act 1935* and the Federal Housing Administration (FHA).

The SEC was given the task of enforcing new securities regulation in US equity markets. Congress later enacted similar legislation for US commodity markets.[21] The SEC regulated initial public offerings of securities on federal exchanges through the *Securities Act 1933*, whilst the *Securities Exchange Act 1934* was designed to regulate the issue of securities on secondary markets. The SEC would regulate all federal exchanges, as well as broker dealers and companies that were listed on the New York Stock Exchange. The overall aims of the Securities Acts and the SEC were to ensure market integrity and to promote investor confidence for exchange-traded securities. The SEC was to achieve these aims by preventing corporate abuses and fraudulent activity through the enforcement of civil and criminal penalties which had been enacted as part of the enhanced securities regulation.

The Federal Deposit Insurance Corporation was a New Deal initiative designed to improve depositor confidence with banks and other deposit-taking institutions. President Roosevelt established the FDIC on the 6 June 1933 when the *Banking Act 1933* was passed into law. Initially, the Banking Act provided that deposits of up to $US2,000 per depositor were guaranteed under the standard maximum deposit insurance (SMDI) from 1 January 1934. This was later increased to $US5,000 in 1935 with the *Banking Act 1935*. The SMDI was further increased in 1950 to $US10,000. In 1966 the SMDI was increased again to $US15,000 per depositor and in 1974 it was further increased to $US40,000. By 1980 the SMDI was set at $US100,000 and was further temporarily extended to $US250,000 per depositor in 2005 by the *Federal Deposit Insurance Reform Act 2005*. Following the current GFC, the $US250,000 limit was extended again by President Obama until 31 December 2013. From 1 January 2014, the SDMI limit will revert back to $US100,000.

The initiatives adopted in the New Deal had a number of important objectives. First, there was acknowledgment at the highest level of government that markets do fail, and without government intervention the US economy would have remained depressed for a considerable period of time. Second, a number of national

---

20   The Securities Exchange Commission was created as part of the New Deal by the *Securities Exchange Act 1934* (US). The SEC enforces the *Securities Act 1933* and the *Securities Exchange Act 1934* (US).

21   Commodity markets were originally regulated by the *Grain Futures Act 1922* (US) and the *Futures Trading Act 1921* (US). *The Futures Trading Act* was later held to be unconstitutional by the US Supreme Court in *Hill v Wallace* 259 US 44 (1922).

infrastructure projects that were initiated by the New Deal brought economic stimulus to an otherwise depressed economic landscape. The construction of the Hoover Dam from 1931 created much needed work and stimulus to thousands of otherwise unemployed workers and helped develop infrastructure in the form of hydroelectric power. Despite their success, the economic stimulus delivered by the New Deal initiatives had limited impact on the overall high levels of unemployment experienced in the United States. It was not until World War II and the massive rearmament of the military in the US and Europe that unemployment was driven down to more sustainable levels.

A third important initiative of the New Deal was the wave of regulation that was introduced with the aim of restoring market integrity and investor and depositor confidence in the US financial system. New securities regulations of equity markets and the creation of an independent watchdog in the form of the Securities and Exchange Commission (SEC) were vital in restoring investor confidence with securities exchanges. The SEC was charged with the task of preventing corporate abuses, and licensing exchanges, such as the New York Stock Exchange, and broker–dealers. All of these changes were designed to safeguard trading in the securities of listed companies.

Lessons from the Great Depression

The lessons learnt from the Great Depression helped shape the policy response for the current crisis. At the height of the crisis following the collapse of Lehman Brothers, governments all over the world began to undertake a number of initiatives which were designed to restore investor confidence in global financial markets. The quick response from the US Federal Reserve and the US Treasury, as well as other regulators in the UK and Europe, was clear recognition that financial markets left to their own devices might not have overcome their inherent structural weaknesses.

The current crisis, like the Great Depression, has featured a severe recession coupled with a damaged global financial system. As history has shown, a weakened macroeconomic environment along with stressed financial markets exacerbates the decline in economic activity. This is because financial markets are an integral part of a dynamic, robust and interlinked economy. When financial markets fail to operate properly, the downturn in economic activity becomes more pronounced, taking longer to recover. Both the Great Depression and the current crisis have demonstrated how damaged financial markets can prolong declines in economic growth and delay recovery.

The current crisis also shares another important characteristic of the Great Depression. Investor panic and "runs" on financial institutions including banks, credit unions, building societies and investment banks have been a hallmark of both. Like the bank runs in the 1930s, the panic runs by depositors on banks and building societies in 2008 and 2009 were not isolated events, but pointed to a more systemic problem gripping the global banking and financial system. In 2008 the collapse and bailouts of building societies such as Northern Rock, and the Lloyds Banking Group in the United Kingdom, and of Bear Stearns, AIG, Washington Mutual, Freddie Mac and Fannie Mae, and Lehman Brothers in the United States all contributed to heightened systemic risk in international financial markets. The crisis was not limited to Europe or the United States but also affected other financial institutions elsewhere, including investment banks Babcock & Brown and Allco Finance Group in Australia, which collapsed with large corporate debts.[22]

The number of financial institutions that failed in the current crisis seems few, however, when compared to the number of bank collapses during the Great Depression. During the height of the Depression, almost 10,000 small regional and mid-sized banks collapsed, with depositors losing their entire life savings because of the absence of any deposit insurance scheme. The sheer quantity of collapses in the Great Depression caused untold financial loss to millions of depositors and led to significant damage to the US and other Western economies.

Similarly during the GFC the bank, building societies and investment bank collapses, if left unchecked, would have led to a significant loss of confidence for depositors and investors, leaving the entire global financial system on the brink of total collapse. As is discussed in Chapter 5, policy responses by a number of governments and central banks all over the world during 2008–2009 helped alleviate further contagion fallout. Despite the relative success of some of the stimulus measures, other responses, including taxpayer-funded bailouts, proved more controversial. Continued perceptions that Wall Street bankers and top executives had been remunerated far too generously during the boom times led to the view that the executives should bear the ultimate responsibility for the financial costs of their failed institutions.

This time around, governments were acutely aware of the consequences of inaction from their past experiences in the Great Depression. As the current crisis unfolded with the collapse of Bear Stearns and Lehman Brothers the world banking system entered into a credit crisis. Governments in the United States and in Europe embarked on a globally coordinated plan to restore confidence. One important initiative that was adopted by a number of countries to achieve this aim was to give depositors with a government guarantee for their deposits. Although the amount of the guarantee varied from country to country,[23] the initiative was

---

22   Babcock & Brown was Australia's second largest investment bank and was listed on the Australian Securities Exchange. Babcock & Brown collapsed with debts of over $A500 million. Allco Finance Group was Australia's third largest investment bank behind Macquarie Bank and Babcock & Brown. Allco experienced a similar demise to Babcock & Brown after it was forced into liquidation in late 2008.

23   The deposit guarantees were not uniform in amount. For example, some countries in continental Europe such as Spain, Italy, Greece, Portugal and The Netherlands provided a guarantee of €100,000. Ireland provided an unlimited guarantee to its nation's depositors, Germany provided a guarantee of €50,000 and the maximum deposit limit guarantee in

viewed as largely successful because it provided a level of security for depositors who may have otherwise continued their run on the banks.

The OPEC Oil Crisis

If deflation and unemployment were the order of the day during the 1930s Great Depression, the world would be plunged into stagflation in the 1970s, involving a sustained period of rising inflation and unemployment. The OPEC oil crisis, which had its origins in the OPEC oil embargo of 1973, led to a new economic and industrial crisis. OPEC in a communiqué issued in October 1973 announced an oil embargo to the United States and its allies. The OPEC oil embargo was imposed in response to the tensions in the Middle East following the conflict involving Israel, Egypt and Syria in the 1973 Arab-Israeli war.[24] During October 1973, OPEC made a series of announcements and attempted to impose a total oil embargo on the United States. The United States, the prime target of the oil embargo, was being punished by OPEC for its support given to Israel during the Arab-Israeli conflict.

The embargo was later extended to The Netherlands and Portugal for their pro-US stand. The UK was excluded from the embargo because its external affairs position at the time favoured the Palestinians. OPEC was unapologetic about the application of the oil embargo to nations that were deemed to be "hostile." Nations deemed "friendly" would be protected and excluded from the oil embargo.[25] Given oil's importance to a nation's economic prosperity and wellbeing, a number of governments were keen to show their neutrality, or support for the Arab cause. This was made clear by Belgium and Japan.[26]

---

the United Kingdom was £50,000 sterling. In the United States the deposit scheme was lifted from $US100,000 to a temporary limit of $US250,000. In Australia the government announced an unlimited guarantee for bank and building society deposits under $A1,000,000 to be guaranteed without charge. The Australian government guarantee was to operate until 12 October 2011.

24   In a communiqué issued by OPEC in Kuwait on 25 December 1973, the Secretary General provided that "the measures taken should in no way affect friendly countries, thus drawing a very clear distinction between those who support the Arabs, those who support the enemy and those who remain neutral."

25   Ibid.

26   In the 25 December communiqué issued by OPEC, support for Japan's position was evident: "The Arab Ministers present noted the changes which had occurred in Japanese policy towards the Arab cause as demonstrated in several ways, including the visit by the Japanese Deputy Prime Minister to certain Arab countries. They also took account of Japan's difficult economic situation and decided to accord it special treatment, excluding it completely from the application of the general cut in output in order to protect the Japanese economy and in the hope that the Japanese Government will appreciate this position and persevere in its fair and equitable attitude towards the Arab cause."

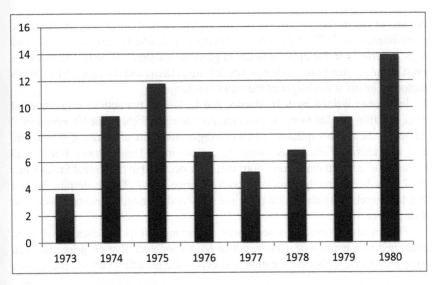

Figure 1.1   Annual inflation rate (CPI) United States 1973–1980

Thus the world was divided between friendly and hostile nations and oil would now be used as leverage in an increasingly tense political as well as economic battle between OPEC and the United States and its allies. The OPEC oil embargo led to considerable uncertainty, given the growing importance of oil for world economic growth. One significant ramification of the crisis was the effect the embargo had on the price of oil and the consequential increase in consumer prices for finished goods. At the time OPEC announced its oil embargo, the price of oil quadrupled to $US12 a barrel from less than $US3 a barrel a year earlier. Figure 1.1 shows the annual inflation rate from the beginning of the oil crisis to the end of 1970s.

As can be seen from the above graph, the annual inflation rate in the United States rose dramatically from just over 3.5% in 1973 to over 9.0% in 1974 and to almost 12.0% in 1975. The rise in consumer prices was largely driven by the simultaneous rise in the oil price following the OPEC oil embargo. As consumer and producer prices rose throughout the 1970s, so did unemployment. Unemployment increased significantly in the United States from 1970 through to the peak in 1982–1983. There were also recorded four economic recessions in the United States during the 1970s: 1970–1971, 1974–1975, 1980 and 1981–1982.

Although the economic consequences of the OPEC oil crisis were severe enough, the oil crisis also had a significant social impact for millions of consumers who were dependent upon oil. In an address to the nation, Richard Nixon, then President of the United States, announced austerity measures designed to conserve the use of oil in the United States. One of the austerity measures involved the establishment in 1973 of the Energy Emergency Action Group, which enforced nightly curfews on the opening hours of gasoline stations.[27] President Nixon went even as far as attempting to change US driving patterns and the dependence of US motorists on oil at the height of the OPEC embargo.[28]

In a paper written by R.B. Barsky and L. Kilian, the authors argue that oil price volatility has led to significant macroeconomic effects on the US economy.[29] Although the authors question whether exogenous political events in the Middle East are capable of causing economic recessions in the United States, Barsky and Kilian conclude that many recessions that have occurred in the United States since 1972 have been directly associated with oil price rises.[30] This is despite the fact that the correlation between oil price volatility and economic downturns was less than perfect.

The macroeconomic consequences following oil price rises have been examined in a number of studies, which have concluded that oil price rises can have an adverse effect on inflation and economic growth.[31] Further, the studies

---

27   On 25 November, 1973 President Nixon announced a range of energy-saving measures, including the closure of gasoline stations at night: "I am asking tonight that all gasoline filling stations close down their pumps between 9pm Saturday night and midnight Sunday every weekend beginning 1 December [...]. Upon passage of the emergency energy legislation before the Congress, gas stations will be required to close during these hours. This step should not result in any serious hardship of any American family. It will, however, discourage long-distance driving during weekends." US Government 1973. (National energy policy. The President's address to the nation announcing additional actions to deal with the energy emergency. Weekly Compilation of Presidential Documents, 1 December 1973, No. 48, Vol. 9).

28   In the same address, President Nixon states: "We can achieve substantial additional savings by altering our driving habits. While the voluntary response to my request for reduced driving speeds has been excellent, it is now essential that we have mandatory and full compliance with this important step on a nationwide basis. And therefore, the third step will be the establishment of a maximum speed limit for automobiles of 50 miles per hour nationwide as soon as our emergency energy legislation passes the Congress. We expect that this measure will produce savings of 200,000 barrels of gasoline per day. Intercity buses and heavy duty trucks which operate more efficiently at higher speeds, and therefore, do not use more gasoline will be permitted to observe a 55 mile per hour speed limit." Ibid., p. 1364.

29   Barsky, R.B. and Kilian, L. 2004. Oil and the macroeconomy since the 1970s. *Journal of Economic Perspectives*, Vol. 18, Fall 2004, pp. 115–34.

30   Ibid., p. 117. Barsky and Kilian provide that although the correlation between recessions and oil price rises is less than perfect, the recessions that began in the United States in 1973 and 1990 occurred just before major oil price rises.

31   Barsky, R.B. and Kilian, L. Do we really know that oil caused the Great Stagflation? A monetary alternative, in *NBER Macroeconomics Annual*, ed. Bernanke, B.S. and Rogoff, K. (Cambridge, MA: MIT Press, 2001), pp. 137–48.

conclude that an exogenous oil price shock is capable of producing inflation and the causal link is unambiguous.[32] According to Barsky and Kilian, the prospect of stagflation in the form of declining economic growth and rising inflation following an oil price rise was to be expected.[33]

With rising unemployment and simultaneous rising inflation, the United States and the rest of the developed world had entered into a sustained period of stagflation. Stagflation proved to be difficult for policymakers to tackle and created indecision among central bankers and government. Governments around the world were grappling with the rising tide of unemployment, yet had limited ability to stimulate domestic demand without adding to inflationary pressures. Automatic stabilizers, which ordinarily would have created budget deficits and the desired stimulus, were largely offset with restrictive monetary policy by central banks and higher interest rates for borrowers.

The inconsistent macro policy settings by central banks and governments added to the confusion and lack of policy direction. The world had entered into uncharted waters, as it had at the time of the Great Depression, with differing ideologies laying fault and blame and proposing inconsistent policies for the problem of stagflation. The monetarists argued that stagflation was the by-product of an increase in the money supply largely caused by burgeoning fiscal deficits. Keynesians, on the other hand, argued that unemployment was the root of all evil and that restrictive monetary policy was harming, not aiding, the current economic environment.

Eventually both the monetarists and the Keynesians won out, which saw a dramatic reversal of unemployment and inflation in the mid-1980s, particularly in the United States and the United Kingdom. Much of the reversal was credited to the policies of President Ronald Reagan in the United States and Prime Minister Margaret Thatcher in the United Kingdom, which countries adopted supply-side economic policies. Supply-side policies, commonly called "Reaganomics," largely consisted of reduced taxes on businesses and consumers along with cuts in government expenditure.

The central concept of Reaganomics was to decrease the level of government involvement and regulation in the economy. The idea had its origins in the belief that markets were most efficient at allocating scarce resources and should not be subjected to stifling bureaucracy and unhelpful government interference. As prices eased and unemployment fell during the mid-1980s all seemed well for a while, until the 1987 stock market crash. This created a new panic that undermined economic security and wellbeing and ushered in a new era of economic instability.

---

32 Rotemberg, J.J. and Woodford, M. Imperfect competition and the effects of energy price increases on economic activity. *Journal of Money, Credit and Banking*, Part 1, November, 28(4), 1996, pp. 550–77.

33 Barsky, R.B. and Kilian, L., Ibid., (n. 29), p. 124.

The 1987 Stock Market Crash

The crash of October 1987 heralded a new era of volatility for equity markets all over the world. Between 13 and 19 October 1987, the Dow Jones Industrial Average fell 769 points. In just four days of trading the Dow Jones lost almost $US1 trillion dollars in market capitalization. On 19 October 1987 the Dow Jones collapsed by 508 points or over 22% of total market capitalization. This represented the largest market decline in a single day and eclipsed the Great Crash of 1929.

The significant market declines were not limited to the Dow Jones and New York. All over the world investors panicked, selling stock at unprecedented speed and volume. Stock indices in Australia, New Zealand, Hong Kong and Singapore were especially hard hit, with average indices falling over 40%. Bourses in Europe were also savaged, with stock exchanges in London, Brussels, Copenhagen, Frankfurt, Amsterdam, Switzerland, Madrid and Paris all recording large declines, some exchanges falling by nearly 50%.

Global central bankers were keen to avoid a repeat of the economic fallout from the Wall Street Crash of 1929. In a speech on the settings of monetary policy, former US Federal Reserve Chairman Alan Greenspan commented on the effect of the 1987 stock market crash:

> In the event, the crash in October 1987 was far more traumatic than any of the possible scenarios we had identified. Previous planning was only marginally useful in that episode. We operated essentially in a crisis mode, responding with an immediate and massive injection of liquidity to help stabilize highly volatile financial markets. However, most of our stabilization efforts were directed at keeping the payments system functioning and markets open. The concern over the possible fallout on economic activity from a sharp a stock price decline kept us easing into early 1988. But the economy weathered that shock reasonably well, and our easing extended perhaps longer than hindsight has indicated was necessary. That period was followed by a preemptive tightening that brought the federal funds rate close to 10 percent by early 1989. In the summer of that year, we sensed enough softening of activity to warrant beginning a series of rate reductions.[34]

It was clear from Alan Greenspan's statement that the fallout from the 1987 stock market crash had resonated with the US Federal Reserve. Greenspan took the market panic on Wall Street and other bourses around the world very seriously. There was good reason for the US Federal Reserve and other central banks to

---

34   Greenspan 2004 (Risk and uncertainty in monetary policy. Remarks by Alan Greenspan at the Meeting of the American Economic Association, San Diego, California, 3 January 2004. The Federal Reserve Board). Available at: <http://www.federalreserve.gov/boarddocs/speeches/2004/20040103/default.html>.

be concerned with the equity market collapse. Reflecting the events that led to the Great Depression, the 1987 stock market collapse could trigger a widespread systemic crisis in financial markets and the banking sector. To avoid further fallout from the crash of 1987, central bankers all over the world resorted to increasing liquidity in financial markets. The measures taken by central bank governors in reducing interest rates and pump-priming the economy were designed to avoid widespread damage and fallout.

Shortly after the 1987 collapse, a Presidential Task Force was established to investigate the causes and ramifications flowing from the crash.[35] The Presidential Task Force (commonly called the 'Brady Commission'), was provided with terms of reference which included instructions to:

> review relevant analyses of the current and long-term financial condition of the Nation's securities markets; identify problems that may threaten the short-term liquidity or long-term solvency of such markets; analyze potential solutions to such problems that will both assure the continued functioning of free, fair and competitive securities markets and maintain investor confidence in such markets; and provide appropriate recommendations to the President, to the Secretary of the Treasury, and to the Chairman of the Board of Governors of the Federal Reserve System.[36]

The Presidential Task Force gathered and analysed primary transaction data from a range of sources, including the New York Stock Exchange (NYSE), the Chicago Mercantile Exchange (CME), the Chicago Board of Trade (CBOT), the American Stock Exchange (AMEX) and the Chicago Board Options Exchange (CBOE). The Task Force also analysed and cross-checked data supplied by the Securities and Exchange Commission (SEC), the Commodity Futures Trading Commission (CFTC) and a number of investment banks. The Task Force also conducted interviews with hundreds of market participants and investors with the aim of providing a more comprehensive understanding of the events that took place in October 1987.

After examining and analysing all of the data, the Brady Commission concluded that the precipitous decline in securities markets in October 1987 was largely characterized by "large sales by a limited number of institutional investors throughout the interrelated system of markets – stocks, futures and stock options. The massive volume, violent price volatility, and staggering demands on clearing and credit raised the possibility of a full scale financial system breakdown."[37] The Brady Commission also concluded that "stocks, stock index futures and options

---

35   See US Department of the Treasury 1988. Report of the Presidential Task Force on Market Mechanisms. Washington, DC: G.P.O.

36   Ibid., p. 1.

37   Ibid., p. 69.

constitute one market, linked by financial instruments, trading strategies, market participants and clearing and credit mechanisms."[38]

It was clear from the conclusions of the Brady Commission that the regulation of financial markets and, in particular, securities markets had become out of date and fallen well behind market practices. In part this was inevitable, given the advances in financial innovation which led to the creation of new and diverse financial products and financial markets. The Presidential Task Force concluded that securities markets were interlinked with other financial markets, reinforcing the perception, if not the reality, that extreme price movements on equity markets were capable of causing other distortions in the financial system.

This was confirmed with the Brady Commission's finding that:

> to a large extent the problems in mid-October can be traced to the failure of these market segments to act as one. Institutional and regulatory structures designed for separate marketplaces were incapable of effectively responding to intermarket pressures. The activities of some market participants, such as portfolio insurers, were driven by the misperception that they were trading in separate, not linked, marketplaces.[39]

According to the Brady Commission, the inescapable conclusion to draw from the experiences of the 1987 October stock market crash was "that the system grew geometrically with the technological and financial revolution of the 1980s. Many in government and industry and academia failed to understand fully that these separate marketplaces are in fact one market."[40]

The Brady Commission was also highly critical of the concentrated nature of securities markets. In the opinion of the Commission, concentration did not create a strong, robust and resilient marketplace. Instead, high levels of equity ownership concentrated in the hands of a few created vulnerabilities and intensified weaknesses when panic set in: "[the fact that] the market break was intensified by the activities of a few institutions illustrates the vulnerability of a market in which individuals directly own 60% of the equities. The experience underscores the need for immediate action to protect the equity market and financial system from the destructive consequences of violent market breaks."[41] In response to these findings, the Brady Commission made a number of recommendations for reforms to market practices, including to the regulation of securities markets.[42]

---

38 Id.
39 Id.
40 Id.
41 Id.
42 The recommendations for reform included the following: (1) One agency to coordinate the few, but critical, regulatory issues which have an impact across the related market segments and throughout the financial system; (2) Clearing systems should be unified to reduce financial risk; (3) Margins should be made consistent to control speculation and

Despite the significance of the October 1987 stock market crash and the findings of the Brady Commission, new panics and crises have continued to confront international financial markets and the global economy. The current crisis and its associated Great Recession have led to heighted systemic risk and instability in the global economy. As the International Monetary Fund commented, economic recessions that are associated with stressed financial markets are often much deeper and last a lot longer then average downturns. The forerunner to the current global crisis may well have been the systemic crisis that hit the fast-growing Asian economies in the late 1990s.

The Asian Currency Crisis

For some time the Asian tiger economies were seen as the new economic miracle in what was once the dominion of the West. The economies of South East Asia and East Asia enjoyed higher economic growth rates and lower levels of unemployment relative to the rest of the developed world. The perception for most was that the economies of South Korea, Thailand, Indonesia, Malaysia, Philippines, China, Singapore, Vietnam and Hong Kong all enjoyed strong economic fundamentals.

Certainly, from the outside all appeared to be well, with most of the Asian economies reaping the rewards of higher growth rates, flexible labour markets and high levels of productivity. The high levels of GDP were also underpinning rises in the standard of living for their citizens. Most commentators believed that these so-called Asian tiger economies would account for a new golden era in economic growth and prosperity.[43]

The optimism was short-lived. In 1997 the Asian financial and currency crisis erupted, with damaging consequences for the Asia Pacific region. The currency crisis in Asia began when Thailand was forced to devalue its currency, the Thai baht, in order bring the currency into line with its balance of payments and trade deficits. The devaluation ignited panic among foreign investors, who almost immediately sought to expatriate capital out of Thailand. The same occurred later in Indonesia and Korea. Foreign investors, who had supported the high-growth strategy of Thailand, Indonesia and South Korea in the 1980s and 1990s by

---

financial leverage; (4) Circuit breaker mechanisms (such as price limits and coordinated trading halts) should be formulated and implemented to protect the market system; (5) Information systems should be established to monitor transactions and conditions in related markets.

43   See, for example, analysis by commentators at the International Monetary Fund who discuss the relative success of South East Asian economies in the early 1970s to the late 1990s (International Monetary Fund 1998: Economic Crisis in Asia, Address by Shigemitsu Sugisaki, Deputy Managing Director of the International Monetary Fund, at the 1998 Harvard Business School, 30 January 1998).

pumping large amounts of capital in the form of short-term loans into the Asian economies, reversed their actions almost overnight.

The reversal of capital flows occurred because doubts emerged about the solvency of Asian debtors and their ability to repay the loans.[44] Most of the borrowings that had flowed into South East Asia were used for speculative purposes by investors and borrowers to buy into residential and commercial real estate. The excessive speculation led to inflated house prices and a bubble began to emerge in a number of Asian economies.

Since most of the capital that had flowed into Asia had been used unproductively, and Asian currencies had been fixed and pegged to the US dollar, overall competitiveness in South East Asia declined significantly. The decline in competitiveness, in turn, led to a decline in export activity which caused currencies to come under further pressure.

What had started as an isolated event in Thailand soon erupted into a much broader and systemic problem for the Asian region. With exports declining and trade deficits increasing, problems in Asia began to cause concerns in other nations that had become reliant on trade with South East Asia.[45] There are similarities between the Asian currency crisis and the recent sovereign debt crisis currently affecting Europe, where a handful of relatively small economies, including Greece, Portugal and Ireland, helped trigger a collapse of confidence in the euro. In 2010 and 2011, confronted with a possible wider systemic and contagion effect on the euro, the European Union and the International Monetary Fund decided to provide bailout money to prop up Greece, Ireland and Portugal to help them avoid defaults on their sovereign borrowings.

Conclusion

Some parallels can be drawn between previous crises and the current GFC. Like the 1930s Great Depression, the current crisis had its genesis in financial markets that had become dislocated and dysfunctional. As the bank runs heightened in the late 1920s and Wall Street experienced its largest declines of all time, investors continued to panic, leading to further disruptions and market volatility. Confusion as to the appropriate policy response to the Great Depression made things much worse than might otherwise have been the case.

Confronted with the realization that the current crisis could potentially develop into a new Great Depression, policymakers, governments and central banks all over the world decided to become more proactive. The painful experiences of the Great Depression had a silver lining, in that lessons learnt from them could be applied to the current crisis. In the 1930s, markets could not self-correct their

---

44   Ibid., p. 4.

45   See Corsetti, G., Presenti, P. and Roubini, N. What caused the Asian currency and financial crisis? *Japan and the World Economy*, 11 (1999), pp. 305–73, see pp. 309–10.

various failures; government intervention was needed. Consequently, in 2008 there was a belief that left to their own devices, financial markets might not have had the ability to return to normality.

The later Asian currency crisis also has parallels with today's financial crisis. The Asian currency crisis was triggered by a currency devaluation in the Thai baht. The Thailand economy was, and remains today, a relatively small economy. Nevertheless the devaluation in Thailand led to wider disruptions in the Asian region. As Greece, Ireland and Portugal demonstrate today, problems with a relatively small economy can have significant reverberations in other, larger economies which, in turn, could have adverse consequences for the wider international community.

Chapter 2
Triggers of the Crisis

Introduction

The triggers of the current economic and financial crisis continue to attract much attention and publicity. There have been a number of theories or explanations that have been put forward concerning the possible causes that have led to the greatest financial crisis since the Great Depression. It has been suggested that one key catalyst for the crisis was the aggressive build-up in many developed economies in household debt that was channeled into unproductive and speculative investments such as residential housing. The build-up in risk led to a bubble initially in the US housing market, which contributed significantly to the build-up of risk within the US economy and later spread to financial markets globally.

When US household debt was repackaged and securitized in the form of collateralized debt obligations (CDOs) and sold off to international investors, government entities, municipal councils, equity funds, pension funds, banks and investment banks, what initially commenced as a US problem spread globally to become truly international. The bursting of the US housing bubble was no doubt a significant contributing factor in explaining the current financial crisis. However, to simply assert that the US housing bubble caused the global financial crisis (GFC) would amount to an oversimplification of the current crisis. As is discussed in Chapter 1, previous crises have occurred throughout the world, including in the US, which have had various causal factors.

Perhaps a somewhat unique feature of the current crisis was the speed at which the Western world appeared to be engulfed by a catastrophic series of interrelated events. There is little doubt that the apparent dislocation of global financial and credit markets manifested themselves in the creation of an almost perfect storm. What is less clear is whether the dislocation of financial markets contributed to the current crisis or whether financial markets were merely symptomatic of a deteriorating global economic cycle that had already commenced.

Some commentators have suggested that financial markets are responsive to economic events, whilst others are of the view that financial markets have a more profound effect on the world economy. In any event, it is clear from the lessons of previous crises that economies that are confronted with recessions and downturns which are coupled with damaged or stressed financial systems ordinarily take a long time to heal. Certainly this was the case with the Great Depression in the 1930s and it appears to be the somewhat dismal conclusion of analyses of the current crisis. Described by the International Monetary Fund (IMF) as the "Great

Recession," this downturn will take a considerable time and sustained effort to
unwind.

The United States Financial Crisis Inquiry Report

In the immediate aftermath of the GFC, a number of enquiries, public and private,
were established to investigate, analyse and provide considered responses to the
crisis. These enquiries have included some set up by international bodies such
as the Group of Thirty (G30);[1] the Financial Stability Forum;[2] the Center for
Financial Studies;[3] the International Monetary Fund;[4] and the US Treasury.

Perhaps one of the most influential commissions set up to investigate the causes
and consequences of the GFC was the Financial Crisis Inquiry Commission, which
was established to "examine the causes of the current financial and economic crisis
in the United States."[5] The Final Report prepared by the Financial Crisis Inquiry
Commission was delivered to the President of the United States, the US Congress
and the American people in January 2011.[6]

A key finding of the Financial Crisis Inquiry Commission was that the GFC
could have been avoided.[7] According to the Commission, the GFC "was the
result of human action and inaction, not of Mother Nature or computer models
gone haywire."[8] This was an interesting finding from the Commission because
it appeared to be concluding what was obvious. Yet despite this, suggestions had
been made that human error was not the only cause of or contributing factor to
the current crisis. Some believed that the crisis had been made worse because
of computer modeling and the over-reliance by financial markets on the use of
mathematical algorithms.

---

1   G30 Working Group on Financial Stability 2009. Financial reform: A framework
for financial stability. Washington, DC: Group of Thirty.

2   Financial Stability Forum 2008. Report of the Financial Stability Forum on
enhancing market and institutional resilience. Basel: Financial Stability Board, Bank of
International Settlements. 7 April.

3   Center for Financial Studies 2009. White Paper No. I and White Paper No. II. New
financial order recommendations by the Issing Committee, Part I (October 2008) and Part
II (March 2009) (London: CFS, White Paper Series, February 2009).

4   International Monetary Fund 2009a. Lessons of the financial crisis for future
regulation of financial institutions and markets and for liquidity management (New York:
IMF, 4 February 2009).

5   Financial Crisis Inquiry Commission of the United States, Final Report of the
National Commission on the Causes of the Financial and Economic Crisis in the United
States, (Washington, DC: G.P.O.).

6   The Financial Crisis Inquiry Commission was established by the *Fraud Enforcement
and Recovery Act* (P.L. 111–21) *2009* (US).

7   Ibid., (n. 5), p. xvii.

8   Id.

The suggestion that computer modeling and limitations associated with algorithms contributed to the crisis may sound far-fetched and lack substance. However, the former Chairman of the US Federal Reserve, Alan Greenspan, did express a view that the current crisis may not have been anticipated because of limitations in the risk management paradigm that was in place during the global crisis.[9] Greenspan further asserts that reliance by market regulators as well as the US Federal Reserve on little or no meaningful data meant that authorities could not make informed decisions regarding the potential consequences and fallout resulting from a major corporate collapse, including the collapse of Lehman Brothers.[10] So-called "tail risks" from a large-scale corporate collapse were not properly analysed or readily quantified.

Indeed, there is much force in the argument that the failure of market regulators to appreciate the fallout arising from the collapse of the Lehman behemoth did in fact make the crisis worse than might otherwise have been the case. As is discussed in Chapter 4, a key challenge for market regulators in dealing with the Lehman Brothers collapse and other large-scale corporate disasters concerned the issue of moral hazard. Market economics informs us that investment losses lie where they have fallen and are part of the risk return paradigm. If governments were to intervene and compensate investors for losses every time a company went broke, an unfair burden would be placed on taxpayers. Hence, it was not unsurprizing that taxpayer-funded bailouts in the form of the Troubled Assets Relief Program (TARP) in the United States proved controversial to say the least.[11]

---

9   According to Alan Greenspan, the limitations with computer models and algorithms may have constituted a "fatal flaw:" "It is in such circumstances that we depend on our highly sophisticated global system of financial risk management to contain market breakdowns. How could it have failed on so broad a scale? The paradigm that spawned winners of the Nobel Prize in economics was so thoroughly embraced by academia, central banks, and regulators that in 2006 it became the core of global regulatory standards (Basel II). Many quantitative firms whose number crunching sought to expose profitable market trading principles were successful so long as risk aversion moved incrementally (which it did much of the time). But crunching data that covered only the last two or three decades prior to the current crisis did not yield a model that could anticipate a crisis. Mathematical models that calibrate risk are, however, surely superior guides to risk management than the 'rule of thumb' judgments of a half century ago. To this day it is hard to find fault with the *conceptual* framework of our models as far as they go. The elegant option pricing proof of Fisher Black and Myron Scholes is no less valid today than a decade ago. The risk management paradigm, nonetheless, harboured a fatal flaw." Greenspan 2010a (The crisis, 15 April 2010), p. 11.

10   Greenspan commented: "In the growing state of high euphoria, risk managers, the Federal Reserve, and other regulators failed to fully comprehend the underlying size, length, and impact of the negative tail of the distribution of risk outcomes that was about to be revealed as the post-Lehman crisis played out. For decades, with little, to no, data, most analysts, in my experience, had conjectured a far more limited tail risk, arguably the major source of the critical risk management system failures." Ibid., pp. 11–12.

11   The TARP program in the US was initially set up by the Bush Administration under the Emergency Economic Stabilization Act of 2008 and was designed to assist in the

The key finding from the Financial Crisis Inquiry Commission that the GFC was caused by human error and not by Mother Nature or by artificial means raises a number of interesting possible triggers. Importantly, there is no single factor or trigger that can explain the cause of the GFC. Instead, the GFC had a number of triggers, and while contributory factors on their own may have been insignificant, when combined they had widespread and long-lasting effects on the international financial markets and the global economy.

Trigger 1: The United States and the Global Housing Bubble

There is little doubt that the housing bubble in the US and other economies had a sizeable adverse impact on the crisis. Years of relatively cheap money channelled into largely unproductive and speculative housing investment contributed to inflated residential house prices. As interest rates remained low through the monetary policy settings of the Federal Reserve in the United States and in central banks in other countries, investment and construction in residential housing began to take off. This led in turn to higher residential real estate prices, which attracted the attention of investors and lenders worldwide.

The era of low interest rates at the beginning of 2001 in the United States and other parts of the developed world coincided with the 9/11 terrorist attacks in New York. Concerned that the terrorist attacks would induce a recession in the United States, the US Federal Reserve aggressively reduced key benchmark interest rates 11 times, so that the official cash rate stood at 1.75% at the end of 2001.[12] According to the Financial Crisis Inquiry Commission, at the end of 2001 the United States had the "lowest [cash rate] in 40 years."[13]

The US Federal Reserve was not alone in aggressively reducing interest rates in the immediate aftermath of the 9/11 terrorist attacks. Central banks in the United Kingdom, Australia and the European Union reduced interest rates over the same period. In the UK, the Bank of England reduced the official interest rate from a high of 6.00% in February 2000 to a 30-year low of 3.50% in May 2003.[14] There was a similar aggressive reduction in interest rates in Australia, with the Reserve

---

orderly purchase by the US government of "troubled" or distressed assets from the private sector, principally held by US banks and investment banks. The total troubled asset buy-back was to be from $US700 billion and was to take place in stages coordinated and paid by the US Treasury. Initially, the TARP program was to be used to purchase toxic mortgage-backed securities flowing from US sub-prime mortgages. As time passed, monies from the TARP program were also used to prop up and bail out segments of the US automotive industry.

12   Ibid., (n. 5), p. 84.
13   Ibid.
14   See the Bank of England Official Bank Rate history. Available at: <http//www.bankofengland.co.uk/mfsd/iadb/Repo.asp>.

Bank of Australia reducing the official cash rate from a high of 6.25% in August 2000 to a 30-year low of 4.25% in December 2001.[15] The European Central Bank cut its official bank rate for EU member states from 3.75% in 2000 to 1.00% in 2003.[16]

Before the Financial Crisis Inquiry Commission, former US Federal Reserve Chairman Alan Greenspan testified that he had expressed his concerns about the state of the US housing market as early as 2002 in the Federal Open Market Committee.[17] The current Chairman of the Federal Reserve, Ben Bernanke, also raised similar concerns regarding the excessive growth of leverage and household debt in the United States and its consequential adverse effect on house prices.[18]

As is discussed in Chapter 1, the current crisis has interesting parallels with previous economic catastrophes, particular with the Great Depression of the 1930s. With the Great Depression there had been a large build-up in household debt in

---

15 See the Reserve Bank of Australia Official Cash Rate statistics. Available at: <http://www.rba.gov.au/statistics/cash-rate.html>.

16 See the European Central Bank Monetary Rate Policy settings. Available at: <http://www.ecb.int/stats/monetary/rates/html/index.en.html>.

17 Alan Greenspan, then Chairman of the Federal Reserve, expressed concern about the potential of a housing price bubble emerging in the US: "In 2002, I expressed concerns to the FOMC, noting that 'our extraordinary housing boom [...] financed by very large increases in mortgage debt – cannot continue indefinitely.' It did continue for longer than I would have forecast at the time, and it did so despite the extensive two-year-long tightening of monetary policy that began in mid-2004. The house price bubble, the most prominent global bubble in generations, was engendered by lower interest rates, but, as demonstrated in the Brookings paper I previously provided to the Commission, it was long term mortgage rates that galvanized prices, not the overnight rates of central banks, as has become the seeming conventional wisdom." Greenspan 2010b. (Testimony of Alan Greenspan before the Financial Crisis Inquiry Commission, 7 April 2010, Stanford, CT: Stanford Law School), p. 5.

18 In providing testimony before the Financial Crisis Inquiry Commission, Ben Bernanke also expressed concerns regarding the excessive growth in leverage and household debt, particularly in the US housing market: "Excessive leverage is often cited as an important vulnerability that contributed to the crisis. Certainly, many households, businesses, and financial firms took on more debt than they could handle, reflecting in part more permissive standards on the part of lenders. A notable example was the decline in down payments required of many home purchasers, which, together with the increased use of exotic mortgage instruments and the availability of home equity lines of credit, resulted in some homeowners becoming highly leveraged. When house prices declined, the equity of those homeowners was quickly wiped out; in turn, 'underwater' borrowers who owed more than their houses were worth were much more likely to default on their mortgage payments. Nonfinancial firms, in contrast, do not seem to have become overleveraged before the crisis; collectively, these firms did see a small increase in debt-to-asset ratios from 2006 to 2008, but these ratios tend to be volatile, and the short-term increase was superimposed on a two-decade-long downward trend." Bernanke 2010c (Ben Bernanke. Statement before the Financial Crisis Inquiry Commission. Stanford, CT: Stanford Law School), pp. 8–9.

the period leading up to the Great Crash of 1929. Most household borrowings had been channelled into speculative and largely unproductive investments in stocks on Wall Street. As stock prices continued to rise, an increasing number of investors with higher debt levels were required to continue to propel stock prices higher. When the great bull run of the 1920s ended, the stock price bubble also ended and precipitated the Great Crash on Wall Street in 1929 and then again in 1932.

Both the Great Depression and the current crisis were underpinned by excessive leverage and speculation in unproductive assets. The lure of higher prices led investors and lenders into a dangerous feedback loop whereby asset prices (stock prices in the 1920s and house prices between 2000 and 2007) were pushed ever higher, with alarming levels of debt. We know from our history that asset bubbles do not always go in one direction – upwards. By definition, a bubble must deflate at some point in time. The Great Depression followed the Crash of 1929 on Wall Street, which deflated stock prices suddenly in one day. Similarly, the equally spectacular sub-prime mortgage implosion in the United States in 2007 and 2008 led to a great crash in residential house prices in most developed countries.[19]

The current US Federal Reserve Chairman, Ben Bernanke, investigated the link between US house prices and easy monetary policy.[20] Other economists have also explored the link.[21] According to Bernanke, US house prices rose strongly in the 1990s in the period prior to the easing of monetary policy. Similarly, house prices rose in other countries over the same period. Hence, when previous periods are taken into account, the link between house prices and monetary policy is less convincing.[22] Bernanke suggests that a much stronger relationship may in fact

---

19   The house price decline has been felt in a number of countries, including the United States, Spain, Portugal, Ireland and the United Kingdom. A number of states in the USA have experienced severe price falls and foreclosures, which have increased the stock of vacant houses. The Comptroller of the Currency Administrator of National Banks reported that a number of cities across the USA had foreclosure rates for sub-prime mortgage loans of over 20%. Not only were cities within a manufacturing centre such as Detroit and Cleveland hit particularly hard but also high-end "service" cities such as Las Vegas and Miami suffered significant foreclosures. US Department of the Treasury 2010. Comptroller of the Currency Administrator of National Banks. The importance of preserving a system of national standards for national banks, OCC White Paper. Washington, DC: OCC, Department of the Treasury, Attachment 1.

20   Bernanke 2010b. Monetary policy and the housing bubble. Speech by Ben Bernanke, Chairman of the Board of Governors of the Federal Reserve System, delivered at the Annual Meeting of the American Economic Association, Atlanta Georgia, 3 January 2010.

21   See Del Negro, M. and Otrok, C. 2007. 99 Luftballons: Monetary policy and house price boom across US states. *Journal of Monetary Economics*, 54(7), pp. 1962–85; Jarocinski, M. and Smets, F. 2008. House prices and the stance of monetary policy. *Federal Reserve Bank of St Louis Review*, 90(4), pp. 339–65.

22   According to Bernanke, "when historical relationships are taken into account, it is difficult to ascribe the house price bubble either to monetary policy or to the broader economic environment." Ibid., (n. 20), p. 7.

exist between US house prices and capital inflows from emerging markets, which may well have been channelled into US housing and residential construction, and this might provide a better explanation for the rise in US house prices.[23]

What we also know from our history of previous crises is that not all deflating bubbles lead to, or contribute to, economic recessions or depressions. Sometimes a bubble will burst and asset prices deflate over time, or remain flat, and the economic consequences tend to be somewhat benign or inconsequential. Economists often refer to such occurrences as a "soft landing." The corollary to a soft landing is a "hard landing," which by its very nature conjures more severe consequences, often leading to recessions, higher unemployment and bouts of deflation. The severity of the ensuing recession following a deflating asset bubble varies from mild – as is evidenced by the dot-com bubble bursting in early 2000 – to the more severe, such as the Great Depression of the 1930s and the current Great Recession.

It is not known for certain what makes a bubble burst, nor is it clear why some deflating bubbles lead to inconsequential outcomes for the wider economy, whilst others lead to significant, widespread and systemic downturns. The supporters of Keynesian theory have suggested that government intervention can smooth out erratic business cycles through expansionary fiscal policy. Taking this one step further, expansionary monetary policy can also aid in providing additional stimulus to a depressed economy. Supporters of this approach have argued that through expansionary measures the economy can overcome the debilitating effects of a deflating bubble.

As is discussed in Chapter 5, the use of scarce taxpayer funds to prop up or bail out investors, entities and public and private pension funds is not without controversy. Arguments that are used in support of such strategy usually involve considerations of balancing the needs of society on the one hand with the desire to maintain appropriate moral hazard standards on the other. If governments become too liberal in their support of investors and provide full or partial compensation for their current losses, investors can lack sufficient discipline to properly scrutinize future investments. In this sense a hazard is created, because investors could take excessive risks with their investment decisions, comfortable in the knowledge that if an investment does not turn out as they had expected, governments would subsidize any losses they incur.

The ongoing debate as to whether the US Federal Reserve, the US Treasury, or any other governmental authority should step in to bail out distressed entities, or purchase toxic assets from private banks and investors, further contributed to unnecessary delay. Delay, and even inaction, in turn exacerbated the crisis. As is discussed in Chapter 3, the decision by the US Treasury and the US Federal Reserve not to bail out Lehman Brothers was possibly the single largest contributory factor undermining confidence in financial markets.

---

23 Bernanke 2005. The global savings glut and the US current account deficit. Remarks by Governor Ben S. Bernanke at the Sandridge Lecture, Virginia Association of Economics, Richmond, Virginia, 10 March 2005.

Trigger 2: The Collapse of Lehman Brothers and the Global Credit Freeze

The collapse of Lehman Brothers was, in a word, enormous. In the early part of 2000, Lehman Brothers epitomized the Masters of the Universe analogy. The firm appeared to be successful, profitable and engaged in developing and actively participating in innovative financial products and markets. The firm delivered to its clients sophisticated financial solutions and, at the same time, delivered itself significant windfall gains. What was not clear at the time was the inherent build-up of risk the firm was absorbing, a situation most likely made worse by rising asset prices fuelled by low interest rates.

At the time Lehman was on the brink, the US Federal Reserve and the US Department of the Treasury frantically worked on a strategy to prevent the firm from filing for bankruptcy.[24] Part of the strategy involved Barclays Bank in the UK purchasing the net assets of Lehman Brothers; with this buyout Lehman Brothers would avoid filing for bankruptcy. Initially it appeared that Barclays and Lehman had both agreed to the buyout and as a result Lehman would avoid filing for bankruptcy. However, the buyout between Lehman Brothers and Barclays did not occur. It appeared that Barclays was required under UK law to obtain the approval of the market regulator, the Financial Services Authority (FSA). The FSA refused to approve the deal allowing Barclays Bank to acquire Lehman Brothers. According to the Financial Crisis Inquiry, the main stumbling block to the prearranged deal concerned the issue of a guarantee. The Federal Reserve required Barclays to "guarantee Lehman's obligations from the sale until the transaction closed."[25] According to UK law, Barclays was required to seek shareholder approval before it could proceed to acquire Lehman Brothers and provide the necessary guarantee. In any event, the FSA did not want Barclays to take on the guarantee, fearing that Barclays could be burdened with Lehman's debts and future repayment obligations for years to come.

Instead of providing approval for the buyout, the FSA proposed that the US Federal Reserve provide the guarantee as a necessary precondition for the deal to go ahead. With the US Federal Reserve guaranteeing Lehman's future obligations Barclays and, more importantly, Barclays shareholders, would be provided with greater financial certainty regarding Lehman's outstanding obligations. The US Federal Reserve and the US Treasury refused to take on the guarantee. As there was a stalemate between the FSA, the US Federal Reserve and the US Treasury, Lehman was left with no choice but to file for bankruptcy. And file it did.

---

24   The former US Treasury Secretary Henry Paulson (2010a) reveals the frantic conversations and meetings that were held with Barclays in an attempt to put together a rescue package for Lehman Brothers in H.M. Paulson, *On the Brink: Inside the Race to Stop the Collapse of the Global Financial System* (New York: Business Plus 2010), pp. 194–214.

25   Ibid., (n. 5), p. 335.

On 15 September 2008 Lehman Brothers issued a press statement announcing that it intended to file for bankruptcy under Chapter 11 of the United States Bankruptcy Code with the United States Bankruptcy Court for the Southern District of New York.[26] Lehman's bankruptcy was the largest in US corporate history, with estimated debts of over $US600 billion.

Lehman's bankruptcy was felt immediately on stock markets all over the world. The Dow Jones Industrial Index fell by over 500 points in a single day. Similar falls were recorded on bourses all over the world, including in Europe, Asia and Australia. What would be less clear at the time of Lehman's collapse was the effect it would have on credit and debt markets and, in particular, the effect its collapse would have on the availability and supply of credit all over the world.

Almost immediately, from the time Lehman collapsed, credit and debt markets began to seize up. The freezing of credit markets worldwide resulted in devastating consequences in the real economy. What began as isolated events now had systemic implications. As the German Chancellor, Angela Merkel, remarked in early 2009, there was now a vital need to restore trust and confidence in the world's financial markets.[27]

The freezing of credit markets at the beginning of 2009 continued unabated throughout the first half of 2010. The functioning of credit markets was distorted because lenders restricted and in some cases refused to lend money, on the basis that the borrowers might not have the ability to repay their loans. Following the decline in real estate and asset prices, collateral had become next to worthless as banks tightened lending standards. Confronted with the spectre of significant losses, lenders withdrew from credit and debt markets and tightened further their lending standards. This, in turn, restricted lending to many businesses and investors began to panic, bringing a number of businesses, including investment banks and other financial institutions, to the brink of failure.[28]

In a speech delivered in 2009, the US Federal Reserve Chairman, Ben Bernanke, attempted to give proper meaning to the extraordinary events in 2008, including the collapse of Lehman Brothers and its dramatic effect on global markets.[29] Bernanke asked "How should we interpret the extraordinary events

---

26   Lehman Brothers 2008. Press release, 15 September 2008. Lehman Brothers Holdings Inc. Announces it intends to file Chapter 11 Bankruptcy Petition. New York: LBHI.

27   Speaking at a G8 Summit, Angela Merkel commented on the importance of restoring trust and confidence in financial markets. Similar statements were made by other leaders, including Australia's Prime Minster, Kevin Rudd, who described the global financial crisis as a "rolling national security crisis."

28   Bernanke 2009c. On the outlook for the economy and policy. Speech by B.S. Bernanke, Chairman of the Board of Governors of the US Federal Reserve System, delivered at the Economic Club of New York, New York, 16 September 2009.

29   Bernanke 2009d. Reflections on a year in crisis. Speech by B.S. Bernanke, Chairman of the Board of Governors of the US Federal Reserve System, delivered at the

of the past year, particularly the sharp intensification of the financial crisis in September and October?"[30] He essentially answered the question by describing the events as reminiscent of a "classic panic," which can be described as "collectively irrational," but "entirely rational at the individual level."[31] As Bernanke correctly pointed out, the actions are rational at the individual level because "each market participant has a strong incentive to be among the first to the exit."[32]

According to Bernanke, the world's financial markets, including those in the United States, exhibited features of panic. The crisis following Lehman Brothers' collapse led to a freezing of credit markets. Financial markets had become dislocated. Without proper functioning of credit markets, the availability of short-term credit began to dry up. The rapidly reducing supply of credit led to even larger declines in asset prices. As asset prices began to fall, banks were reluctant to lend, which in turn affected short-term liquidity. Hence, a feedback loop had emerged with diminishing available credit and reduced liquidity causing ever-greater declines in asset prices.

Trigger 3: Systemic Market Failure

There is little doubt that the GFC demonstrated significant market failure. This was especially the case at the time of Lehman's collapse. Financial markets all over the world became dislocated. Credit markets were frozen, lenders withdrew funding and tightened lending standards, short-term liquidity dried up and asset prices continued to fall.

There are several strands of market failure that epitomized the GFC. First, there was the initial US and global housing bubble, which resulted in significant house price rises, particularly during the 1990s and up to 2007, culminating in the formation of a formidable bubble. Second, the collapse of Lehman Brothers, as well as other notable collapses (or near collapses) in the United States, including mortgage originators Fannie Mae and Freddie Mac, AIG, Bear Stearns, Washington Mutual, Wachovia Bank and other regional US banks. In the United Kingdom, the collapse of Northern Rock undermined consumer and investor sentiment. In Australia the collapse of Babcock and Brown (the second largest investment bank) and Allco Finance Group (the third largest investment bank) adversely affected market sentiment.

Third, the creation of exotic and opaque financial products, including credit default swaps and CDOs, all continued to make the financial crisis much worse. The markets for these products were largely non-transparent, confusing and perhaps

Federal Reserve Bank of Kansas City's Annual Economic Symposium, Jackson Hole, Wyoming.
30   Ibid., p. 5.
31   Id.
32   Id.

even misleading, especially for ordinary retail investors. Even sophisticated institutional investors fell victim to the complexity of such instruments.[33]

All of these events were evidence of private market failure. Instead of there being an orderly resolution of the deflating housing bubble and associated corporate collapses, investors panicked and markets became dysfunctional and dislocated. The fear that gripped financial and credit markets in September and October 2008 did not demonstrate properly and orderly functioning financial markets. Instead, as Bernanke rightly points out, the markets were panic stricken. Reminiscent of the Great Depression, the so-called "run" had begun with the collapse of Lehman Brothers. Banks on Main Street were now under strain, along with millions of businesses that relied on properly functioning credit markets. Financial and credit markets operated irrationally and soon became dislocated as trust and confidence were replaced in the marketplace with fear and loathing.

Without government intervention, financial and credit markets may have continued on their downward spiral, bringing down with them the entire world economy. The immediate policy response by the US Federal Reserve and the US Treasury, along with governments and central banks in the UK, the EU and elsewhere, would now be crucial in ensuring that the world's major industrialized economies would be protected from systemic risk and contagion and from the spectre of complete collapse.

Trigger 4: Sovereign Debt Risk

As is discussed in Chapter 3, the panic and fear was not limited to the private market or private investment banks. The sovereign debt of a number of countries would become the next formidable issue on the horizon. Countries exposed to large sovereign debt were now also vulnerable to market and investor scrutiny. Nations such as Greece, Ireland, Portugal, Spain and Italy were the next in line to face the fury of the market. Greece's public finances had been in a mess for decades. The country had insufficient tax revenues, a very generous retirement age and pension system, and a bloated and inefficient public service. All of this led to the country borrowing unsustainable amounts of debt to fund its relatively expensive lifestyle.

The catastrophic events on the world's financial and credit markets were soon to engulf vulnerable nations with parlous fiscal positions such as Greece. But Greece was not the only nation struggling with its fiscal imbalances. Ireland also succumbed to its burgeoning public debt and suffered the indignity of having to

---

33   The recently enacted *Dodd–Frank Wall Street Reform and Consumer Protection Act 2010* (Pub.L. 111–203, H.R. 4173) introduced a number of provisions to reform the regulation of swap markets. The newly enacted amendments were introduced in response to collective criticism of OTC Derivatives Markets, including swap markets, credit default swaps and CDOs.

rely on bailout money from the EU. Ireland required in excess of €90 billion from the EU and the IMF to avoid defaulting on its loans and to save its banking sector from complete collapse.

The rising risk of sovereign debt default added a new and dangerous dimension to the ongoing crisis. Already fragile financial markets were now required to adjust to the prospect that the state of fiscal deficits could lead to a renewed bout of panic and fear among bondholders and market participants. The concerns had already spread from Greece to affect other European nations, including Ireland, Portugal, Spain, Italy, Iceland and Belgium. Fearing a repeat of the extraordinary events of September and October 2008, the EU and the IMF acted quickly to implement an unprecedented bailout package, first for Greece, then Ireland and later Portugal.

The EU member states and their institutions, the European Parliament and the European Commission, along with the International Monetary Fund were concerned that left unchecked, the sovereign debt risk of Greece, Ireland and Portugal could develop into widespread systemic risk and lead to a run on the euro. Not only would European currency and financial markets be adversely affected but contagion risk could also spill over, to undermine the world's financial and currency markets.

Trigger 5: Opaque Financial Markets

As is discussed in Chapter 4, the world's financial markets also played an important contributing role in the current crisis. Arguably, the evidence tends to suggest that the build-up in inherent risk in the US and global housing bubble was a major factor which led to the crisis in the first place. However, the housing bubble alone did not solely cause the widespread systemic panic in financial markets in 2008. The creation of exotic and complex financial instruments caused confusion among investors who had purchased billions of dollars of securitized residential mortgage securities that were now worthless.

Advances in financial engineering and innovation in the lead-up to the global financial crisis GFC saw the creation of new and complex financial products, including the credit default swap and the CDO. These two instruments alone allowed what might have been an otherwise unremarkable deflating housing bubble to become a truly global and devastating event. As the housing bubble began to deflate in the United States, the inherent build-up of risk had already been exported to investors, banks, investment funds, municipal authorities and pension funds all over the world. Investors in CDOs had unwittingly purchased a piece of the American housing nightmare. The purchasers and holders of the credit default swaps, CDOs and other exotic financial derivative products had little knowledge of their current financial exposures and were certainly not acutely aware of their future obligations.

All of this had been effectively covered up by the rising valuations of asset and stock prices in the period immediately preceding the crisis. The extent of the distrust in credit and equity markets following the collapse of Lehman Brothers was now evident in bondholders and investors who requested guarantees before purchasing any more securitized structured financial products. The guarantee sought by bondholders and investors in financial markets was essentially an indemnity from any future losses flowing from the fallout of the now fast-deflating global housing bubble.

The toxic residential mortgage-backed securities, which had their genesis in financial markets in the United States, had been re-engineered, repackaged and even relabeled, and exported to investors all over the world. Now investors and bondholders sought guarantees for protection against future unidentifiable losses. As is discussed in Chapter 5, the request for an indemnity to be supplied by taxpayers for future losses was contentious to say the least. Never in the history of modern capitalism could investors and bondholders receive such a blanket guarantee in the absence of fraud or misleading or deceptive conduct. Even when fraud was involved, civil redress was normally a private affair, involving the aggrieved party commencing civil action against the alleged perpetrator.[34]

Governments all over the world were left to pick up the pieces of yet another devastating and bursting bubble. This time the bubble had widespread systemic consequences flowing to international financial markets. The widespread use of structured financial instruments, which had been created on the back of rising house prices, spread default risk all over the world.

Although governments were willing to provide a limited guarantee to retail investors for their bank deposits, which also included a wholesale guarantee to banks to participate in global credit and debt markets, there would be no further indemnity provided to individual market participants holding toxic assets. Instead, only through the Troubled Asset Relief Program (TARP) did the US government offer institutions the ability to offload the toxic assets they had stored on their balance sheets.[35]

---

34 A good recent example of this point is the Bernie Madoff affair, where US prosecutors prosecuted Bernie Madoff for operating the world's largest ponzi scheme involving over $US60 billion in defrauded client accounts. Madoff pleaded guilty to the securities fraud and was imprisoned for 150 years. The ponzi scheme that Madoff operated left a number of investors with devastating losses and a trustee which sought to recover assets from the Madoff estate.

35 US TARP was established by the Bush Administration and the US Treasury through the enactment of the *Emergency Economic Stabilization Act of 2008* (P.L. 110–343; H.R.1424). TARP provided up to $US700 billion to be used to purchase toxic or troubled sub-prime mortgage-related assets from US financial institutions, including Freddie Mac and Fannie Mae. The Act provides a wide mandate for the US Treasury to purchase toxic assets, however they are defined, so as to ensure US economic stability is not jeopardized. Under TARP the Treasury can use funds to purchase toxic assets in a graduated roll-out involving three tranches: (1) $US250 billion at any one time; (2) $US350 billion at any one time, provided there is Presidential certification to Congress; (3) $US700 billion at any one

As Bernanke pointed out, TARP illustrated a useful and valuable policy response by the US government to stabilize a US economy suffering from the destabilizing effects of toxic mortgage- related assets. In addition to TARP, the US Federal Reserve was also active in providing additional liquidity to financial markets in an attempt to stabilize money markets, including the commercial paper market.[36] The US Federal Reserve had also become active in coordinating policy responses at the international level.[37]

As is discussed in Chapter 4, the Over-the-Counter (OTC) swaps markets had been heavily criticized for its opaqueness and non-transparency. OTC derivatives markets had routinely been blamed in the past for a number of financial crises, largely because the markets were not centrally cleared or settled. Instead, most OTC derivatives markets were bilaterally cleared between two or more counterparties. Concentration of market activity among a relatively small number of financial intermediaries, broker–dealers and sophisticated investors added to the mystique and suspicion of OTC derivatives markets.

In contrast to exchange-traded markets, including securities and futures markets, OTC derivatives markets in the United States were not subject to the same regulation and supervisory oversight by regulatory agencies. Further, OTC derivatives were largely transacted between sophisticated market participants and hence were not subject to consumer or retail investor protection provisions that were written into US securities and commodity futures laws.

Swaps and other OTC financial instruments could be re-engineered so that the inherent risk of the financial instrument would be recalibrated. This meant that the holder of the instrument would not fully understand or appreciate the precise level of risk exposure the investor had acquired. Obligations under an OTC derivatives agreement such as a swap could also run for a number of years, creating further confusion and uncertainty. This was especially the case if the initial swaps agreement began to unravel or, alternatively, counterparty defaults occurred during the life of the agreement.[38]

---

time, on condition that there is an approved plan provided by the President to Congress: *Emergency Economic Stabilization Act of 2008* (P.L. 110–343; H.R.1424): sec. 115.

36   As Bernanke states, on 19 September 2008 the US Federal Reserve announced the creation of a Commercial Paper Funding Facility, which had as one of its key objectives the stabilization of money market mutual funds. B.S. Bernanke. Ibid., (n. 18), p. 3.

37   The US Federal Reserve with the European Central Bank, the Swiss National Bank and other central banks established temporary swap lines to assist liquidity in the short-term money market. The Federal Reserve further reduced interest rates in a coordinated move with other central banks in October 2008. B.S. Bernanke. Ibid., (n. 28), p. 3.

38   Bernanke acknowledged that OTC derivatives clearing and settlement practices were severely inadequate. The complexity and opaqueness of a number of derivatives products also proved problematic, as "financial firms sometimes found it quite difficult to fully assess their own net derivatives exposures or to communicate to counterparties and regulators the nature and extent of those exposures." Bernanke 2010c. Statement of Ben S.

The report of the Financial Crisis Inquiry Commission also concluded that OTC derivatives markets had contributed significantly to making the financial crisis much worse than might otherwise have been the case.[39] According to the Commission's findings, OTC derivatives markets contributed to the GFC in three main ways. First, the use of credit default swaps added fuel to an already overheated housing bubble in the United States. Through the use of financial instruments such as credit default swaps, additional liquidity and leverage had been introduced into financial markets, allowing borrowers and other market participants access to short-term credit. Easy credit conditions, in turn, were channelled into an already inflated housing bubble.[40]

Second, OTC derivatives markets had become vehicles to develop and re-engineer exotic or synthetic derivatives, which included the synthetic credit default swap. The main use of these exotic derivatives was essentially to provide purchasers with additional leveraged bets on the US housing bubble.[41] Third, the Commission was of the view that when the US housing bubble popped, OTC derivatives "were in the centre of the storm."[42]

As is discussed in Chapters 4 and 5, the GFC led to calls for significant reforms to be made to the way financial markets were regulated. The recent reforms in the United States have introduced regulation into the previously unregulated swaps markets. Many of the reforms have concentrated on improving transparency, settlement and clearing processes, and financial reporting of outstanding liabilities with OTC derivatives.[43] In addition to OTC derivatives markets, a number of reforms were also introduced to improve market transparency and investor and consumer protection[44] for market participants involved with the trading of

Bernanke, Chairman of the Board of Governors of the Federal Reserve System before the Financial Crisis Inquiry Commission, Washington, DC, 2 September 2010, p. 11.

39   Financial Crisis Inquiry Commission of the United States 2011. Final Report of the National Commission on the Causes of the Financial and Economic Crisis in the United States. Washington D.C.: G.P.O., p. xxiv.

40   According to the Financial Crisis Inquiry Commission, almost $US79 billion was channelled into AIG alone; it was then redirected to borrowers for additional loans, utilizing housing as collateral. Ibid., (n. 39), p. xxiv.

41   The Financial Crisis Inquiry Commission revealed that Goldman Sachs sold over $US73 billion in synthetic derivatives such as credit default swaps in the three years between 2004 and 2007. Ibid., (n. 39), p. xxv.

42   Ibid., (n. 39), p. xxv.

43   The *Dodd-Frank Wall Street Reform and Consumer Act 2010* (Pub.L. 111–203, H.R. 4173) (hereinafter called "the *Dodd-Frank Act 2010*" introduced a number of key reforms to swaps markets regulation and the regulation of security-based swap markets, as well as reforms to the payment, clearing and settlement supervision of OTC financial derivatives. A more detailed discussion of these reforms is presented in Chapter 4.

44   See Title X of the *Dodd-Frank Act 2010*, which provides for the establishment of a bureau of consumer financial protection designed to provide additional and new protective measures for consumers of financial products and financial instruments, including mortgages

securities.[45] The regulatory reforms have also introduced regulation of hedge fund advisers,[46] implemented new standards for corporate governance,[47] accountability and executive compensation,[48] and introduced restrictions on proprietary trading by financial institutions.[49]

Trigger 6: Ineffective Market Regulation

Not all bubbles will produce widespread, systemic and devastating consequences on the scale of the GFC. Understanding and providing a rational explanation as to why the global and US housing bubbles contributed to a significant deterioration in the world's financial markets has recently been the subject of enquiry and investigation.

A number of enquiries have concluded that financial markets played a significant part in the current crisis.[50] Credit markets froze, market participants panicked and OTC derivatives markets were used as an additional source of fuel to fan the flames of an already raging financial fire. Households had become considerably indebted as investors participated in one of the largest housing bubbles the world has ever seen. Sovereign risk for a number of countries rose as fiscal discipline was abandoned and replaced with lower taxes and higher expenditure by governments. Markets became dislocated and ceased to function properly and market discipline and order were replaced by panic and fear.

There is much force in the argument that all these events were probably all that was required to engineer one of the most spectacular financial catastrophes since the Great Depression. However, just as in the Great Depression, there was

---

and loans. Consumer protection measures, particularly for consumers of financial products such as housing loans, private loans and credit card debts, had been left largely void because many of the credit providers had been operating in the shadow banking system, which was largely unregulated by US Federal authorities.

45   The *Dodd-Frank Act 2010* introduced a number of additional protections for investors involved in trading securities in US securities markets. These reforms were aimed at providing greater protection to investors, including whistleblower protection (see section 922), enhanced application of anti-fraud provisions (see section 929L) and improvements in the asset-backed securitization process (see sections 941–46).

46   See sections 401–16 of the *Dodd-Frank Act 2010*.

47   See sections 971 and 972 of the *Dodd-Frank Act 2010*.

48   See sections 951–57 of the *Dodd-Frank Act 2010*.

49   See section 989 of the *Dodd-Frank Act 2010*, which provides for the Government Accountability Office to undertake a study to investigate inter alia whether proprietary trading presents a "material systemic risk to the stability of the United States financial markets, and if so, the costs and benefits of options for mitigating such systemic risk."

50   See, for example, the Financial Crisis Inquiry Report which concluded that deregulation in financial markets had contributed to lax standards and a build-up of excessive risk in the US. Ibid., (n. 5), pp. 52–6; pp. 59–61; pp. 64–6.

another important factor warranting further inquiry. The role government played in regulating financial markets and managing the crisis after the GFC took hold is pivotal in providing a comprehensive understanding of the current crisis.

The absence of effective regulation in providing sound, safe and robust financial markets is often cited as another major contributing factor of the GFC. The Financial Crisis Inquiry Commission was even more scathing of the role of regulation in contributing to the crisis. The Commission concluded that the "government was ill prepared for the crisis."[51] However, the Commission did appreciate the efforts made by the key market regulators in attempting to stabilize the economy and world financial markets under the most trying of circumstances.[52]

In testimony provided before the Financial Crisis Inquiry Commission, the current US Treasury Secretary Timothy Geithner acknowledged the limitations of the current regulatory and supervisory framework in the United States. As Geithner points out, "this regulatory system did not evolve to keep pace with growth and innovations in our financial services industry."[53] The limitations and constraints that existed in financial markets regulation and supervisory oversight in the United States appeared to severely undermine and restrict the ability and capacity of the regulatory framework to prevent the crisis in the first place. Moreover, these constraints adversely affected the government's ability to properly manage the crisis once it took hold.

The US Treasury Secretary provides one possible explanation as to why the regulatory framework failed so spectacularly in the GFC. According to Geithner, the US was operating a parallel banking system, which was largely unregulated, side by side with the standard banking system, which is subject to a high level of regulation.[54] The parallel banking system is often called the "shadow" banking system. But as Geithner correctly points out, the parallel system was not hidden from view; it operated in "broad daylight and [was] financed by sophisticated institutional investors with bonds issued under the disclosures and protections of the securities laws."[55]

The parallel banking system has been largely unregulated and, unlike the "official" banking system, was not subjected to proper supervisory oversight by any of the key market regulators or government agencies. The lack of supervision of the parallel banking system begs the obvious question: Why was there a lack

---

51   Financial Crisis Inquiry Commission Report. Ibid. (n. 5), p. xxi.

52   The Financial Crisis Commission praised the efforts of former US Treasury Secretary Henry Paulson, US Federal Reserve Chairman Ben Bernanke and the new US Treasury Secretary, Timothy Geithner, in attempting to stabilize the US financial system and economy. Ibid., (n. 5), pp. xxi–xxii.

53   T.F. Geithner, Testimony before the Financial Crisis Inquiry Commission, Causes of the financial crisis and the case for reform, 6 May 2010. Press Centre, US Department of the Treasury.

54   Ibid., p. 3.

55   Ibid.

of government regulation and supervisory oversight of the parallel system? The answer, according to Geithner, was that in the case of the parallel system, "no regulator or supervisor had the legal authority to look across the financial system and take action to prevent the diversion of activity away from regulation."[56]

Hence, there was no regulation of the parallel system because insufficient legal authority was given to federal regulators. The lack of authority for regulators and prudential supervisors created the necessary incentive and environment for the private market to create the parallel system, which coexisted with the much more highly regulated official system. The build-up of risk in the parallel and unregulated system exposed the structural weaknesses that existed in financial markets in the United States. Not only were the weaknesses exposed but also the entire regulatory and supervisory system may have been undermined because of the build-up of risk in the parallel system, which later spilled over into the conventional banking sector during the global crisis.[57]

The solution, according to Geithner, was obvious. There needed to be reform of financial markets regulation with the aim of enhancing and improving supervisory oversight of the shadow banking system.[58] Only by doing this could the US, and perhaps the world, avoid a repeat of the GFC. Importantly, reform was also required to enhance consumer protection, particularly for consumers of financial products such as mortgage loans, private loans and credit card debts. This was because many consumers who obtained their loans from credit providers operated in the shadow banking system. Consumers of the loans that had originated in the shadow banking system did not receive the protections afforded to consumers who had obtained loans from regulated banks.[59]

The parallel banking system theory also drew support from the former US Treasury Secretary, Henry Paulson, when he testified before the Financial Crisis Inquiry Commission. According to Paulson, the shadow banking system and the traditional banking system had both failed to keep pace with advances in financial innovation and both systems had now become "archaic and outmoded."[60]

---

56   Ibid.

57   Geithner was acutely aware that if market regulators had had the legal authority to properly regulate the parallel system, the build-up of risk that had occurred in the parallel system might have been avoided in the first place. Ibid., (n. 53), p. 4.

58   Ibid.

59   The deficiencies in consumer protection for consumers of loans, mortgages and other credit was recognized in the *Dodd-Frank Act 2010*. As is discussed in Chapter 7, the *Dodd-Frank Act* introduced a number of provisions designed to enhance consumer protection measures for consumers who participated in the shadow banking system. Importantly, the *Dodd-Frank Act 2010* introduced a new Bureau of Consumer Financial Protection (see Title X of the Act). The new Bureau has broad powers to investigate breaches, including unfair, deceptive, or abusive acts or practices by any credit provider (Section 1031).

60   Paulson 2010b (Testimony by Henry M. Paulson Jr, before the Financial Crisis Inquiry Commission, US Government, 6 May 2010), p. 3.

Former US Federal Reserve Chairman Alan Greenspan also provided a sobering assessment of the regulatory framework in the United States. According to Greenspan, even with market failure and the associated breakdown in private risk management and private counterparty surveillance, the financial system would still have managed to function effectively provided there was an effective regulatory framework.[61]

However, the regulatory system in the US did not hold up as well as it probably should have, and it effectively became comprised when investor panic took over following the collapse of Lehman Brothers. According to Greenspan, regulators had not properly appreciated the fallout from Lehman's collapse.[62] This was primarily due to the fact that for decades, insufficient financial data was available to regulators to enable them to make a proper and informed assessment of any major failure.[63] In other words, federal regulators had not properly quantified the tail risks associated with the collapse of a large and interconnected firm such as Lehman Brothers.

Hence, US regulators were handicapped by a parallel banking system which had been largely unregulated and allowed to operate outside the normal regulatory and supervisory framework that applied to the traditional banking system. Moreover, regulators were placed further behind the eight ball with an outdated regulatory framework, which relied too heavily on limited, inadequate and out-of-date financial data. Regulators could not make any meaningful assessment of any potential fallout from a major default such as Lehman Brothers. Instead, regulators were constrained in making a proper assessment because the financial intelligence they had received was unreliable.[64]

Regulators and government agencies in the United States, as well as other parts of the world, had also been grappling with the spread of systemic risk associated with a large-scale collapse. The potential spread of systemic risk throughout the financial system served to highlight the limitations and challenges associated with the regulatory framework, which had been compromised by the largely

---

61 Greenspan 2010b (Testimony of Alan Greenspan before the Financial Crisis Inquiry Commission, Causes of the Financial Crisis and the Case for Reform, 7 April 2010, at Stanford Law School, Stanford, CT), p. 8.

62 Greenspan stated in his testimony before the Financial Crisis Inquiry Commission, "The risk management paradigm nonetheless harboured a fatal flaw. In the growing state of euphoria, managers at financial institutions, along with regulators including but not limited to the Federal Reserve, failed to fully comprehend the underlying risk, length, and potential impact of the so-called negative tail of the distribution of risk outcomes that was about to be revealed as the post-Lehman Brothers crisis played out." Ibid., (n. 61), p. 7.

63 Greenspan stated that "for decades, with little or no data, almost all analysts, in my experience, had conjectured a far more limited tail risk." Ibid., (n. 16), p. 7.

64 This was confirmed by the Financial Crisis Inquiry Commission, which revealed that "just a month before Lehman's collapse, the Federal Reserve Bank of New York was still seeking information on the exposures created by Lehman's more than 900,000 derivatives contracts." Ibid., (n. 5), p. xxi.

unregulated shadow banking system.[65] The shortcomings that were evident with regulatory frameworks in not adequately managing the crisis were not limited to the United States. Weaknesses also existed with frameworks in continental Europe, the United Kingdom, Iceland, Ireland and South East Asia.

Bernanke was also of the view that a number of regulatory gaps existed with regulation of the financial and banking sectors in the United States.[66] One such gap was the emergence of the shadow banking system which operated parallel to and in competition with the traditional banking system. The largely unregulated shadow banking system did have some market-based controls, including reputation and branding and market pricing. However, these measures proved to be insufficient to prevent and manage the build-up of systemic risk which occurred with non-regulated shadow banks, hedge funds and mortgage originators, some of which operated as special purpose vehicles.[67]

Bernanke identified another important limitation with financial markets regulation and the supervisory framework in the United States and elsewhere.[68] According to Bernanke, financial markets regulation and prudential supervision did not provide sufficient focus on the central issue of systemic risk.[69] Instead, regulatory and supervisory frameworks were more likely to enforce measures aimed at promoting market integrity, but ignore, or give little weight to the issue of financial stability.

The lack of macro prudential focus of the statutory regulatory framework represents a fundamental weakness in providing effective regulation of financial markets, particularly in times of extreme volatility and market stress. If regulation is not focused on preventing or managing systemic risk or promoting financial stability, financial markets may well be vulnerable to a sharp and sudden downturn.

Conclusion

The triggers of the GFC are not definitive and are still the subject of ongoing debate. However, it would appear that the contributing factors discussed in this

---

65   See, for example, Cox 2010: Testimony of Christopher Cox, former Chairman of the US Securities and Exchange Commission before the Financial Crisis Inquiry Commission, May 5, 2010, in which the former chairman stated that "The shadow banking system helped to spread this contagion to institutions in every sector – from commercial banks and thrifts such as Wachovia, Washington Mutual, and Indy Mac, to investment banks such as Bear Stearns and Lehman Brothers, to the government-sponsored enterprises Fannie Mae and Freddie Mac, as well as the nation's largest insurance company."

66   Bernanke 2010c (Statement of Ben Bernanke, Chairman of the Board of Governors of the Federal Reserve System before the Financial Crisis Inquiry Commission, Washington, DC, 2 September 2010), p. 12.

67   Ibid., pp. 12–13.

68   Ibid., p. 13.

69   Ibid.

chapter have shed some light on the issue. What has been clear is that the GFC produced devastating consequences for the real economy, and revealed severe shortcomings with the functioning of the market, as well as regulation.

There is little doubt that the US and global housing bubbles played a significant part in the creation of the GFC. The bubbles induced a significant number of investors, homeowners and consumers to take out large loans, which became unaffordable when interest rates were reset higher from honeymoon rates. When the bubble popped and the sub-prime mortgage crisis took hold, the seeds were sown for a major catastrophe. That calamity occurred with the corporate collapses of Bear Stearns, Indy Mac, Wachovia, Washington Mutual and Lehman Brothers, and the mortgage originators Freddie Mac and Fannie Mae.

As history has shown, federal regulators did not appreciate the full extent of the fallout from the collapse of Lehman Brothers. This had a lot to do with the structural weaknesses in the regulatory framework and with regulators who relied upon inadequate financial data and modeling. Inaccurate financial information led to mistakes being made and insufficient appreciation of the tail risks associated with the collapse of Lehman Brothers.

With the emergence of a shadow banking system that was largely unregulated and operated in parallel and in competition with the traditional banking sector, regulatory authorities were constrained in what they could do. As the run commenced in the shadow banking system, the traditional banking sector was soon infected with the fallout from the housing virus. Now both the shadow banking system and the traditional banking sector were at the mercy of investors and nervous bondholders.

As the panic and fear set in, the regulatory framework that was supposed to provide protection and promote stability became exposed. Financial markets did not help to restore market order, since investors and bondholders lost trust and confidence in their everyday dealings. All of the limitations came together to form the perfect storm. The shadow banking system and traditional banking sector were placed under extraordinary stress following the collapse of Lehman Brothers. Regulators failed to properly quantify and assess the tail risks associated with a large-scale collapse, whilst investors and bondholders exercised their legal and financial rights in cutting their losses and running away from the now bursting housing bubble.

Chapter 3

The Crisis Goes Global

Introduction

The GFC has already proved itself a truly global and historic event. Although its genesis may well have been the US housing bubble, the GFC affected both developed and emerging nations. The crisis did not discriminate on any basis. Put simply, the consequences of the crisis have been devastating. The GFC has been responsible for destroying financial systems and government budgets, undermining market confidence and security in financial markets, and ushering in one of the most severe recessions since the Great Depression.

The GFC destroyed economic growth and real wealth. Unemployment rose to double-digit proportions in the United Sates and parts of Europe. Worldwide industrial production plummeted, bankruptcies rose and deflation began to take hold. The credit crisis that led to a freezing of short-term credit in money markets led to further home foreclosures and corporate collapses in the United States. The damage was not limited to the United States but spread to other parts of the world. The collapse of investment banks in the United Kingdom and Australia began to take their toll on investor sentiment, which was reflected in substantial falls in equity markets.

Banks and thrifts (retail deposit-taking institutions) also collapsed as the crisis moved from the shadow banking system and the sub-prime mortgage market to the mainstream banking sector. In the United States, mortgage originators Freddie Mac and Fannie Mae defaulted and required immediate government assistance to prevent their complete demise. Global investment banks Bear Stearns and Lehman Brothers collapsed under the weight of debt and investor uncertainty. Banks and thrifts, including the Wachovia Corporation, AIG and the Washington Mutual, all suffered a similar fate and were acquired by other major banks for a fraction of their previous market values.

The story of collapse, demise and rationalization was repeated in other developed countries, including the United Kingdom, Australia, Iceland, Ireland, Spain and Portugal. Neither were emerging economies spared the effects of the GFC, nor nations with large sovereign debt risk such as Ireland, Greece and Portugal. All of these events served to highlight the destructive nature of the global crisis.

The United States

US Sub-prime Mortgages: Freddie Mac and Fannie Mae

The United States was the epicentre of the GFC and the genesis of the crisis. Sub-prime mortgages that were sold to unsuspecting consumers were later repackaged and relabelled as "investments," and sold to investors through the use of OTC swaps and synthetic derivatives. Sub-prime mortgages largely operated in the shadow banking system, with credit providers supplying mortgages to consumers who could ill afford the repayments. The sub-prime loans were essentially non-recourse, which meant that consumers could literally walk away from their mortgage by simply allowing the mortgagor to foreclose on the borrower's home when the borrower fell behind with repayments.

Once defaults began, the house of cards that had been built on the sub-prime fault line began to unravel. Corporate collapses followed soon thereafter. At first, the giant mortgage originators Freddie Mac and Fannie Mae collapsed. These two entities alone accounted for over $US2 trillion worth of mortgages. Both Freddie Mac and Fannie Mae were highly active in the sub-prime mortgage market. As Wall Street investment banks began selling sub-prime mortgage-backed securities, Freddie Mac and Fannie Mae, along with other investors, were highly active in the market, purchasing billions of dollars of mortgages.[1]

Both Freddie Mac and Fannie Mae were no strangers to controversy. In 2007, following an investigation by the US Securities and Exchange Commission (SEC), Freddie Mac[2] agreed to pay a $US50 million penalty for alleged securities fraud and related alleged violations in connection with misstating earnings,[3] including alleged accounting irregularities.[4] According to the SEC, the alleged securities

---

1   According to testimony provided to the Financial Crisis Inquiry Commission, Wall Street investment banks increased sales of sub-prime mortgages from $US87 billion in 2001 to $US465 billion in 2005. See Financial Crisis Inquiry Commission 2011 (Final Report of the National Commission on the Causes of the Financial and Economic Crisis in the United States. Washington, DC: G.P.O.), p. 123.

2   In the settlement, both the SEC and Freddie Mac agreed, without admitting or denying the allegations, to enter into final judgment.

3   The SEC complaint alleged that "Freddie Mac engaged in a fraudulent scheme that deceived investors about its true performance, profitability, and growth trends. According to the complaint, Freddie Mac misreported its net income in 2000, 2001 and 2002 by 30.5%, 23.9% and 42.5%, respectively. Furthermore, Freddie Mac's senior management exerted consistent pressure to have the company report smooth and dependable earnings growth in order to present investors with the image of a company that would continue to generate predictable and growing earnings." US Securities and Exchange Commission 2007. Freddie Mac, four former executives settle SEC action relating to multi-billion dollar accounting fraud. Press release, 28 September 2007). Available at: <http://www.sec.gov/news/press/2007/2007-205.htm>.

4   Following the investigations into Freddie Mac by the SEC, the corporate regulator alleged that Freddie Mac had engaged in violations in the implementation of accounting

violations were a direct result of a corporate culture at Freddie Mac "that placed emphasis on steady earnings, and a senior management that fostered a corporate image that was touted as 'Steady Eddy' to the marketplace."[5]

Further, The US Financial Crisis Inquiry Commission reported that the Office of Federal Housing Enterprise Oversight (OFHEO) had also called Fannie Mae into question for alleged violations and accounting irregularities.[6] The OFHEO prepared a very detailed report into an investigation that it had initiated into the earnings announcements made by Fannie Mae and filed with the SEC between 1998 and 2003.[7]

According to the specially commissioned report, "a large number of Fannie Mae's accounting policies and practices did not comply with General Accepted Accounting Principles (GAPP)."[8] Further, the OFHEO report found that "the Enterprise also had serious problems of internal control, financial reporting, and corporate governance."[9] The OFHEO also reported that Fannie Mae had taken on significant risk related directly to its operations and reputation.[10] The build-up in risk, in turn, ultimately weakened both entities and exposed shareholders and taxpayers to considerable financial losses at the time of their collapse.

Banks and Thrifts: Wachovia and Washington Mutual

The demise of US banks Wachovia and Washington Mutual also served to highlight the damage brought about by the GFC. The liquidity crisis that emerged from the collapse of Lehman Brothers in September 2008 led to a funding crisis for both Wachovia and Washington Mutual Bank. Both banks were exposed to the toxic assets resulting from the acquisition and supply of sub-prime mortgages to its retail borrowers. In the final week of September 2008, both banks experienced a run on their deposits from anxious customers who were concerned about their potential collapse.

---

standard SFAS 133, which relates to accounting for derivatives instruments and hedging activities. These alleged accounting irregularities included: "the improper change in valuing the company's 'swaptions' portfolio at year-end 2000; the improper use of derivatives to shift earnings between periods; the improper use of a reserve in connection with the company's application of SFAS 91; the use of certain transactions to nullify the effects of an accounting pronouncement known as Emerging Issues Task Force Issue 99–20; and the maintenance and reporting of a reserve for losses on loans materially in excess of probable losses." Ibid., pp. 1–2.

5   Ibid., p. 1.
6   Ibid., (n. 1), p. 122.
7   Office of Federal Housing Enterprise Oversight 2006. Report of the Special Examination of Fannie Mae, May 2006. Available at: <http://www.fhfa.gov/webfiles/747/FNMSPECIALEXAM.pdf>.
8   Ibid., Summary of the Report of the Special Examination of Fannie Mae.
9   Ibid.
10   According to the OFHEO, Fannie Mae "consistently took a significant amount of interest rate risk and, when interest rates fell in 2002, incurred billions of dollars in economic losses." Ibid.

Wachovia and Washington Mutual were also placed under additional liquidity stress when their unsecured and secured borrowing capacity was further restricted.[11] Market conditions for both banks deteriorated when investors and bondholders withdrew their support in financial markets, which led to considerable falls in their market value. The falls in the value of their securities led to a corresponding rise in their credit default swaps as lenders demanded higher returns for the banks' higher expected risk.[12] Meanwhile overnight funds and counterparties involved in short-term money markets and OTC swap markets demanded greater collateralization from both banks before they would resume lending.[13]

On 25 September 2008 Washington Mutual closed its doors. The FDIC organized a transfer of Washington Mutual's retail deposit book, including its other assets, to JP Morgan Chase.[14] On 26 September 2008 Wachovia approached the Federal Deposit Insurance Corporation (FDIC), claiming that it was unable to secure additional liquidity from the short-term money market to operate its business or loan book. The FDIC approached the US Treasury, requesting authorization for the FDIC to provide assistance to Citigroup, in order to enable Citigroup to purchase the net assets of Wachovia.[15] The terms of the sale of Wachovia's assets and its branches required Citigroup to provide an asset guarantee. The asset guarantee required Citigroup to cover $42 billion in initial losses and the FDIC to cover for any further losses beyond that amount.[16]

The collapse and subsequent asset transfers of both Wachovia and Washington Mutual underscore the gravity and systemic ramifications flowing from the GFC. Both banks were victims of the liquidity crisis that existed in short-term money markets. The GFC had now become systemic, moving initially from the US sub-prime mortgage market to infect the broader US financial sector, claiming mainstream banks as its new victims.

---

11   See Bair 2010 (Statement of Sheila C. Bair, Chairman of Federal Deposit Insurance Corporation on "Systemically important institution and the issue of too big to fail" before the Financial Crisis Inquiry Commission, 2 September 2010), p. 5.

12   According to Bair, a number of counterparties and money market fund operators declined to advance any further money to Wachovia. Ibid., p. 6.

13   Bair states that "on the evening of Thursday, 25 September, two regular counterparties refused to lend to Wachovia." Ibid., (n. 8).

14   According to Bair, the transfer took only one day and involved over 2,300 branches. Ibid., (n. 8). A remarkable achievement given the size and complexity of Washington Mutual's assets and retail deposit book.

15   Bair, Ibid., (n. 11), p. 9.

16   Id. According to Bair, "while the aggregate losses on these assets were projected by FDIC staff to range between $35 billion to $52 billion" losses falling within that range would have resulted in no loss to the FDIC.

Investment Banks: Bear Stearns, AIG and Lehman Brothers

Bear Stearns was a global investment bank with its headquarters in New York. Founders Joseph Bear, Robert Stearns and Harold Meyer established the bank in 1923. Bear Stearns survived the Great Crash on Wall Street in 1929 and the Great Depression in the 1930s and became a global giant in merchant and investment banking in the 1980s and 1990s.

At the beginning of 2002 Bear Stearns became an active participant in the securitization of sub-prime mortgages. All appeared to be well for a while, as US house prices continued to rise and investors poured more of their capital into residential mortgages. However, like Lehman Brothers, Bear Stearns began to suffer a liquidity crisis in 2007. At the time the US bubble popped, investors, bondholders and counterparties in Bear Stearns became nervous and began to demand greater collateralization from the investment bank, threatening to restrict lending if their demands were not met. Swap spreads on Bear Stearns' debt began to rise as concerns were raised that the investment bank would not have sufficient liquid assets to repay creditors in the case of default.

With heightened default risk, creditors demanded greater security as well as higher returns on the firm's credit default swaps in OTC markets. Bear Stearns held vast sums of toxic sub-prime mortgages, which ran into billions of dollars. As the markets became nervous of sub-prime mortgages following the housing bubble meltdown, investors turned their focus to firms, which held potentially large write-downs of toxic assets.

In March 2008, Bear Stearns began to feel the acute pressure of the short-term money markets, with credit default swap spreads rising sharply. Its short-term liquidity position also deteriorated as the firm's counterparties withdrew or restricted the provision of credit lines. Bear Stearns approached the Federal Reserve Bank of New York (FRBNY) for assistance. On 16 March 2008 the FRBNY released a statement,[17] announcing that it would establish a Primary Dealer Credit Facility (PDCF),[18] which was "intended to improve the ability of primary dealers to provide financing to participants in securitization markets and promote the orderly functioning of financial markets more generally."[19]

Under the facility, announced on 24 March 2008, the FRBYN provided short-term financing to JP Morgan Chase for the purpose of facilitating JP Morgan's

---

17   Federal Reserve Bank of New York 2008a. Press release, 16 March: Federal Reserve Announces Establishment of Primary Dealer Credit Facility. Available at: <http://www.newyorkfed.org/newsevents/news/markets/2008/rp080316.html>.

18   According to the FRBNY, the facility was designed to provide short-term overnight funding to primary dealers. The funding was to be provided in exchange "for a specified range of collateral, including all collateral eligible for tri-party repurchase agreements arranged by the FRBNY, as well as investment-grade corporate securities, municipal securities, mortgage-backed securities and asset-backed securities." Ibid.

19   Ibid.

purchase of Bear Stearns. The FRBYN would acquire a portfolio of assets from Bear Stearns valued at $US30 billion and the portfolio would be used as collateral to secure $US29 billion in short-term financing. Under the proposed acquisition agreement between J.P. Morgan and Bear Stearns and facilitated by the New York Federal Reserve, J.P. Morgan would absorb the first $US1 billion of any losses associated with the portfolio of Bear Stearns assets and any realized gains would accrue to the New York Fed. The portfolio of Bear Stearns assets, which included the toxic sub-prime mortgage-backed securities, would be managed by BlackRock Financial Management under strict guidelines administered by the FRBYN.[20]

American International Group (AIG) was another global financial, investment and insurance giant which would have suffered a similar fate to Bear Stearns had it not had assistance from the Federal Reserve Bank of New York. From about late August to early September 2008, the FRBNY considered that AIG's short-term liquidity position had deteriorated as a result of volatile market conditions. The FRBNY quickly decided to act and on 16 September 2008 the US Federal Reserve announced that with the support of the US Treasury, the FRBNY would lend $US85 billion to AIG.[21] The loan would be secured against assets belonging to AIG so as to provide protection to the US government and the American taxpayers in the case of any default by AIG.[22]

According to the Federal Reserve, the loan to AIG was necessary given the current circumstances, and to avoid "a disorderly failure of AIG, which could add to already significant levels of market fragility and lead to substantially higher borrowing costs, reduced household wealth, and materially weaker economic performance."[23]

On 23 September 2008 AIG signed the loan agreement with the Federal Reserve Bank of New York to obtain access to the $US85 billion credit facility. The terms of the agreement allowed AIG access to the credit facility for a two-year period and interest would be at the LIBOR rate plus an additional 850 basis

20   Federal Reserve Bank of New York 2008d. Press release, 24 March 2008. Statement on financing arrangement of J.P. Morgan Chase's acquisition of Bear Stearns. Available at: <http://www.newyorkfed.org/newsevents/news/markets/2008/rp080324.html>.

21   Board of Governors of the Federal Reserve System 2008e. Press release, 16 September 2008. Available at: <http://www.federalreserve.gov/newevents/press/other/200 80916a.html>.

22   The loan and its terms and conditions were made pursuant to section 13(3) of the *Federal Reserve Act of 1913* (12 U.S.C. ch 3). The US government was to receive a 79.9% equity interest in the net assets of AIG and in addition had the right to veto the payment of dividends to both common and preference shareholders.

23   Ibid., (n. 21). The Board of AIG also released a press release on the same day agreeing to receive the assistance of the Federal Reserve and the US Treasury. See American Insurance Group 2008b. AIG Statement on announcement by Federal Reserve Board of $85 billion secured revolving credit facility addresses liquidity issues and policyholder concerns, 16 September 2008, New York.

points (8.50%).[24] Under the credit facility the New York Federal Reserve would borrow up to $US37.8 billion in investment-grade securities from AIG in return for providing cash under the facility.[25]

The actions of the Federal Reserve Bank of New York and the US Treasury in providing the much-needed line of credit to AIG were absolutely necessary given the circumstances at the time. Without these support measures, AIG would have faced considerable liquidity stress. The credit facility helped to stabilize AIG, providing the organization with sufficient short-term liquidity and enough time to enable AIG to sell assets in an orderly manner. The actions of the Federal Reserve and the US Treasury were designed to prevent the spread of systemic risk[26] flowing from any further market-related disruptions that would undermine the stability of AIG.[27]

Lehman Brothers, a giant in the global investment bank arena, was also in major financial difficulties following the volatile market conditions in 2008. Concerns started to emerge after Lehman announced a $US2.8 billion loss in the second quarter of 2008.[28] The earnings loss came after Lehman Brothers had attempted to strengthen their liquidity position by offering a $US4 billion public sale of its common stock in June 2008, as well as a $US2 billion public offering of preferred stock. In June 2008, the FRBYN undertook liquidity stress-testing of Lehman Brothers and concluded: "Lehman's weak liquidity position is driven by its relatively large exposure to overnight CP, combined with significant overnight secured funding of less liquid assets."[29]

------

24   American Insurance Group 2008a. AIG signs definitive agreement with Federal Reserve Bank of New York For $85 billion credit facility. Press release, Business Wire, 23 September 2008. New York.

25   Board of Governors of the Federal Reserve System 2008f. Press release, 8 October 2008. Available at: <http://www.federalreserve.gov/newsevents/press/other/200 81008a.htm>.

26   In a press release by AIG on 10 November 2008 the Chairman and CEO of AIG, Edward M. Liddy, acknowledged the assistance provided by the Federal Reserve and the US Treasury through the credit facility. Liddy also commented on the possibly systemic consequences if AIG were to file for bankruptcy: "The $85 billion emergency bridge loan was essential to prevent an AIG bankruptcy, which would have caused incalculable damage to AIG, our economy and the global financial system." American Insurance Group 2008b. Press release, 10 November 2008. US Treasury, Federal Reserve and AIG Establish Comprehensive Solution for AIG.

27   Federal Reserve Bank of New York 2008b. Press release, 29 September 2008. Statement by the Federal Reserve Bank of New York regarding AIG transaction. Available at: <http://www.newyorkfed.org/newsevents/news/markets/2008.html>.

28   Lehman Brothers Holdings, 2008. Press release, 16 June 2008. Lehman Brothers Reports Second Quarter Results, New York. Available at: <http://www.lehman.com/press/qe/past/2_08qe.htm>.

29   Federal Reserve Bank of New York 2008c. Primary dealer monitoring: Liquidity stress analysis, 25 June 2008. Available at: <http://www.newyorkfed.org/>.

As is discussed in Chapter 2, the attempts by the Federal Reserve and the US Treasury to prevent Lehman Brothers from filing for bankruptcy failed. Following the breakdown in talks with Lehman's suitor, Barclays, Lehman Brothers filed for bankruptcy on 15 September 2008. As the Vice President and General Counsel of the Federal Reserve Bank of New York described the events leading up to Lehman's bankruptcy:

> By Monday, 15 September, Lehman faced a total erosion of market confidence, and so the Federal Reserve would have been lending into a classic run. Had Lehman not filed for bankruptcy on September 15, but opened as if it were business as usual, creditors and counterparties would have rushed to protect their positions, using all legal remedies, causing the liquidity crisis to spread throughout Lehman's organization.[30]

One of the main sticking points for a successful deal for Lehman's net assets with Barclays concerned the provision of a guarantee. The day immediately preceding Lehman's bankruptcy, Barclays informed the Federal Reserve that it could not provide a guarantee for Lehman's trading obligations without first obtaining a shareholder resolution. The shareholder vote was a requirement under UK law. Obtaining such a resolution could take considerable time, which Lehman and the Fed could ill afford. The Federal Reserve then enquired whether the UK market regulator, the Financial Services Authority (FSA), could waive the requirement that a guarantee be provided so as to facilitate the merger transaction between Lehman and Barclays.

The FSA refused to waive the requirement for Barclays to obtain shareholder approval for Lehman's liabilities and continuing contractual obligations. Barclays suggested that in order for a deal to be completed the Federal Reserve would have to guarantee all of Lehman's current and future liabilities. The precedent had been established for providing assistance with the rescue of Bear Stearns and AIG. With the bailout of Bear Stearns and AIG the Federal Reserve had provided significant financial resources to both entities in the form of loan agreements and the provision of credit facilities.[31]

However, as was pointed out by Baxter from the Federal Reserve Bank of New York, the Federal Reserve Board of Governors did not have the legal authority to provide a "naked guarantee."[32] As Baxter further pointed out, even with the passage of the *Emergency Economic Stablization Act 2008*, US law provides only the US Treasury with the legal authority and capacity to issue a guarantee.[33] The Act does not provide the Federal Reserve with such powers.

---

30   Baxter 2010 (Statement by Thomas C. Baxter, Executive Vice President and General Counsel Federal Reserve Bank of New York, before the Financial Crisis Inquiry Commission, 1 September 2010), p. 11.

31   Ibid., p. 8.

32   Ibid., p. 9.

33   Ibid., p. 9. See also Section 102(c)(4) of the *Emergency Stabilization Act 2008*.

The reaction by the world's financial markets to the Lehman Brothers bankruptcy was immediate. Credit markets froze, credit default spreads rose, equity markets fell sharply and investors panicked. The loss of confidence by investors and depositors in turn led to runs on a number of banks and financial institutions in the US and other countries, including the United Kingdom, Australia, Ireland, Spain, Portugal, Iceland, The Netherlands and Belgium.

The United Kingdom

The United Kingdom was not spared the fallout from the Lehman Brothers' bankruptcy, nor was it immune from the economic consequences of the bursting US and global housing bubble. In September 2007, the UK began witnessing the first runs on the retail deposits of a UK bank since the reign of Queen Victoria.[34] The run commenced on the British building society, Northern Rock plc.[35] Northern Rock had started from humble beginnings in the 1990s to become a substantial player in the UK residential mortgage market. At the end of 2006, Northern Rock's balance sheet recorded the value of its assets at over £100 billion sterling, with over 89% of the bank's assets in residential mortgages.[36]

The large number of residential mortgages held by Northern Rock created a perception in the minds of investors and customers that Northern Rock could potentially collapse. With the issue playing on the minds of customers, a run on Northern Rock's retail deposits began on the morning of 13 September 2007. As was described by the Parliamentary Enquiry into Northern Rock, the day had witnessed long queues of Northern Rock customers anxiously waiting for the branch doors to open so they could withdraw their deposits.[37]

34 UK Parliamentary Enquiry into Northern Rock 2007, Select Committee on Treasury Fifth Report. Available at: <http://www.publications.parliament.uk/pa/cm200708/cmselect/cmtreasy/56/5604.htm#a4>. In Victorian times a number of runs took place on British banks, especially in the 1860s. In 1866 investor panic led to the collapse of the regional bank Overend, Gurney & Co. For a history of runs on British banks in the 1860s, see: Elliott, G. *The Mystery of Overend & Gurney: A Financial Scandal in Victorian London* (London: Methuen, 2006); Collins, M. and Baker, M. *Commercial Banks and Industrial Finance in England and Wales, 1860–1913* (Oxford: Oxford University Press, 2003) and Bagehot, W. *Lombard Street: A Description of the Money Market* (London: Henry S. King, 1873).

35 Northern Rock Plc demutualized on 1 October 1997 and the building society described itself as "a specialized lender, whose core business is the provision of UK residential mortgages funded in both the retail and wholesale markets." Northern Rock Community Report 2006, p. 9; and UK Parliamentary Enquiry into Northern Rock 2007. Ibid., (n. 34), Chapter 2, paragraph 13.

36 Northern Rock Annual Report 2006, p. 82.

37 According to the Parliamentary Enquiry into Northern Rock, whilst wholesale funding grew strongly there had not been a commensurate rise in retail funding. Ibid., (n. 34), Chapter 2, paragraphs 14.

Despite the run by depositors, evidence tendered before the Parliamentary Enquiry suggested that the asset book of Northern Rock had been of high quality. The problems experienced by Northern Rock were not caused by its asset book but, rather, its liabilities as represented by the way the bank had chosen to fund the purchase of its assets. Northern Rock had relied heavily on borrowings from wholesale markets to finance its aggressive growth in its asset base, including its market share of UK residential mortgages.[38]

The proportion of Northern Rock's assets that were funded by wholesale markets instead of through retail deposits meant that Northern Rock had become increasingly dependent on funding through money markets.[39] When the wholesale credit markets became dislocated as a result of the US sub-prime mortgage market, Northern Rock suffered a liquidity crisis because it faced increased difficulty in sourcing sufficient funding and credit in Britain's money markets.[40]

The Parliamentary Enquiry concluded:

> The directors of Northern Rock were the principal authors of the difficulties that the company has faced since August 2007. It is right that members of the Board of Northern Rock have been replaced, though haphazardly, since the company became dependent on liquidity support from the Bank of England. The high-risk, reckless business strategy of Northern Rock, with its reliance on short and medium term wholesale funding and an absence of sufficient insurance and a failure to arrange standby facility or cover that risk, meant that it was unable to cope with the liquidity pressures placed upon it by the freezing of international capital markets in August 2007.[41]

The build-up of risk in Northern Rock's funding model meant that Northern Rock would be vulnerable if market conditions deteriorated. The situation was made worse in August 2007 because of excessive market volatility and the fact that Northern Rock did not have a viable alternative funding model in place to overcome any deterioration in market conditions. The Chancellor of the Exchequer had no choice but to authorize the Bank of England to provide credit support facilities to Northern Rock so that it would stabilize Northern Rock's operations.[42]

---

38   Ibid.
39   The Parliamentary Enquiry revealed that by the end of 2006, Northern Rock's retail deposit book had grown from approximately £9.9 billion sterling in 1997 to just £22.6 billion in 2007. In contrast, Northern Rock's wholesale funding grew sixfold over the same period. Ibid. (nn. 7 and 8).
40   By August 2007, Northern Rock's traders had noted a "dislocation in the market" for its short-term funding. Ibid. (n. 34), Chapter 2, paragraph 23.
41   Parliamentary Enquiry into Northern Rock. Ibid., (n. 34), Chapter 2, paragraph 31.
42   On 19 November 2007 the Chancellor of the Exchequer informed Parliament: "I can tell the House that Bank of England lending is secured against assets held by Northern Rock, which include high-quality mortgages with a significant protection margin built in

In order to provide additional stability and to maintain investor certainty in Northern Rock's retail deposits, the UK government further announced that it would guarantee all retail deposits in Northern Rock's accounts.[43] The retail deposit guarantee was widely viewed as necessary to restore depositor confidence in Northern Rock. The deposit guarantee was also designed to prevent any future runs on the bank and to safeguard the UK financial sector from the spread of systemic risk caused by the collapse of a major building society in the form of Northern Rock.[44]

Australia

The effects of the GFC did not remain in the US or the UK, but were felt right across the world as far as Australia. Australia's second and third largest investment banks, Babcock & Brown Ltd. and Allco Finance Group Ltd. collapsed under the strain of mounting debts and hostile credit markets. Both investment banks were listed on the Australian Securities Exchange (ASX) and at the height of the debt-infused boom had market capitalizations that ran into the billions of dollars.

Babcock & Brown was floated on the ASX in 2004. Its issue price for each share was $A5.00, giving the company a market capitalization upon listing of over $A1.5 billion. Babcock & Brown's operating activities included funds and asset management, securitization, aviation leasing, syndicate financing and investing. At the top of the equity boom, Babcock's share price had risen almost sevenfold and its market capitalization by 2007 was over $A10 billion. Babcock & Brown operated as a global investment bank with operations in North America, Europe and South East Asia, and at its height employed almost 1,500 employees worldwide.

---

and high-quality securities with the highest quality of credit rating. The Bank is the senior secured creditor." Ibid., (n. 34), Chapter 9, paragraph 333.

43   On 17 September 2007, the Chancellor of the Exchequer stated, "when I announced the guarantee, I wanted to be pretty clear what exactly I was announcing because people would want to know beyond doubt what the position was." The initial guarantee announced on 17 September covered "all the existing deposits in Northern Rock" and was set for the duration of "the current instability in the financial markets." Ibid., Chapter 9, paragraph 335.

44   The Parliamentary Enquiry into Northern Rock arrived at this conclusion: "The guarantee on Northern Rock's retail deposits was necessary to stop the run on those deposits. The guarantees issued in September and October to categories of wholesale deposits with Northern Rock assisted with the stability of the company during that period and since. One effect of the various Government guarantees issued in September and October has been to reinforce the incentive for the Government to help to ensure that Northern Rock remains a going concern that honours its commitments to depositors." Ibid., Chapter 9, paragraph 340.

Allco Finance Group Ltd. was Australia's third largest investment bank, behind Macquarie Bank Ltd. and Babcock & Brown Ltd. Allco was also listed on the ASX and since its listing in 2001 had enjoyed similar success to Babcock & Brown. Allco was involved in structured financing, investing in businesses and infrastructure assets, leasing, funds management, underwriting and securitization.

The operations of Babcock and Allco came crashing down with the collapse of the US sub-prime mortgage market. With the failure of Lehman Brothers in September 2008, the die had been cast for both investment banks. Both listed entities were heavily leveraged and dependent upon wholesale markets, short-term money markets and a consortium of banks to fund their aggressive business models.

Allco was the first to suspend its securities from trading on the ASX. Its parent company and subsidiaries then went into voluntary administration.[45] Administrators and receivers were appointed to the company to oversee a sale of its assets located in Australia and North America. Following the asset sales, the receivers appointed to Allco advised that there would be no distributions made to shareholders.[46] It was later resolved on 26 May 2009 to have the company wound up at a creditor's meeting.

A similar fate was awaiting Babcock & Brown. The board of Babcock & Brown appointed administrators in early 2009 and on 12 June 2009 the administrators announced that there would be no distribution to shareholders. The company's listing on the ASX was also terminated on the same day, following an announcement to the company's shareholders. On 24 August 2009 the creditors of the company resolved to place the company into liquidation.

Both investment banks suffered a similar fate to their North American counterparts, Bear Stearns, AIG and Lehman Brothers. Allco and Babcock & Brown pursued a high-growth strategy utilizing excessive leverage to finance their ambitious business models. When credit markets became dislocated following the US sub-prime mortgage crisis and the collapse of Lehman Brothers, Allco and Babcock & Brown found it difficult to rollover their loans. The difficulty in raising wholesale funds in turn triggered breaches in the company's debt covenants, which allowed lenders the right to exercise their powers to make calls on the loans under the various agreements.

South East Asia, China and India

The fallout from the GFC also had an adverse impact on South East Asia, China, Japan, Singapore, Malaysia, Korea, Taiwan and India. However, good

---

45   Allco went into voluntary administration on the 4 November 2008 pursuant to section 436A of the *Corporations Act 2001* (Cth).

46   The administrators appointed by Allco made the declaration on 25 May 2009, following the sale of Allco's aviation business to an international consortium involving investors from China and New York.

fundamentals in the region's economies meant that the consequences were more limited relative to the United States and parts of Europe. Ben Bernanke, Chairman of the US Federal Reserve, noted that the GFC affected the South East Asian regional economies predominantly through international trade.[47]

International trade had been somewhat adversely affected because of the disruptions to international credit markets.[48] Hence, countries that were dependent upon trade for their economic growth and income suffered a decline in export income when their share of international trade had been disrupted or restricted. According to Bernanke, some Asian economies had experienced considerable decline in their GDP growth in a similar experience to the previous Asian financial and currency crisis in the 1990s.[49] Even in the fastest-growing Asian countries, China, India and Indonesia, where real GDP growth remained positive throughout the GFC crisis, growth in industrial output had been lower relative to previous periods.[50]

Bernanke made an interesting observation concerning the relative financial openness of an economy and its decline in economic output. Asian economies which operated open financial systems suffered greater declines in industrial output during the GFC relative to economies that were not so open.[51] According to Bernanke, Taiwan, which had a relatively open financial system, suffered significant declines in industrial output and real GDP, whereas in China, Indonesia and India, which operate less open financial systems, the falls in industrial output were more modest.[52]

The correlation appears to suggest that with more open financial systems there is a greater likelihood that the domestic economy may suffer larger shocks if there is an associated downturn in the international economy. The same applies with domestic economies that are dependent upon properly functioning international financial markets. The interlinkages between a nation's domestic economy and the world's financial systems tend to support Bernanke's observation.[53] Hence, it

---

47 Bernanke 2009a. (Asia and the global financial crisis. Speech by B.S. Bernanke, Chairman of the Board of Governors of the US Federal Reserve System, presented at the Federal Reserve Bank of San Francisco's Conference on Asia and the Global Financial Crisis, Santa Barbara, California, 19 October 2009), p. 2.

48 Bernanke noted that "The turmoil in credit markets doubtless exacerbated the sharp decline in demand for durable goods, and thus in trade volumes, as purchases of durable goods typically involve some extension of credit." Ibid., p. 3.

49 Bernanke reported that relative to the period immediately preceding the GFC, the Asian economies, including Japan, recorded declines in real GDP growth of between 13% and 20%. Id.

50 Ibid., (n. 47), pp. 3–4.

51 Ibid., (n. 47), p. 4.

52 Ibid.

53 Indeed, Bernanke goes on to suggest that "these powerful economic linkages, as well as the importance of the United States and Asia in the global economy, underscore the need for consultation and cooperation in addressing common issues and concerns." Ibid., (n. 47), p. 7.

is not surprizing to see the link supported by recent disruptions to international financial markets.[54]

Latin America

The interlinkages between the global financial system and Latin American economies has meant that the fallout from the GFC also affected developing countries in Central and South America. A speech delivered by the Governor of the Bank of Mexico, G. Ortiz, confirmed that countries such as Mexico, which had a strong trade association with the United States, also experienced significant material declines in export income and real GDP.[55] Ortiz also observed that nations with a relatively higher degree of openness suffered greater declines in exports and industrial production compared with Latin American countries that had more robust internal or domestic markets.[56]

This is a similar conclusion to Bernanke's observation concerning the relative openness of a country's financial system. In both cases, it appears that globalization of trade and capital flows may not have provided an effective safe harbour but may have instead exacerbated the problem. Ordinarily, the benefits of globalization and international trade far outweigh any perceived risks. These benefits generally occur when the world economy is booming. However, if the international economy is suffering a material decline, or if disruptions exist within international financial markets, then negative spillover will normally occur to adversely affect domestic economic growth and income.

One theory that was put forward to explain the initial resilience of emerging economies during the GFC was that they had become decoupled from the US economy. The theory suggested that the emerging giants, China and India, with their relatively robust domestic economies, had been largely insulated from the fallout of the crisis and would emerge to be the dominant economies in the following decades. However, as Bernanke and Ortiz correctly pointed out, the "de-coupling" theory would soon falter with the demise of Lehman Brothers. The emergence of the global financial catastrophe led to an international recession, which, in turn,

---

54 A conclusion that Bernanke reaches is that both the US economy and the global economy have benefitted significantly from Asia's rapid development, growth and integration into the global economy. Similarly, the benefits flowing to the Asian economies in terms of rising standards of living, integration and development have also been substantial. Ibid., (n. 47), p. 7.

55 Ortiz 2009. The global financial Crisis – a Latin American perspective. Speech by G. Ortiz, Governor of the Bank of Mexico and Chairman of the Board of Directors of the Bank for International Settlements, delivered at the conference, Financial globalization: culprit, survivor or casualty of the great crisis? held at Yale University, New Haven, CT, 13 November 2009.

56 Ibid., p. 3.

caused a material decline in export volumes and industrial production in both developed and emerging nations.[57]

South East Europe

In the immediate aftermath of the collapse of Lehman Brothers, countries in South East Europe also began to feel the ramifications of the GFC. Sensing that there could be serious consequences following the fallout from the GFC, the Governing Council of the European Central Bank (ECB) reduced its key interest rate by 100 basis points in seven months. The ECB had been concerned with the potential slowdown in the European Union member states.

Despite the stimulus provided by the ECB, it had been noted that the ECB's monetary policy might not be completely effective, especially during times of extreme stress.[58] The ECB would also have to implement a number of unconventional measures designed to improve the effectiveness of its policy responses when confronted with an international crisis and extreme market volatility. With this in mind the ECB implemented a number of measures which included: improving domestic banks' liquidity needs by charging EU banks a fixed rate if they chose to borrow from the ECB; the provision of long-term refinancing structures to maturity for member states' banks; ECB purchases of covered bonds; and expanding the list of assets by the member banks to be used as collateral.[59]

Clearly, the ECB felt that it was necessary to implement expansionary measures designed to stimulate liquidity in the immediate aftermath of the collapse of Lehman Brothers. The Central Bank felt the need not only to implement expansionary monetary policy but also to adopt unconventional measures designed to improve the overall effectiveness of its initial policy response. In addition to the measures adopted by the ECB for its member states, the Central Bank also attempted to provide support to non-Eurozone members, including Denmark, Sweden, Poland and Hungary.[60] In conjunction with the ECB, the

57 Ortiz makes the point that the global recession, which was brought about by the GFC, caused a marked decline in output for developing countries in Latin America, particularly for Mexico, because it introduced both an "external demand shock," and an "external financial shock." Ibid., (n. 55), pp. 2–3.

58 Provopoulos 2009. (Key challenges for South East Europe in light of the crisis. Opening address by G. Provopoulos, Governor of the Bank of Greece, delivered at the Conference of Bank of Greece and Oxford University, Challenges and prospects of South East European economies in the wake of the financial crisis, held in Athens, 16 October 2009), p. 1.

59 According to Provopoulos, the ECB undertook these non-standard measures in order to improve credit flows to money markets and to stimulate credit and money markets so as to improve short-term liquidity. Ibid., pp. 1–2.

60 The ECB entered into swap and repo arrangements which were designed to improve market liquidity for these European countries. Ibid., p. 2.

International Monetary Fund (IMF) provided further financial assistance to other nations located in South East Europe.[61]

Despite the policy responses adopted by the ECB and the IMF, considerable uncertainty remained about a number of European countries, including Greece, Spain, Italy, Portugal and Ireland. For Greece, the main economic challenge was how to deal with its sovereign debt crisis, which flared up in mid-2010. Burdened by large fiscal deficits, investors and bondholders turned their attention to Greece, which had for years become increasingly reliant upon and vulnerable to international money markets and lenders.[62]

Concern soon spread through financial markets that Greece's public debt and fiscal deficits were no longer sustainable. In April 2010, Greece's stock market declined markedly and credit default swaps for Greek bonds rose sharply. The rating agencies Moody's and Standard & Poor's continued to downgrade Greece's public debt, which caused yields to rise as bondholders demanded higher returns.[63]

Fearing an imminent collapse in its ability to repay its loans, Greece sought assistance from the EU and the IMF. The IMF agreed to provide Greece with an emergency loan, initially of up to €45 billion. The package would assist Greece with its attempts to refinance its various loans when they fell due. In return for the IMF loan, Greece was required to enact strict austerity measures designed to dramatically reduce the country's fiscal deficit and bring it into line with the requirements of EU membership. The emergency loan from the IMF was later increased to €110 billion by contributions from the EU.

To assist in the process of stabilizing Greece's fiscal position, the Greek parliament enacted the *Economy Protection Bill* in March 2010. The Bill was designed to save €4.8 billion in austerity measures. The implementation of government expenditure cuts and increases in taxation had been one of the key requirements imposed by the EU and the IMF in granting financial assistance to Greece. The austerity measures included finding savings by reducing salaries to Greece's public servants, increasing the retirement age of workers to 65 years of age and increasing a number of state taxes, excise duties and VAT. The austerity measures proved unpopular and many of Greece's workers vented their anger, frustration and disappointment at the plight of their nation's finances.

Added to Greece's woes, the EU also had to deal with a crisis in confidence in its currency, the euro. After witnessing for months the weakness and volatility in the US dollar, the EU was now confronted with a volatile euro. At the height of the GFC, there had been suggestions that the US dollar would no longer be the

---

61   The IMF provided emergency loans and sponsored gold sales, as well as other measures, to assist Belarus, Bosnia-Herzegovina, Hungary, Iceland, Latvia, Poland, Romania, Serbia and the Ukraine. See Provopoulos (Ibid., (n. 58)), p. 2.

62   It was estimated that the Greek fiscal deficit for 2009–2010 was over 13% of GDP.

63   On 16 December 2010 Standard & Poor's downgraded Greece's public debt from A minus to BBB plus. On 22 December Moody's downgraded its rating for Greece from A1 to A2.

world's reserve currency and would be replaced by the euro. After all, the euro had experienced little volatility and appeared to be both stable and robust relative to the US dollar.[64]

However, the temporary stability in the euro masked a more troubling and challenging issue confronting the EU. The sovereign debt crisis affecting first Greece and later Ireland, Portugal and Spain began to undermine markets and reintroduce heightened volatility into international currency markets. The euro was now viewed as particularly vulnerable, since the EU had control over monetary policy but had no say in the fiscal policy of its member states. The EU could only utilize interest rate policy or implement other non-standard monetary policy measures to influence economic activity in its member states.

Fiscal policy was left to each of the member states to determine the appropriateness of the nation's fiscal position. The absence of a coordinated or uniform approach to fiscal policy among EU member states presented a problem for the euro in the international currency markets. With the outbreak of the sovereign debt crisis involving first Greece and later Ireland and Portugal, considerable volatility had been reintroduced into international currency markets, which adversely affected both the underlying value and overall stability of the euro.

Ireland

The sovereign debt crisis that began with Greece's fiscal imbalances was to claim Ireland as its new victim. After experiencing considerable market volatility with Ireland's equity market and banking sector and the euro, Ireland requested financial assistance from the IMF and the EU under the Exceptional Access Policy and Emergency Funding Mechanism. Under the emergency funding arrangement, the IMF provided Ireland with access to €22.5 billion, comprizing part of an overall financing package worth €85 billion.

The IMF reported in February 2011 that market reaction to the approval of the emergency funding arrangement had been positive. According to the IMF, spreads on sovereign bonds had fallen on the days when the ECB had entered into the market to buy sovereign paper.[65] The funding arrangements came at a time of considerable turbulence for Ireland, both politically and economically. In January 2011 the Prime Minister of Ireland declared an end to his coalition government. The Irish Parliament was dissolved on 1 February, with elections scheduled for

---

64   See for example, Nowotny 2009. The Euro – a stability anchor in turbulent times. Speech by E. Nowotny, Governor of the Austrian National Bank, delivered at the John Hopkins University, Bologna, 10 September 2009.

65   International Monetary Fund 2011. Ireland: Extended Arrangement Interim Review under the Emergency Financing Mechanism. IMF Country Report No. 11/47 (Washington, DC: IMF, February 2011), p. 3.

25 February 2011. The IMF further noted that the Irish banking sector remained under stress as bank asset quality declined in line with falling residential real estate prices.[66] Ireland's banks also remained heavily dependent upon the emergency funding arrangement for short-term liquidity, since short-term money market funding had all but collapsed in late 2010 and early 2011.[67]

The International Economy

The GFC was responsible not only for causing damage to the world's financial system; the severe consequences flowing from the ongoing market turmoil and credit crisis also helped induce a major downturn in industrial output and world growth. Described by the IMF as the "Great Recession,"[68] the GFC brought about the largest decline in economic activity since World War II and the Great Depression. According to the IMF, even with proactive policy action by governments all over the world, global output declined by 1.3% in 2009, which "would represent by far the deepest post-World War II recession."[69] The Great Recession was also truly global, since output measured on a per capita basis would decline in "countries representing three-quarters of the global economy and growth in virtually all countries has decelerated sharply from rates observed in 2003–07."[70]

The IMF was also deeply concerned with the period of economic growth post the current economic downturn. According to the IMF, recessions that are coupled with damaged financial systems can take longer to heal. With dislocated and dysfunctional financial markets credit lending and credit growth are severely reduced, which leads in turn to lower business investment and lower consumer expenditure.[71] The IMF also issued a warning on the current sovereign debt crisis confronting Europe. According to the IMF, "large fiscal deficits will need to be rolled back just as the population aging accelerates in a number of advanced economies."[72]

In terms of adopting appropriate policy measures, the IMF had been acutely aware of the dangers of adopting protectionist measures. Keen to avoid a repeat of the damaging policy responses during the Great Depression, the IMF advocated for greater international coordination. This time the policy responses by governments

---

66   Ibid., p. 3.
67   Ibid., p. 3.
68   International Monetary Fund 2009b. World Economic Outlook: Crisis and Recovery (Washington, DC: IMF World Economic and Financial Surveys, April 2009), p. xvi.
69   Ibid., p. xvi.
70   Id.
71   Ibid., (n. 69), p. xvii.
72   Ibid.

all over world would be designed to support and stimulate consumer demand, international trade, global growth and bank lending.[73]

As part of a coordinated policy response, the IMF encouraged central banks to ease monetary policy and cut official interest rates. Adopting expansionary monetary policies would be critical in avoiding the devastating effects of falling asset prices and deflation. Even where a nation's key interest rates are set at or near zero, non-standard expansionary measures should also be explored. The use of monetary policy to accommodate additional liquidity and stimulate demand should occur "for as long as it takes."[74] Central banks should also engage in quantitative easing in circumstances where interest rates were at zero or close to zero, and the "central bank's own balance sheet could support credit intermediation."[75]

Importantly, the IMF viewed private credit creation as an important component contributing to the overall health of global credit markets. Moreover, the credit risk associated with credit intermediation should be minimized particularly as it relates to the central bank's balance sheet and credit risk profile. Adopting quantitative easing measures along with accommodative interest rates would help restore liquidity to credit markets, which, in turn, would help stimulate consumer demand and business investment.

Expansionary monetary policy should also be duly coupled with expansionary fiscal stimulus to help underpin global demand and world growth. The stimulus measures would be designed to overcome the significant decline in private household wealth caused by sharp falls in international equity markets and declining real estate prices.

Although the world has seen deflating bubbles in the past, the current downturn in house prices in the United States, the United Kingdom and other countries around the world has spilled over into the banking and financial system. The spillover has occurred because "excesses and failures" were at the core of the financial system.[76] The ramifications from the fallout of the excesses would be felt by both developed and emerging nations as the rapidly deteriorating global economy exacerbated weaknesses in domestic economies. The current downturn had witnessed declines in global GDP by as much as 6% in annual terms.[77]

---

73   The IMF stated as much: "Policymakers must be mindful of the cross-border ramifications of policy choices. Initiatives that support trade and financial partners – including fiscal stimulus and official support for international financing flows – will help support global demand, with shared benefits. Conversely, a slide towards trade and financial protectionism would be hugely damaging to all, a clear warning from the experience of 1930s beggar-thy-neighbour policies." Ibid. (n. 69), p. xvii.

74   Ibid., (n. 69), p. xviii.

75   According to the IMF, an increasing number of central banks would need to resort to non-conventional expansionary measures, including quantitative easing. Ibid. (n. 69), p. xviii.

76   Ibid., (n. 69), p. 3.

77   According to the IMF, overall global GDP declined by over 6%, for developed economies the decline was in excess of 7%, whilst for developing nations the fall in real GDP was over 4%. Ibid., (n. 69), p. 4.

The rapid deceleration in global demand and real GDP had already made the situation much worse for developed countries such as Japan, which was in the midst of a 20-year deflationary cycle. Japan had battled the serious consequences of a bursting housing and investment bubble in the 1990s without much success. For the Japanese, who had grown accustomed to high levels of growth and low unemployment, deflation now brought misery to millions of unemployed Japanese workers. The same scenario was now beginning in the United States and Europe, as millions of workers were being laid off, with closures of businesses and factories a common occurrence at the height of the GFC.

Conclusion

Whether the international economy could pull itself out of a seemingly similar deflationary debt spiral was a major concern for governments in the United States and Europe. The US had been hit particularly hard with the millions of foreclosures affecting US homeowners. The rapid decline in trade and export volumes had hit Asia and Western Europe hard, due to their reliance on export income to fund economic growth.[78] Developing nations in Latin America, India and the subcontinent, and Eastern Europe also suffered considerable economic pain as international trade fell sharply in response to declining consumer demand and business investment.

High levels of unemployment would be the unpleasant by-product of the nasty excesses emerging from the global housing bubble. With globalization of trade and capital flows, no country would be spared the adverse effects of the GFC and the associated global recession. As with previous great crises, the world would again be confronted with the challenges of low economic growth, high unemployment and deflating asset prices. To emerge from the current downfall, governments all over the world would need to coordinate their policy responses and stimulus measures.

The major challenge for policymakers was to stimulate global demand within an environment of low interest rates and fiscal imbalances. Sovereign risk would soon emerge as a major headwind for European policymakers as the GFC continued to undermine vulnerable nations with large fiscal imbalances.

---

78   Id.

Chapter 4
Financial Markets and the GFC

Introduction

The world's financial markets were at centre stage of the GFC. The crisis was very much a financial crisis, as it had its genesis in a global and US housing bubble fuelled by low interest rates in developed economies and a global savings glut in emerging countries. Financial markets acted as transmission channels for the crisis, spreading the housing virus throughout the international economy, infecting financial and credit markets all over the world.

OTC derivatives markets served to highlight the importance of having robust and responsive regulatory frameworks. However, most OTC derivatives markets around the world were largely unregulated and inadequately supervised. As was discussed in Chapter 2, the emergence of a shadow banking system that operated in parallel and in competition with the conventional banking sector served to undermine the overall effectiveness of financial markets regulation. The use of the parallel system by bankers, investment banks, mortgage originators and broker–dealers in sourcing credit and developing sophisticated OTC financial products led to a build-up of risk. When the housing bubble burst, the parallel system was placed under significant stress as securitized sub-prime mortgage loans became almost worthless and subsequently toxic.

The collapse of Lehman Brothers and the bailout of other investment banks undermined consumer trust and investor confidence in the US financial system. Short-term credit markets seized up, leading to a chronic shortage of liquidity in wholesale money markets. The seed was now sown for the perfect financial storm. Over-leveraged banks, investment banks and mortgage originators that used short-term credit to fuel their aggressive growth strategies and business models were now made extremely vulnerable to changes in market sentiment.

Financial Markets, the GFC and the Great Recession

It is now beyond argument that the world's financial markets were at the centre stage of the current crisis. All financial markets, particularly equity and credit markets, reacted adversely to the global meltdown. In some cases, certain financial markets became dislocated and ceased to function in a rational manner. The financial stress, which restricted the proper functioning of credit markets, was particularly damaging, as credit flows became restricted and short-term liquidity all but dried up.

The ensuing financial crisis and market dislocation, in turn, caused banks, mortgage originators and credit providers to restrict the availability of credit to millions of small and large businesses. The severe shortage of liquidity and available credit led to a dangerous feedback loop, which encouraged deflation in asset prices. As credit dried up, so did the availability of investors, which placed further pressure on an already fragile housing market.

In 2008 the IMF investigated the relationship between financial markets, the GFC and the global recession and came to the following conclusions:[1]

- Recessions which are accompanied by severe financial turmoil often are more protracted and deeper compared with other economic downturns.
- There is a stronger likelihood that a downturn or recession will accompany an episode of financial turmoil if house prices and aggregate credit rise in the period immediately preceding the downturn.
- Countries which have more open financial systems are generally more vulnerable to sharper contractions in global growth because their financial systems are more procyclical, with their innovations in financial instruments and financial markets. Conversely, countries with less open financial systems are less vulnerable to global economic downturns because their banking sector is less procyclical in respect of financial innovation.
- Countries with strong financial stability frameworks can help alleviate economic downturns through clear policy direction designed to strengthen and restore the capital bases of financial intermediaries, including banks, broker–dealers, hedge funds, investment banks and mortgage originators.
- The relationship of asset prices and aggregate credit in the United States during the current crisis appears to replicate previous episodes that were later followed by recessions.[2]

The conclusions reached by the IMF suggest that the current crisis, which had its genesis with the US sub-prime mortgage and global housing boom, rapidly escalated to a credit and liquidity crisis in the world's financial markets. The liquidity crisis continued unabated, which led to severe dislocation in wholesale interbank lending markets. According to the IMF, the associated dislocation in credit and interbank lending markets led the supply of credit to dry up further.

---

1 International Monetary Fund 2008 (World Economic Outlook. Financial Stress, Downturns, and Recoveries. IMF World Economic and Financial Surveys), pp. 130–31.

2 The IMF noted that the pattern of net household borrowings in the United States closely tracked the trajectories of previous recessions. The IMF further commented that "nonfinancial firms entered the turmoil with a relatively strong position. Combined with the large losses sustained by core banking institutions, these factors suggest that the United States continues to face considerable recession risks, even though real interest rates are low by the standards of financial stress-driven recessions." Ibid., p. 131.

Interbank providers who did have funds refused to lend to counterparties because of concerns relating to potential default and creditworthiness.[3]

Problems with market dislocation, liquidity and credit squeezes are not new. As is discussed in Chapter 1, the October 1987 global stock market crash induced dislocation in equity markets and reduced household wealth considerably. The collapse of hedge fund Long-Term Capital Management in 1998 also introduced considerable stresses to short-term cash, credit and equity markets.[4]

However, this time around financial markets appeared to exacerbate the crisis, acting like transmission channels and spreading the US sub-prime virus throughout the world. Financial innovation played an important role in making the crisis systemic, as financial markets and financial instruments, including OTC derivatives, were being used to expose investors and market participants to further a downturn in residential house prices.

OTC Derivatives Markets

Bernanke noted that derivatives markets had a mixed record throughout the crisis.[5] In most cases derivatives were used by entities to hedge risk and to better manage their risk positions.[6] However, in some instances financial intermediaries also used OTC credit derivatives "as a tool for taking excessive risks."[7] According to Bernanke, excessive risk-taking through the use of credit derivatives occurred with the American International Group (AIG).[8] AIG took large positions in credit derivatives without appropriate hedges in place. Hence, when the credit positions were unwound, AIG was left with insufficient capital to guard against the "large, correlated risks that it was taking."[9]

The lack of transparency and market concentration of OTC derivatives also posed problems for the world's financial markets. Since OTC derivatives markets were traditionally not centrally cleared or settled, market participants may not have had a proper understanding or enough appreciation to "fully assess their own

---

3   According to the IMF, the dislocation in interbank lending markets affected commercial banks, investment banks, universal banks and broker–dealers. This was despite the fact that some of these institutions had the ability to raise funds from retail depositors. Ibid., p. 132.

4   Ibid., p. 132.

5   Bernanke 2010c (Statement by Ben S. Bernanke, Chairman of the Board of Governors of the Federal Reserve System before the Financial Crisis Inquiry Commission, Washington, DC, 2 September 2010), p. 10.

6   Ibid., p. 11.

7   Id.

8   Bernanke notes that the problems associated with AIG had to do much less with the actual derivatives instruments and more with a failure with risk management practices. Ibid., (n. 5), p. 11.

9   Id.

net derivatives exposures or to communicate to counterparties and regulators the nature and extent of those exposures."[10]

The Financial Crisis Inquiry Commission raised concerns relating to the use and abuse of OTC derivatives during the crisis, including within the period immediately prior to the crisis. In his opening remarks, the Chairman of the Financial Crisis Inquiry Commission commented on the exceptional rate of growth of the OTC derivatives markets. OTC derivatives trading grew from $88 trillion in 1999 to $684 trillion in 2008.[11] Similar growth was experienced by credit derivatives, which grew notionally from less than $1 trillion in 2000 to be over $58 trillion in 2007.[12]

The Chairman of the Commodity Futures Trading Commission (CFTC) was less forgiving on the role OTC derivatives played in the current crisis.[13] According to Gensler, in 2008 the financial system failed, the financial regulatory system failed, and "derivatives played a central role."[14] The CFTC was also of the view that regulated financial markets such as futures markets and securities markets were more transparent because price was established through supply and demand and listed on an approved exchange.[15] By improving transparency through the regulation of clearing houses it was further argued that systemic risk would be reduced.[16] This is because a regulated and approved clearing house would not only

---

10   Id. According to Bernanke, the complexity of certain derivatives instruments had drawn the US Federal Reserve's attention in the past. In September 2005 the Federal Reserve Bank of New York hosted a meeting with representatives and participants in OTC derivatives markets. The purpose of the meeting was to discuss a number of issues concerning the processes relating to OTC derivatives. See Federal Reserve Bank of New York 2005. Press release, 15 September 2005. Statement Regarding Meeting on Credit Derivatives. Available at: <http://www.newyorkfed.org/newsevents/news_archive/markets /2005/an050915.html>. See also Bernanke 2010c, p. 11.

11   Financial Crisis Inquiry Commission 2010a (Opening Remarks of Phil Angelides, Chairman of the Financial Crisis Inquiry Commission, At the Hearing on "The Role of Derivatives in the Financial Crisis," 30 June 2010, Washington, DC), p. 1.

12   The use of notional values for OTC derivatives has somewhat limited meaning, since notional values do not correspond to actual cash flows or liability amounts which are owed by counterparties on settlement.

13   See Gensler 2010 (Testimony of Gary Gensler, Chairman of the Commodity Futures Trading Commission, before the Financial Crisis Inquiry Commission, 1 July 2010. Commodity Futures Trading Commission). Available at: <http:// www.cftc.gov/pressroom/ speechestestimony/opagensler-48.html>.

14   Ibid., p. 1.

15   Ibid., p. 15.

16   I wrote an article in 2004 on precisely this issue, namely, whether trading in financial derivatives leads to an increase in systemic risk. After reviewing a number of academic studies which investigated the issue, I concluded that trading in financial derivatives by intermediaries did not increase systemic risk. In fact a number of academic studies demonstrated that trading in financial derivatives in fact reduced market volatility as measured by market variance. See T. Ciro, Trading in financial derivatives: Does it increase

be more transparent but would also be more liquid and would guard against the risk of counterparty default.

With exchange-traded derivatives, all derivatives instruments use a standardized contract which allows for transferability. The fungible nature of a futures contract allows in turn for the trading of futures contracts on designated exchanges. Since exchange-traded derivatives are open to retail market participants it was thought appropriate that futures contracts should be regulated under a statutory framework and by a market regulator. In the United States, futures exchanges are regulated and supervised by the CFTC, whilst the Financial Services Authority (FSA) is responsible for the regulation of futures markets in the United Kingdom. Similar market regulators and frameworks exist in overseas jurisdictions.

Unlike futures contracts, sophisticated investors almost exclusively use OTC derivatives. Since there is no retail use of OTC derivatives it was thought that formal regulation was not required because there were no "consumers" as such. Sophisticated market participants who were well versed on the underlying risks of OTC derivatives did not require consumer-type protections afforded by regulation. Instead, it was thought that regulation would only increase the underlying costs without necessarily providing any tangible benefits.

However, as is discussed in Chapter 7, all of this has now changed. OTC derivatives and, in particular, swap contracts will now be regulated as provided by the recent amendments enacted by the *Dodd-Frank Act 2010*. The Act introduces a number of groundbreaking reforms, including the regulation of swaps, along with the requirement that swap contracts be centrally cleared on an organized exchange.[17]

The reforms were designed to enhance consumer protection for users of derivatives products. The reforms were also a response to one of the key findings of the Financial Crisis Inquiry Commission. The Commission concluded that OTC derivatives "contributed significantly to this crisis."[18] According to the Commission's Report, the passing by Congress of the *Commodity Futures Modernization Act 2000* (*CFMA*) effectively deregulated OTC derivatives markets because it removed the CFTC and the Securities and Exchange Commission (SEC) from regulatory oversight functions with OTC derivatives markets in the United States.[19]

The Commission reported that as a result of the reforms introduced by the *CFMA*, OTC derivatives markets activity not only in the United States but also in

---

market volatility and systemic risk? *Company and Securities Law Journal* 22(1) 2004, 23, pp. 43–5.

17   See also further discussion in Chapter 7 on new proposals regarding centralized derivatives clearing and settlement facilities.

18   Financial Crisis Inquiry Commission of the United States 2011. Final Report of the National Commission on the Causes of the Financial and Economic Crisis in the United States. Washington, DC: G.P.O., p. xxiv.

19   Ibid., p. 48.

the rest of the world, boomed. From the time the *CFMA* was passed by Congress in 2000, OTC derivatives markets in the United States had a notional value of $US95.2 trillion and a market value of $US3.2 trillion.[20] By 2008, the OTC derivatives market had increased by over 700%.[21]

The *CMFA* did more than simply deregulate OTC derivatives markets from supervisory oversight. The Act introduced important reforms, which were designed to clarify the legal status of OTC derivatives.[22] One of the key reforms introduced by the *CMFA* concerned clarifying the legal status of hybrid derivatives. With hybrid derivatives such as synthetic securitized swaps, the derivative can have the features of a futures contract, a security or an OTC derivative. The uncertainty in terms of the proper characterization of an OTC derivative was illustrated in the decision of *Transnor (Bermuda) Ltd v BP N America Petroleum*.[23] The case decided that OTC derivatives in the form of bilaterally negotiated energy contracts had the characteristics of futures contracts and hence should be regulated as such, notwithstanding that the contract was not traded on a registered futures exchange.[24]

The *Transnor* decision led to a great deal of uncertainty for OTC derivatives traders, as it remained unclear as to whether their instruments would be characterized as a futures contract and regulated by the *Commodity Exchange Act 1936*. There were similar concerns regarding the proper characterization of OTC derivatives in other jurisdictions, including the United Kingdom, and Australia.[25] A number of decisions in the UK had mischaracterized derivatives instruments as illegal and void gaming contracts.[26]

The Financial Crisis Inquiry Commission was also somewhat critical of Federal Reserve Chairman Alan Greenspan's support for the deregulation of the

---

20   Id.

21   The Commission reported that by June 2008, OTC derivatives had increased to $US672.6 trillion and their gross market value was $US20.3 trillion representing a 700% increase from 2000. Ibid., (n. 18), p. 48.

22   See President's Working Group on Financial Markets 2009. Report on over-the-counter derivatives markets and the Commodity Exchange Act (President's Working Group, Washington, DC, November 2009).

23   738 F Supp 1472 (SDNY 1990).

24   See also Ciro 2004 (n. 16), p. 43.

25   In Australia, the High Court in *See v Cohen* (1923) 33 CLR 174 held that the *Gaming and Betting Act 1912* (NSW) was not relevant to an OTC forward contract to purchase wheat. For a discussion of the various gaming statutes that were pleaded by losing counterparties involved in OTC derivatives transactions, see T. Ciro, *Derivatives Regulation and Legal Risk* (London: Euromoney, 2004), pp. 51–2 and T. Ciro, Gaming laws and derivatives, *Company and Securities Law Journal*, 17(3), (1999), pp. 171–86.

26   See, for example, the Court of Appeal (UK) decision in *re Gieve* [1899] 1 QB 794 and the House of Lords (UK) decision in *Universal Stock Exchange v Strachan* 40 WR 494. Even after the passing of the *Financial Services Act 1986* (UK), losing counterparty defendants would plead the various gaming legislation, claiming that their derivatives contracts were illegal gaming ventures and unenforceable in a court of law.

OTC derivatives markets in the United States.[27] Greenspan had been supportive of deregulated OTC derivatives markets in the United States in the late 1990s and into the new millennium. Greenspan was of the view that regulation in OTC derivatives markets had not provided any discernible benefit.[28] OTC markets had functioned well without any of the benefits of regulation under the *Commodity Exchange Act*.[29] Further, regulation would impose considerable costs and burdens on OTC market participants.

Whether OTC derivatives such as swaps markets should or should not be regulated would now be only of academic interest, since the recent legislative reforms in the form of the *Dodd-Frank Act 2010* had introduced both regulation and centralized clearing of swap contracts.[30] One important issue left for consideration concerned the overall effectiveness of the regulatory reforms. Would regulation and centralized clearing introduced by the recent reforms in the United States reduce the perceived risks associated with OTC derivatives? There is little doubt that centralized clearing will reduce counterparty risk, since the bilateral settlement process with OTC derivatives will now be replaced with centralized clearing and settlement. Transparency will also be improved for the pricing of swaps, since the process of price discovery will now be effectively determined and "advertised" on an organized exchange.[31] This is to be contrasted with pricing in OTC derivatives markets, where prices are determined through the process of confidential negotiation and are not generally revealed to other market participants.

The current crisis served to highlight another important issue for consideration, namely whether systemic risk will be reduced through regulation and centralized clearing of swaps. There is little actual evidence to demonstrate that increased regulation and centralized clearing will in fact lead to greater financial stability. Supporters of enhanced regulation have argued that if OTC derivatives markets

---

27   Financial Crisis Inquiry Report (Ibid., n. 18), pp. 48–9.

28   See Greenspan 1999. Financial derivatives. Remarks by Chairman Alan Greenspan before the Futures Industry Association, Boca Raton, Florida, March 19, 1999. The Federal Reserve Board. Available at: <http://www.federalreserve.gov/boarddocs/speeches/1999/19990319.htm> (accessed 1 October 2010).

29   Ibid., p. 1.

30   See Chapter 7 for a fuller discussion of the regulatory reforms introduced by the *Dodd-Frank Act 2010*.

31   In testimony before the Financial Crisis Inquiry Commission, the former Secretary to the US Treasury, Henry Paulson, was of the view that improved regulation of OTC derivatives would help mitigate risk. "Better regulation of these products is clearly needed. Standardized derivatives should be traded on a public exchange, and non-standardized contracts should be centrally cleared and should be subject to more regulatory scrutiny, transparency, and greater capital charges. Such regulations will encourage standardization, promote transparency, and penalize excessive complexity with capital charges, thereby restoring these products to their proper function – mitigating, not enhancing, risk." See Paulson 2010b (Testimony by Henry M. Paulson Jr before the Financial Crisis Inquiry Commission, 6 May 2010), p. 6.

are subject to regulation and supervisory oversight, overall risk will decline. However, it remains unclear whether regulation and centralized clearing of financial derivatives will in fact deliver more optimal outcomes in times of severe market stress.

It should be remembered that at the height of the financial crisis and following the collapse of Lehman Brothers, all financial markets, whether they were regulated or not, had become dislocated and dysfunctional. In fact, most if not all financial markets had become dislocated at the height of the financial crisis in late 2008 and early 2009. Securities markets and futures markets were highly regulated and were subject to prudential as well as supervisory oversight by a number of regulatory bodies and did not function well at the height of the GFC.

Structured Financial Products: Wrapped, Synthesized, Securitized and Collateralized

In the period preceding the financial crisis, intermediaries created, marketed and sold complex financial instruments which were designed to exploit the growing demand for leveraged financial products. Two types of financial instruments that were typically sold en masse to investors included residential mortgage-backed securities (RMBSs) and collateralized debt obligations (CDOs).[32] As part of the marketing strategy to enhance their appeal more broadly in the investment community, both instruments were "wrapped" with a credit default swap and securitized.

Providing credit default swap protection to CDOs and RMBSs allowed these instruments to achieve a higher credit rating than would have otherwise been the case. According to the Financial Crisis Inquiry Commission, between 2000 and 2007 the rating agency Moody's had issued ratings for $US4.7 trillion in RMBSs and $US736 billion in CDOs.[33]

A key finding by the Commission of Inquiry into the Financial Crisis was that many of the RMBSs and CDOs attracted AAA credit ratings, which had indirectly contributed to the crisis.[34] According to the Commission the

---

32   RMBSs and CDOs are examples of structured financial products which typically involve the pooling of assets such as mortgage securities. The mortgage securities initially belong to mortgage originators, but are rebundled or pooled and transferred to a special purpose investment vehicle. The mortgage securities are then typically issued with credit default swaps, which are rated at an investment grade level. The securities are now ready to be sold to investors, who essentially purchase a set of future cash flows offering higher yields than the interbank funding rate of interest.

33   Financial Crisis Inquiry Commission 2010b. Preliminary Staff Report: Credit Ratings and the Financial Crisis, 2 June 2010, p. 3.

34   According to the Commission, "the credit rating agencies abysmally failed in their central mission to provide quality ratings on securities for the benefit of investors [...]. Despite the leveling off and subsequent decline of the housing market beginning in 2006,

"inflated ratings may have enabled the issuance of more subprime mortgages and mortgage-related securities by increasing demand for RMBS and CDOs. If fewer of these securities had been rated AAA, there may have been less demand for risky mortgages in the financial sector and consequently a smaller amount originated."[35]

In late 2007 and early 2008 the rating agencies began to aggressively downgrade mortgage-backed securities. According to the Commission's Final Report, by 2008 the rating agencies would downgrade over 80% of the AAA-rated mortgage-backed securities and almost the entire Baa-rated securities.[36] The mortgage-backed securities had been rated in essentially three separate tranches or classes, namely AAA, AA and BBB. By separating the classes of securities through different ratings, the structured mortgage securities could be subordinated.

Through the process of subordination, the structured products could be marketed to different investors, depending on their risk profiles, investment needs and requirements. Hence, investors, including government authorities, that required higher credit ratings on their purchases of collateralized debt would typically buy AAA-rated tranches of mortgage-backed securities. The senior tranches of securities and collateralized debt would provide the holder of the securities with greater creditor protection in the event of mortgage default.

However, when the underlying sub-prime mortgages began to lose value, so did the overall value of the mortgage-backed securities and collateralized debt obligations. The decline in value in the structured financial products became even more pronounced when the rating agencies began to downgrade the RMBSs and CDOs to junk status in 2007 and 2008.[37]

The synthetic nature of some of the structured financial products also created its own set of problems. Since most of the mortgage-backed securities and CDOs had been bundled together with credit default swaps and pooled into special purpose vehicles, investors who purchased the synthetic structured products may not have fully appreciated their underlying inherent risk.

---

securitization of collateralized debt obligations (CDOs), CDOs squared, and synthetic CDOs continued unabated, greatly expanding the exposure to losses when the housing market collapsed and exacerbating the impact of the collapse on the financial system and the economy." Financial Crisis Inquiry Commission Report (Ibid., (n. 18)), p. 212.

35   Ibid., (n. 18), p. 3.

36   Ibid., (n. 18), pp. 222–3.

37   The Commission of Inquiry into the Financial Crisis found that the rating agencies downgraded 83% of all the 2006 Aaa-rated mortgage-backed securities tranches and all of the Baa tranches. Moreover, of the mortgage-backed securities issued in 2006 over 75% had been downgraded and nearly all of the securities issued in 2007 were downgraded to junk status. Ibid., pp. 222–3. The Commission of Inquiry also found that nearly all of the CDOs that had been issued had also been downgraded to junk status by 2008. Ibid., (n. 18), pp. 223–4.

The Shadow Banking Sector

The problems created with complex and opaque mortgage securities, CDOs and other structured financial products have led to calls for the industry to be subject to greater regulation and supervision. One of the main areas of concern was the parallel nature of the structured finance industry and its potential to cause systemic risk throughout domestic and international financial markets.

Market regulators, including the SEC and the CFTC, expressed concern with the shadow banking system that had been operating in parallel to the traditional banking industry in the United States. As is discussed in Chapter 2, the parallel banking system was largely unregulated and not subject to the regulatory controls or prudential oversight of standard US retail banks.

The shadow banking industry played a central role in the period leading up to the financial crisis.[38] The parallel system also made the financial crisis much worse in both its duration and its intensity. The build-up in risk in the parallel system had been due to market failure and the lack of regulation and supervision of market activity and market participants. Since the shadow banking system had been unregulated there was no clear strategy of managing or limiting the underlying inherent systemic risk that had largely gone unchecked.

According to the current US Treasury Secretary, Timothy Geithner, the parallel banking system in the United States had grown to become almost as large as the entire traditional banking industry: "At its peak, this alternative banking system financed about $8 trillion in assets. Many of these assets were financed with short-term obligations and in institutions or funding vehicles with substantial leverage – leaving them with relatively thin cushions of resources to protect against the probability of loss."[39]

As Geithner pointed out, the sheer size, volume and nature of activity associated with the parallel system should have been concern enough for market regulators. However, there was also the added problem that much of the activity in the shadow banking industry had been unregulated, with little or no prudential oversight of market participants and market activity. The parallel system had also relied heavily on traditional financial markets, including short-term money markets, mutual funds and commercial paper markets, to provide much-needed finance to develop structured financial products which were at the core of the financial crisis.

---

38   The Financial Crisis Inquiry Commission also concluded that the shadow banking system contributed to the systemic risk now confronting the entire global financial market. According to the Commission, the shadow banking system was "very fragile due to high leverage, short-term funding, risk assets, inadequate liquidity [...]." Ibid., (n. 18), p. 255.

39   Geithner 2010 (Testimony before the Financial Crisis Inquiry Commission. Causes of the financial crisis and the case for reform. Press Centre, US Department of the Treasury, 6 May 2010), p. 2.

Systemic Risk Concerns

Although the shadow banking system had operated in parallel to the traditional banking industry, the two systems were interlinked. The interlinkages between the parallel and traditional banking systems introduced an added level of complexity to the financial crisis. With a largely unregulated and unsupervised system in operation, not only was the shadow banking industry in competition with the traditional banking sector but the parallel system had also been responsible for transmitting the large build-up of risk to conventional markets.

In effect, the parallel banking industry had been operating as transmission channels for toxic sub-prime structured mortgage securities and CDOs.[40] As toxic securities entered the mainstream banking sector, systemic risk increased for financial markets in the United States as well as for other countries. The Commission of Inquiry into the Financial Crisis concluded:

> that the banking supervisors failed to adequately and proactively identify and police the weaknesses of the banks and thrifts [...]. This failure was caused by many factors, including beliefs that regulation was unduly burdensome [...]. The Federal Reserve realized far too late the systemic danger inherent in the interconnections of the unregulated over-the-counter (OTC) derivatives market and did not have the information to act.[41]

Regulators had noted the increasingly excessive riskiness of the shadow banking system for a number of years. As the Commission discovered, the precise nature of the build-up of risk and its adverse impact on systemic or contagion risk were not well understood or appreciated. The former Treasury Secretary acknowledged the shortcomings of the regulatory framework in effectively dealing with the shadow banking system in testimony that he provided to the Commission.[42]

---

40   The Financial Crisis Inquiry Commission confirmed the interconnectedness of the shadow banking system with traditional financial markets. According to the Commission, when the sub-prime mortgage market collapsed, other financial markets reacted adversely by cutting off the availability of short-term funds, including commercial paper and repo lending markets. The Commission was of the view that "these markets and other interconnections created contagion, as the crisis spread even to markets and firms that had little or no direct exposure to the mortgage market." Ibid., (n. 18), p. 255.

41   Financial Crisis Inquiry Commission 2011 (Ibid., (n. 18)), p. 308.

42   According to Paulson, the regulatory framework in the United States had become outdated and failed to keep pace with the changes in financial markets: "But like all activities in the financial sector, these markets were fueled by the global excesses and regulatory flaws I have already discussed. Inside and outside the traditional banking system, financial institutions overreached, financial services were misused, and financial products were misunderstood. In addition, our regulatory system was balkanized, outdated, and lacked the infrastructure to oversee these markets [...]." Paulson 2010b (Testimony by Henry M. Paulson Jr before the Financial Crisis Inquiry Commission, 6 May 2010), p. 3.

However, the former Federal Reserve Chairman, Alan Greenspan, provided testimony before the Commission that appeared to suggest that the Federal Reserve had been monitoring the activities of sub-prime mortgage originators, particularly when it came to the issue of consumer protection.[43] Whether regulators had provided effective supervision of the activities of mortgage originators in the sub-prime mortgage market was less clear. There was evidence that there had been an excessive build-up in risky practices in the shadow banking system which had been allowed to spill over into mainstream financial markets.

In many ways, the build-up in risk that began in the shadow banking system was then channelled into the traditional banking sector because of the interlinkages that existed between the two systems. Financial intermediaries that operated in the parallel system had developed complex structured financial products. The products were then sold to a number of investors, both retail and sophisticated, in mainstream financial markets.

The values that had been attributed to the structured financial instruments were derived from the underlying value of residential property in the United States. As house prices began to fall, so did the underlying value of the structured financial instruments. When the instruments were later downgraded to junk status they became worthless, leading to a run on credit, equity and other financial markets all over the world. Hence, as the global and US housing bubble popped, causing significant declines in the value of residential real estate asset values, the values of the residential mortgage-backed securities were also, simultaneously, affected.

A similar problem was now emerging with systemic risk at the global level once the traditional banking sector had become infected with toxic sub-prime securities. At the height of the financial panic following the collapse of Lehman Brothers, questions began to emerge as to the safety, soundness and stability of the entire global financial system. By late 2008 and early 2009, evidence had emerged to suggest that financial markets had ceased to operate normally, with many credit and debt markets showing signs of dislocation, excessive volatility and stress.

The interactions of the various financial markets in exacerbating the financial crisis now exposed the flaws in US regulatory policy. For years, regulatory authorities had been concerned with the stability of individual institutions and

---

43   See, for example, Greenspan's statement: "On the broader subject of the Federal Reserve's approach to consumer protection in subprime lending, it is important to keep in mind that the subprime mortgage market evolved and changed dramatically over the past decade – and the Federal Reserve, together with the other banking agencies, carefully monitored those developments and adjusted our supervisory policy to meet the evolving challenges in the marketplace." Greenspan 2010b (Testimony of Alan Greenspan before the Financial Crisis Inquiry Commission, 7 April 2010), p. 15.

financial intermediaries instead of the stability of the financial system as a whole.[44] As the Commission noted in its draft preliminary report on the shadow banking system, the US Federal Reserve, like other central banks, had both a stability mandate and a supervisory mandate.[45] However, neither the Federal Reserve nor any other regulatory authority in the US – or elsewhere for that matter – had a mandate to monitor systemic risk "that could arise from the combined activities of individual companies."[46]

The US Federal Reserve Chairman Ben Bernanke, also recognized the shortcomings and limitations of the Federal Reserve's mandate in dealing with the systemic nature of the crisis: "Although regulators can do a great deal on their own to improve financial regulation and oversight, the Congress also must act. We have seen numerous instances when weaknesses and gaps in the regulatory structure itself contributed to the crisis, many of which can only be addressed by statutory change."[47]

Bernanke was now advocating for legislative reform to tackle any future financial crisis. The GFC had highlighted the importance of strengthening regulatory and supervisory oversight of financial markets by removing gaps within the legislative framework:

> to promote financial stability and to address the extremely serious problem posed by firms perceived as "too big to fail," legislative action is needed to create new mechanisms for oversight of the financial system as a whole; to ensure that all systemically important financial firms are subject to effective consolidated supervision; and to establish procedures for winding down a failing, systemically critical institution without seriously damaging the financial system and the economy.[48]

As is discussed in Chapter 7, the *Dodd-Frank Act 2010* introduced a number of important initiatives to improve financial stability. One such initiative concerned the creation of two new bodies, namely the Financial Stability Oversight Council (FSOC), which had its inaugural meeting in October 2010, and the Office of Financial Research (OFR). Both bodies, which have been enacted under the *Dodd-Frank Act 2010* have as their collective aims:

---

44 Financial Crisis Inquiry Commission 2010c (Preliminary Staff Report: Shadow banking and the financial crisis, 4 May 2010), p. 14.
45 Ibid., p. 14.
46 Id.
47 Bernanke 2009b (Financial regulation and supervision after the crisis – the role of the Federal Reserve. Speech by Chairman Ben S. Bernanke at the Federal Reserve Bank of Boston 54th Economic Conference, Chatham, Massachusetts, 23 October 2009. Board of Governors of the Federal Reserve System), p. 1.
48 Ibid.

1. To identify risks to the financial stability of the United States that could arise from the material distress or failure, or ongoing activities, of large, interconnected bank holding companies (including non-bank financial companies).[49]
2. To promote market discipline, by eliminating expectations on the part of shareholders, creditors and counterparties.[50]
3. To respond to emerging threats to the stability of the United States financial system.[51]

Although the reforms introduced by the *Dodd-Frank Act 2010* were designed to improve systemic risk concerns associated with the collapse of a major financial intermediary, the reforms are limited to the jurisdiction of the United States. Since the global financial market is interlinked with the financial markets of every other country, the overall effectiveness of systemic risk regulation will necessarily involve cooperation and coordination from other international regulatory authorities.[52] Only through the creation of international regulatory authorities and regulatory frameworks will the goal of minimizing systemic risk in all financial markets be realized.[53]

Liquidity and Short-term Money Markets

Another area of concern which was highlighted by the GFC is related to the lack of liquidity in short-term money markets. A number of firms involved in the development and sale of structured financial products such as residential mortgage-backed securities and collateralized debt obligations increasingly relied on the availability of liquidity and funding from short-term money markets, mutual funds and commercial paper markets. The world's banks had also become dependent on short-term markets to source funding for their domestic borrowing needs.

When funding sources for credit dried up following the collapse of Lehman Brothers, borrowers of commercial lines of credit could not rollover their loans. The inability of highly leveraged firms to obtain and source short-term credit in

---

49 See section 112(1)(a) of the *Dodd-Frank Act 2010*.
50 Ibid., section 112(1)(b).
51 Ibid., section 112(1)(c).
52 International coordination by international regulatory authorities will be necessary in order to reduce systemic risk concerns. Bernanke made a similar point at a speech in Massachusetts: "Not much more than a year ago, we and our international counterparts faced the most severe financial crisis since the Great Depression. Fortunately, forceful and coordinated policy actions averted a global financial collapse, and since then, aided by a range of government programs, financial conditions have improved considerably." Bernanke 2009b (Ibid., (n. 47)), p. 1.
53 See Chapter 8, where it is proposed that a new international regulatory agency be created to promote the goal of financial stability in international financial markets.

money markets and commercial paper led to borrowers defaulting on their loans. The stability of short-term money and commercial paper markets were adversely affected by the defaults that had commenced in 2008, leading to further panic and runs on global financial markets.

In October 2010, the President's Working Group on Financial Markets examined the activities in short-term money markets.[54] The Working Group was established to examine further the vulnerabilities of the financial system and to offer suggestions for improvement.[55] In October 2010. the President's Working Group was asked to examine the run on short-term money market funds following the collapse of Lehman Brothers in September 2008.

The Working Group found that money market funds had been susceptible to runs in times of excessive market volatility or stress. The structural weaknesses were exposed by the collapse of Lehman Brothers. According to the Working Group's Report, money market funds were susceptible to runs because shareholders "have an incentive to redeem their shares before others do [especially] when there is a perception that the fund might suffer a loss."[56]

Ordinarily, shareholders who choose to redeem their shares would not cause any real concern. However, the crisis demonstrated that when shareholders act in a herd-type mentality and all shareholders simultaneously redeem their shares, the vulnerability of the short-term money market is exposed. The consequences of excessive volatility in short-term funding markets can also lead to further systemic dislocation as companies and businesses attempt to refinance or rollover commercial lines of credit. The dislocation affecting short-term credit markets could, in turn, lead to damage to the real economy as lending and credit growth would be restricted, causing economic activity to decline.

To overcome some of the vulnerabilities in money market funds, the Securities and Exchange Commission in the United States announced new rules for market participants. As is discussed in Chapter 6, the SEC's rules resulted in regulatory changes to the way money market funds would now be organized. The reforms were designed to mitigate the systemic risks associated with volatility in short-term money and commercial paper markets. The SEC rules aim to mitigate systemic risk by reducing liquidity risk, credit risk and interest rate risks associated with money market funds.[57] In addition, the SEC rules require fund advisers to periodically stress-test their funds' ability to maintain stability given certain

---

54   President's Working Group on Financial Markets. 2010. Report on money market fund reform options. President's Working Group, October 2010. Washington, DC: G.P.O.

55   In 2009, the US Department of the Treasury issued a discussion paper: Financial regulatory reform: A new foundation (Washington, DC, 17 June 2009). The paper recommended the establishment of the President's Working Group on Financial Markets to conduct a study and make recommendations for further reforms designed to mitigate the susceptibility of money market funds to runs.

56   President's Working Group on Financial Markets. Ibid., (n. 54), p. 2.

57   The new SEC rules are discussed in more detail in Chapter 6.

hypothetical events.[58] The new rules also place more stringent restrictions on repurchase agreements that are used as collateral to secure additional borrowings.

Despite the new SEC rules, the President's Working Group recognized that additional reforms were required to reduce the susceptibility of money market funds to the risk of panic runs. Further reforms would be required to mitigate "the risk of runs before another liquidity crisis materializes."[59] The Working Group considered that mitigating risks with money market funds would be "especially important because the events of September 2008 may have induced expectations of government assistance at minimal cost in the case of severe financial stress."[60]

The expectation by market participants that governments will intervene to prevent further distortions flowing to the real economy poses an interesting dilemma. If the expectation is in fact realized through government-funded bailouts, market participants and investors might well engage in further risky market practices with the expectation that governments will intervene to correct any distortions. This poses governments with the challenges of moral hazard, since risky behaviour by market participants will effectively go unpunished.[61]

The expectation that governments will in fact intervene in financial markets, especially short-term money markets, was confirmed by the recent financial crisis and by the President's Working Group: "Market participants know, and recent events have confirmed, that when runs on MMFs occur, the government will face substantial pressure to intervene in some manner to minimize the propagation of financial strains to short-term funding markets and to the real economy."[62]

The interventions would be required not only to protect investors in money markets but also to minimize systemic risk and contagion spreading to the entire financial system. There would be a real need for government authorities to intervene to prevent disruptions to the real economy. Importantly, such interventions would be intended not only to reduce harm to money market fund investors but also to prevent disruptions of markets for commercial paper and other short-term financing instruments, which are critical for the functioning of the economy.[63]

As is discussed in Chapter 6, the President's Working Group recommended that a range of policy options be explored with the aim of further mitigating systemic risk concerns with money market funds. Broadly, the policy options put forward

---

58   President's Working Group on Financial Markets (Ibid., (n. 54)), p. 15.

59   Ibid., (n. 54), p. 16.

60   Id.

61   The problem of moral hazard and expectations was pointed out by the President's Working Group: "Without additional reforms to more fully mitigate the risk of a run spreading among money market funds, the actions to support the money market fund industry that the US government took beginning in 2008 may create an expectation for similar government support during future financial crises, and the resulting moral hazard may make crises in the MMF industry more frequent than the historical record would suggest." President's Working Group on Financial Markets (Ibid., (n. 54)), p. 18.

62   Ibid.

63   Ibid.

by the President's Working Group were designed to improve stability of short-term money markets. By making money markets more stable it was expected that systemic risk would be mitigated or contained so as to minimize the risk of further disruption through the entire financial system.

Counterbalancing the purported benefits of further reform and regulation were investor perceptions that enhanced regulation would increase compliance costs. With increased regulatory cost burdens, investors may choose to become more active in less regulated markets and utilize instead other alternatives. As the Working Group acknowledges, for regulation to be effective the proposed reforms, which are designed to mitigate systemic risks with short-term money markets, would need to be extended to alternative markets, including cash management substitutes.[64]

Conclusion

There is little doubt that financial markets played a central role in the global financial meltdown of 2008 and 2009. Through globalization, financial markets had become interconnected, which in turn increased the risk of systemic or contagion risk spreading throughout the entire financial system following a large-scale market disruption. The shadow banking system, which was largely unregulated and lacked prudential oversight, was now linked to the soundness and stability of mainstream banks.

The shadow banking system had become increasingly popular for financial intermediaries to develop and fund structured financial products in the form of residential mortgage-backed securities and collateralized debt obligations. These two innovative instruments alone accounted for much of the build-up in risk that existed within the shadow banking system. When Lehman Brothers collapsed in September 2008, funding in short-term money markets began to dry up. The lending restrictions on short-term funding led to a crisis in the shadow banking system. Since the parallel system had been largely unregulated, there was no regulatory authority that could prevent the build-up in risk from spilling over into mainstream financial markets. The scene had now been set for the perfect financial storm.

---

64   Ibid., (n. 54), p. 19.

Chapter 5
Rescue Packages and Policy Responses

Introduction

The GFC triggered an unprecedented response by governments all over the world. Not surprisingly, the countries most affected by the crisis, the United States and the member states of the European Union (EU), responded vigorously in their attempts to stabilize their financial systems and mitigate the effects of systemic risk. There remained a number of challenges for governments and policymakers to overcome in order to deal with the crisis effectively. First, there was the challenge of properly understanding and assessing the level of risk confronting the world's financial markets. This would, in turn, require analysis of the underlying sources and triggers of the GFC.[1]

Second, regulatory authorities came to the realization that both conventional and non-traditional methods were required to provide an effective policy response to deal with the consequences of the GFC on the real economy. With economic activity declining at an alarming rate and the rate of unemployment rising in many industrialized countries, central banks adopted expansionary monetary policy by aggressively reducing their key interest rates. However, when interest rates had been reduced to near zero levels, other non-standard policy responses were implemented to further stimulate economic growth.

Third, governments all around the world realized that if they were to provide an effective response to the global crisis, international coordination and cooperation would be required. Without proper coordination and cooperation any proposed regulatory reform or policy response would enjoy limited success.

Finally, there was a need for regulatory authorities and governments to acknowledge the weaknesses and structural vulnerabilities that existed within their own regulatory and supervisory frameworks. The financial crisis had exposed significant gaps that existed between market practices and regulatory frameworks. The gaps were especially apparent with OTC derivatives markets and the shadow banking system, which operated in parallel with the more highly regulated mainstream banking system.

Some countries adopted a more proactive policy response, whilst other domestic regulatory authorities reacted to the crisis in a more measured and reactionary manner. Sometimes governments and regulatory authorities responded with international coordination and cooperation, often with either the

---

1 See Chapter 2 for a discussion of the triggers of the GFC.

United States or the European Union leading the way with policy responses and strategic direction. On other occasions regulatory authorities from each country would adopt unilateral actions designed to prevent any further fallout from the crisis.

The United States

The GFC was particularly damaging to the US economy. As a result of dislocated financial and credit markets, economic activity fell at an alarming rate. In the third and fourth quarters of 2008, industrial production recorded the largest quarterly decline since World War II. The falling levels of aggregate demand and economic activity in turn led to the largest rise in unemployment since the Great Depression and the economic recessions immediately after World War II.

The US government responded to the crisis in October 2008 by passing legislation in the form of the *Emergency Economic Stabilization Act 2008* (H.R. 1424/P.L. 110–343), commonly called the Troubled Assets Relief Program (TARP). The introduction of the TARP program did not have a smooth passage in Congress. The program, which used taxpayers' funds to purchase toxic mortgage assets, was largely viewed as a government-sponsored program to bail out the Wall Street excesses at the expense of "main street" workers and families.

US TARP

The *Emergency Economic Stabilization Act 2008* authorized the US Treasury to purchase billions of dollars of toxic mortgage-backed securities from US mortgage originators and investment banks.[2] The main aim of the program was to ensure that the toxic assets would be effectively flushed out of the US financial system. TARP was designed to provide a safe harbour and protect the American economy, taxpayers and business from the financial fallout from toxic sub-prime mortgages and structured financial products.

The TARP Act provided the legal mandate for Treasury to make funding commitments to purchase troubled assets from any financial institution on terms

---

2   See Section 2 of the *Emergency Economic Stabilization Act 2008* (hereafter referred to as the TARP Act), which provides that the purposes of the Act are:
    (1) to immediately provide authority and facilities that the Secretary of the Treasury can use to restore liquidity and stability to the financial system of the United States;
    (2) To ensure that such authority and such facilities are used in a manner that:
        (a) protects home values, college funds, retirement accounts, and life savings;
        (b) preserves homeownership and promotes jobs and economic growth;
        (c) maximizes overall returns to the taxpayers of the United States; and
        (d) provides public accountability for the exercise of such authority.

and conditions directed by the Treasury Secretary.[3] TARP also enacted a key recommendation of the Treasury Department discussion paper on financial markets reform,[4] which recommended the creation of an Office of Financial Stability and Oversight.[5]

One of the main functions of the Office of Financial Stability will be to provide for proper oversight of the TARP funds to be expended by the Treasury Secretary for the purchase of toxic assets. Included as part of its oversight functions, the Office of Financial Stability will also be responsible for the appointment of financial agents, designing asset classes to be purchased under TARP and providing plans for the use of special purpose vehicles to purchase troubled assets.[6] The Financial Stability Office will also be responsible for reporting any suspected fraud, misrepresentation or malfeasance to the Special Inspector General for TARP or the Attorney General of the United States.[7]

The TARP Act authorizes TARP funds to be used to purchase "troubled assets" from any "financial institution." The term "troubled assets" is broadly defined to include any assets:

> residential or commercial mortgages and any securities, obligations, or other instruments that are based on or related to such mortgages that were issued or originated on or before 14 March 2008, the purpose of which the Secretary of the Treasury determines promotes financial market stability.[8]

Troubled assets can also include:

> any other financial instrument that the Secretary [of the Treasury] after consultation with the Chairman of the Board of Governors of the Federal Reserve System determines the purchase of which is necessary to promote financial market stability.[9]

The term "financial institution" is also broadly defined to include:

> any institution, including, but not limited to, any bank, savings association, credit union, security broker or dealer, or insurance company, established and regulated under the laws of the United States.[10]

---

3 See section 101.

4 See US Department of Treasury 2009 (Financial regulatory reform: a new foundation, rebuilding financial supervision and regulation. Discussion paper, 17 June 2009: Washington, DC).

5 See section 104.

6 Section 104(a)(1)(A).

7 Section 104(a)(1)(B)(3).

8 Section 3(9) (A).

9 Section 3(9)(B).

10 Section 3(5).

Mindful of the fact that taxpayer funds were being used to purchase toxic assets held by financial institutions, the TARP Act provided additional assistance to US homeowners. Under TARP, when acquiring residential mortgages, mortgage-backed securities and other assets secured by residential real estate, the Treasury Secretary needs to implement a plan which seeks to maximize the level of assistance that will be provided to homeowners.[11] Assistance is to be provided in the form of encouraging mortgage providers to minimize foreclosures on family homes, and for the Secretary to use loan guarantees and other credit enhancements to facilitate loan modifications.

In addition, the Treasury Secretary should also where possible allow tenants who are residing in homes and who are not in default on their rent to continue to live in their home.[12] Further assistance will also be provided to home borrowers "to reasonable requests for loss mitigation measures, including term extensions, rate reductions, principal write downs."[13]

The assistance measures are designed to minimize foreclosures so that owners can remain in their homes. In the event of foreclosure, homeowners can receive additional support through other governmental agencies.[14] Foreclosures have been a considerable problem in the United States because most home borrowers have non-recourse loans. This is a peculiar feature of US mortgages which typically have fixed rates of interest, are secured by way of collateral against the residence, and allow the borrower to walk away from any future loan obligations in the event of foreclosure.

Non-recourse loans expose mortgage originators to risk of loss in the event of loan default by the borrower. This is because the borrower with a non-recourse loan can walk away if the mortgage debt exceeds the aggregate value of the collateralized home. The lender has no recourse to make the borrower pay the shortfall. When this occurs, the loan is effectively "under water," because the total value of the loan exceeds the value of the mortgaged asset. This situation is typically known as "negative equity," as the remaining equity in the home falls below zero.

In the event of significant house price declines, the risk of loss following foreclosure will have effectively passed from the borrower to the lender. A direct consequence of the current crisis has been the millions of homes which have been foreclosed in the United States. This has led to the supply of available houses for sale to increase dramatically, which, in turn, has caused significant price declines, and exposed holders of mortgage securities to billion dollar losses.

The homeowner assistance afforded under TARP would have a second important aim, namely to minimize the rate of foreclosure in the United States. If successful, the homeowner assistance would place an effective floor on any

---

11   Section 109.
12   Section 109(b).
13   TARP Act, Section 109(c).
14   TARP Act, Section 110(b)(1).

further decline in prices for residential homes. By reducing the available stock of homes for sale, the expectation would be that there would be a more orderly sale of foreclosed homes, which would stabilize house prices and reduce loan losses.

In addition to providing homeowner assistance, the TARP Act also implemented reforms for the executive remuneration and corporate governance of financial institutions involved in the sale of troubled assets.[15] When the US Treasury purchases equity or takes on the liability obligations of a financial institution which holds troubled assets, the Treasury Secretary shall "require that the financial institution meet appropriate standards of executive compensation and corporate governance."[16] The relevant standard that is required to be applied under the TARP Act continues for the entire duration that the Treasury holds investment in the financial institution, and includes the following criteria:

> limits on compensation that exclude incentives for senior executive officers[17] of a financial institution to take unnecessary and excessive risks that threaten the value of the financial institution; provision for the recovery by the financial institution of any bonus or incentive compensation paid to a senior executive officer based on statements of earnings, gains or other criteria; prohibition on the financial institution making any golden parachute payment to its senior executive officer during the period that US Treasury holds an equity or debt position in the financial institution.[18]

The provisions relating to executive compensation serve an important public aim and are designed to ensure that senior executive officers do not receive disproportionate remuneration at the expense of the American taxpayer. Reconciling the use of public funds to shore up the stability of the US financial sector and not allowing Wall Street investment bankers to be enriched would always prove to be a difficult task. Both the Bush and Obama administrations had strong public support to prevent senior executives at failed financial institutions deriving significant personal returns at the expense of American taxpayers.

Under TARP, the Treasury Secretary is entitled to a graduated system of authorized payments to purchase troubled assets from American financial institutions. Section 115 provides that the Treasury Secretary can purchase troubled assets in three distinct tranches:

---

15   See TARP Act, Section 111. Under section 111, "any financial institution that sells troubled assets to the Secretary under [the TARP Act] shall be subject to the executive compensation requirements."

16   See TARP Act, Section 111(b)(1).

17   The term "senior executive officer" means "an individual who is one of the top 5 highly paid executives of a public company, whose compensation is required to be disclosed pursuant to the Securities Exchange Act of 1934." (TARP Act, Section 111(b)(3)).

18   TARP Act, Section 111(b)(1).

$US250 billion at any one time;[19] $US350 billion at any one time provided the President of the US submits to the Congress written certification that the Treasury Secretary needs to exercise the authority under this provision;[20] $US700 billion outstanding at any one time provided the President of the US provides Congress with a written report detailing the plan of the Treasury Secretary to exercise the authority under this section.[21]

Hence, TARP became known as the $US700 billion bail out fund, designed to be used to purchase toxic mortgage assets from financial institutions located in the US. The overall aim of the bailout package was to promote financial stability in the US financial sector as well as the overall US economy. However, the US government came under increasing pressure to provide assistance to main street businesses, unemployed workers and families who had become victims of the GFC.

US Automotive Industry

With this in mind, President Obama announced that he would provide assistance to the US automotive industry and, in particular, to Chrysler LLC in the United States and Chrysler Canada Inc.[22] Both the US and Canadian governments would contribute $US10.5 billion in funding, including short-term and medium-term capital and debtor-in-possession financing to assist with the court-supervised restructuring of Chrysler LLC.

Out of the total $US10.5 billion in term funding, the United States would contribute $US8.08 billion, whilst the Canadian governments (including the Government of Canada and the Government of Ontario) would provide $US2.42 billion.[23] The investment by both countries would see the United States government obtain 8% equity in the restructured Chrysler entity and the Canadian government would receive 2% in Chrysler. The funding arrangement for Chrysler was conditional on the US government receiving the authority to appoint four independent directors to the Chrysler board, with the Government of Ontario having the authority to appoint one independent director.

In addition to the financial assistance provided by both governments, the US government would also be active in arranging for another international car company, namely FIAT, to partner an arrangement to restructure Chrysler and

---

19   Section 115(a)(1).
20   Section 115(a)(2).
21   TARP Act, Section 115(a)(3).
22   See US Government 2009b (The White House, Office of the Press Secretary, joint press release by President Obama and Prime Minster Harper. United States–Canada support for Chrysler LLC, 30 April 2009. Available at: <http://www.whitehouse.gov/the-press-office/joint-statement-president-obama-and-prime-minister-harper-united-states-canada-supp>).
23   Ibid.

save thousands of jobs. Under the arrangement Fiat would contribute a free licence permitting all of its intellectual property to be utilized with Chrysler in exchange for 20% of the equity in the restructured Chrysler entity. Fiat would also have the right to appoint three additional directors to the reconstituted Chrysler board. Fiat would also obtain an additional 15% in the equity of Chrysler in three installments of 5% each in exchange for satisfying key performance indicators, including: the introduction of a new vehicle to be produced at the Chrysler plant in the US; the provision of a distribution network for Chrysler in numerous foreign jurisdictions; and the manufacture of state-of-the-art, next-generation engines at a US Chrysler factory.[24]

As was reported by the Obama Administration press statement, the new Chrysler entity would also establish an independent trust that would provide health care benefits for Chrysler's retired workers.[25] To pay for these benefits, the trust would be funded by issuing notes of up to $US4.6 billion payable over approximately 13 years with a 9% rate of interest. In return, the trust would receive 55% equity in the new Chrysler and would have the right to appoint one independent director to the new restructured board.[26]

US Monetary Policy

US monetary policy became a key instrument for the US Federal Reserve to use to respond to the GFC. However, some had argued that monetary policy had become a blunt policy instrument that would be incapable of providing an effective and measured policy response to the unfolding crisis. Even the Chairman of the US Federal Reserve, Ben Bernanke, commented that the crisis was "so complex that its lessons are many, and they are not always straightforward [...]. As with regulatory policy, we must discern the lessons of the crisis for monetary policy. However, the nature of those lessons is controversial. Some observers have assigned monetary policy a central role in the crisis."[27]

---

24 See US Government 2009a (The White House, Office of the Press Secretary, Obama administration auto restructuring initiative Chrysler–Fiat alliance, 30 April 2009. Available at: <http://www.whitehouse.gov/the_press_office/Obama-Administration-Auto-Restructuring-Initiative/>).

25 In addition to the funding that would be provided by the Obama Administration, the US government would also provide additional support of approximately $US3.3 billion working capital in the form of debtor possession financing to support Chrysler through its Chapter 11 filing and restructure with Fiat. The US government would also provide a new loan to the new Chrysler entity worth approximately $US4.7 billion in the form of a term loan, with $US2.1 billion due in 30 months and the balance of 50% due on the eighth anniversary of the loan. Ibid., (n. 24), p. 2.

26 Ibid. The Chrysler pension plan for employees of Chrysler will also be preserved with the additional $US600 million contribution from Daimler.

27 Bernanke 2010b (Monetary policy and the housing bubble. Speech at the annual meeting of the American Economic Association, Atlanta, Georgia, 3 January 2010), p. 1.

Despite these uncertainties, monetary policy became the main regulatory policy relied upon by authorities throughout the crisis. From as early as August 2007, the Federal Reserve had noted that financial market conditions had deteriorated, credit conditions from short-term money markets had tightened and increased uncertainty existed about global economic growth.[28]

The first reduction in the US federal funds rate occurred in September 2007, when the Federal Open Market Committee (FOMC) decided to lower its target for the federal funds rate by 50 basis points to 4.75%. According to the FOMC, economic growth had been moderate over the first half of 2007, but the tighter credit conditions that existed, particularly in short-term money markets, had the "potential to intensify the housing correction, and to restrain economic growth more generally."[29]

The federal funds rate was again reduced in October 2007, this time by 25 basis points to 4.5%. According to the Committee, although economic growth was solid in the third quarter of 2007, and strains had eased in financial markets, "the pace of economic expansion [would] likely slow in the near term."[30] In December 2007 the FOMC lowered its federal funds rate by another 25 basis points to 4.25%. The reduction in the key federal funds rate was recommended on the basis of continuing slowdown in economic growth and further intensification of the housing correction. Further strains in financial markets had also occurred, with evidence of tighter credit conditions being played out in short-term money markets.

In January 2008, the US economic outlook weakened further, with appreciable downside risks to overall economic activity. Although short-term money market conditions had improved slightly, the broader financial market outlook had deteriorated. Given the ongoing weakness, the Federal Reserve lowered its target federal funds rate by 75 basis points to 3.5%.[31] This was a significant reduction by the Federal Reserve. The size of the cut in the key federal fund rate indicated that the US economy had slowed dramatically and was headed for a considerable slowdown.

The concern for a sizeable downturn in the US economy was further reflected by the Federal Reserve, which again lowered the federal fund rate by another 50 basis points to 3% in the month of January 2008. According to the FOMC:

---

28   Board of Governors of the Federal Reserve System. 2007a (Press release, 17 August 2007). Available at: <http://www.federalreserve.gov/newsevents/press/monetary /20070817b.htm>.

29   Board of Governors of the Federal Reserve. 2007b (Press release, 18 September 2007). Available at: <http://www.federalreserve.gov/newsevents/press/monetary/200709 18a.htm>.

30   Board of Governors of the Federal Reserve System 2007c (Press release, 31 October 2007). Available at: <http://www.federalreserve.gov/newsevents/press/monetary /20071031a.htm>.

31   Board of Governors of the Federal Reserve System 2008a (Press release, 22 January 2008). Available at: <http://www.federalreserve.gov/newsevents/press/monetary /20080122b.htm>.

[f]inancial markets remain under considerable stress, and credit has tightened further for some businesses and households. Moreover, recent information indicates a deepening of the housing contraction as well as some softening of labor markets.[32]

Unfortunately, the reductions in the key federal fund rate proved to be insufficient on their own to stabilize US financial markets. The markets remained under stress and liquidity pressures continued to build in funding markets. In order to improve liquidity in financial markets, the Federal Reserve with other central banks, including the Bank of Canada, the Bank of England, the European Central Bank, the Bank of Japan and the Swiss National Bank, announced measures to provide term funding of up to $US200 billion to financial intermediaries.[33]

Lending through the Fed's balance sheet is a non-conventional monetary policy response. It was designed to provide additional liquidity to US financial markets, which had been experiencing tighter credit conditions. The Fed's term lending strategy was aimed at overcoming the liquidity crisis in the US banking sector and fostering a more orderly functioning of financial markets. Under the additional lending package announced by the FOMC, the Fed would lend up to $US200 billion of Treasury securities to primary dealers in financial markets for a term of up to 28 days. Further, the Fed would also provide pledges for other securities, including federal agency debt, federal agency residential mortgage-backed securities and non-agency AAA/Aaa-rated private residential mortgage-backed securities.[34]

In addition to increasing domestic lending through the Fed's balance sheet, the FOMC authorized further increases in its existing temporary swap lines with other central banks, including the European Central Bank (ECB) and the Swiss National Bank. These arrangements would provide additional funding to both the ECB and the Swiss National Bank, which are designed to increase liquidity in European financial markets.[35] The Federal Reserve then announced further aggressive cuts to the federal funds rate in March 2008. By the beginning of April the Fed would lower its key interest rate by another 75 basis points to 2.25%.[36]

The Fed was now committed to utilizing its full array of policy options to respond to the crisis in US financial markets along with the emerging downturn in

---

32 Board of Governors of the Federal Reserve System 2008b (Press release, 30 January 2008). Available at: <http://www.federalreserve.gov/newsevents/press/monetary/20080130a.htm>.

33 Board of Governors of the Federal Reserve System 2008c (Press release, 11 March 2008). Available at: <http://www.federalreserve.gov/newsevents/press/monetary/200803 11a.htm>.

34 Ibid.

35 Ibid.

36 Board of Governors of the Federal Reserve 2008d (Press release, 18 March 2008). Available at: <http://www.federalreserve.gov/newsevents/press/monetary/20080318a.htm>.

the US economy. The Fed's policy response would now include a combination of both conventional and non-traditional methods to deal with the crisis. The Fed's conventional response would be to continue to aggressively cut its federal funds rate to the point that the key rate would be reduced to a range between 0% and 0.25%. The Fed would also deploy non-standard measures, including quantitative easing, in the form of lending from the Fed's balance sheet.

Following the collapse of Lehman Brothers and the continuing liquidity shortages in credit and money markets, the Fed implemented a quantitative easing program designed to stabilize US financial markets. In March 2009, the Fed announced that it would purchase an additional $US750 billion in toxic mortgage-backed securities, which would bring the total purchases of these toxic assets to $US1.25 trillion. The Fed would also purchase up to $US300 billion in longer-term Treasury securities, and up to $US200 billion of agency debt by the end of 2009.[37]

By September 2009, the US Federal Reserve received indications that economic activity had slightly improved following the severe downturn experienced in late 2007 and throughout 2008 and early 2009. There were signs that household consumption appeared to be stabilizing and activity in the housing sector had improved from its low base earlier in the year.[38] Although the policy responses by the Federal Reserve appeared to have their anticipated effect in providing much-needed liquidity, job growth remained sluggish and the unemployment rate would continue to climb, to be almost 10% by 2010.[39]

The Federal Reserve acknowledged the weakness in the recovery of the US economy, as well as the continued high levels of unemployment. The situation was about to take a dramatic turn for the worse when, at the time the economic recovery was appearing to take hold and financial markets had been emerging from their crisis, uncertainty and volatility began to intensify in European currency and financial markets.

In response to the unfolding crisis in confidence in the Euro, along with the US dollar, the Fed announced that it would recommence its swap lending facilities with other central banks around the world. The Fed re-established its temporary US dollar swap facilities with the Bank of Canada, the Bank of England, the ECB and the Swiss National Bank.[40] The Fed's temporary swap lines that were coordinated with other central banks were designed to provide much-needed liquidity in US and international financial markets. By improving liquidity the Fed

---

37   Ibid.
38   Board of Governors of the Federal Reserve System 2009 (Press release, 23 September 2009). Available at: <http://www.federalreserve.gov/newsevents/press/monetary/20090923a.htm>.
39   Ibid.
40   Board of Governors of the Federal Reserve System 2010a (Press release, 9 May 2010). Available at: <http://www.federalreserve.gov/newsevents/press/monetary/20100509a.htm>.

hoped its actions would help prevent the spread of systemic and contagion risk to international financial markets.[41]

Despite these proactive policy responses, the pace of recovery in economic activity, growth and employment remained subdued. With ongoing market volatility evident in European financial markets and the euro, there was heightened concern that the recovery in the international economy would be adversely affected. With the volatile market conditions persisting, the US Federal Reserve decided to keep its federal funds rate between the range of 0% and 0.25%, and engage in a new round of quantitative easing.

In November 2010, the Fed announced that it would purchase a further $US600 billion of longer-term Treasury securities by the first half of 2011.[42] This would equate to approximately $US75 billion per month. The additional asset purchases undertaken by the Fed were designed to inject additional liquidity into the US financial system. By improving liquidity credit and lending, markets would begin to stabilize, which, in turn, would encourage lending to businesses and individuals.

The policy responses provided by the Federal Reserve through its expansionary monetary policy agenda had provided much-needed stability to US financial markets. By utilizing both conventional and non-traditional methods, the Fed had been proactive in its policy response and determination to alleviate stress in financial markets and to stimulate economic activity. The expansionary policy response by the Fed had been supported by financial markets and promoted by the US government. The level of support for expansionary monetary policy was to be contrasted with US fiscal policy, which continues to be controversial and subject to much scrutiny and ongoing debate.

US Fiscal Policy

The severe economic recession that followed on from the GFC led to a significant deterioration in the United States' fiscal position. The US, like other countries, had suffered a considerable decline in its collection of tax revenues as a result of higher levels of unemployment and declining profitability from the corporate sector. In many ways the US budgetary position had responded appropriately, given the economic recession the country had been experiencing. When an economy experiences a slowdown, tax collections fall and welfare payments rise. The budget goes into deficit and becomes "automatically" expansionary. The expansionary nature of a fiscal deficit is designed to stimulate economic activity by increasing consumer demand for goods and services.

However, there is also a downside with a fiscal deficit, particularly if it is large and ongoing. In 2010, and 2011, the fiscal position of the United States government

---

41   Ibid.
42   Board of Governors of the Federal Reserve 2010b (Press release, 3 November 2010). Available at: <http://www.federalreserve.gov/newsevents/press/monetary/20101103a.htm>.

deteriorated significantly. According to the Congressional Budget Office (CBO), unless the US government takes active steps to reduce the federal fiscal deficit, the deficit will increase considerably. According to the CBO the federal debt in the United States at the end of 2010 would stand at 62% of GDP,[43] a significant rise from 2007, when the federal debt stood at 36% of GDP.[44]

The rise of the federal fiscal deficit in the United States represents a considerable challenge in US government policy. According to CBO, the rise in the deficit was directly attributable to the GFC. This is because the GFC led to a deep and protracted global recession. The fiscal deficit was also larger due to the expansionary policy responses adopted by Treasury and the US government to deal with the crisis.[45] The size of the current fiscal deficit in the US is also important for another reason. It is the first time since World War II that the US sovereign debt has exceeded 50%. Moreover, CBO has projected the federal debt to rise considerably in the United States over the following two decades. Under current US law the federal debt is expected to rise to be approximately 80% of GDP by 2035.

However, if the proposed changes to US tax laws (including indexation) and Medicare payments are made, then the US federal debt is expected to be nearly 90% of GDP by 2020, 110% by 2025 and a mammoth 180% by 2035.[46] The CBO estimates that if there is no change in tax revenue collections or government expenditure, by 2035 the rise in the fiscal deficit and associated government debt would "pose a clear threat of a fiscal crisis during the next two decades."[47]

Policymakers in the United States now face the daunting challenge of dealing with the high levels of unemployment caused by the Great Recession and the GFC, and the unintended consequence of a potential new crisis flowing from a ballooning fiscal deficit. The CBO has warned that the federal budget deficit in the United States has the potential of creating further uncertainty for financial markets and investors, leading to further destabilization of the US economy. This has happened in other countries that have experienced fiscal crises; these have often made recessions much worse than otherwise would have been the case.[48]

The potential for a new crisis to emerge, this time from an uncontrollable fiscal deficit in the United States, will inevitably limit the effectiveness of budgetary policy as a policy response to the GFC. With limitations on an effective expansionary fiscal policy, the US government is restricted on what actions it can

---

43   US Government 2010 (Congressional Budget Office. Federal debt and the risk of a fiscal crisis. The Congress of the United States, 27 July 2010), p. 2.
44   Ibid.
45   Ibid.
46   Ibid., (n. 43), p. 3.
47   Ibid.
48   Ibid., (n. 43), p. 4. See also Borensztein, E. and Panizza, U. 2008. The costs of sovereign default. Working Paper No. 08-238 (Washington, DC: International Monetary Fund), October.

take to deal with a crisis. However, a more disturbing consequence that could emerge from the fiscal deficit might be if the US government were to prematurely respond to lowering the deficit; the fragile recovery in the United States might stall as fiscal stimulus measures were wound back.

Bernanke makes an interesting observation regarding the current US fiscal deficit and overall fiscal sustainability:

> Expectations of large and increasing deficits in the future could inhibit current household and business spending – for example, by reducing confidence in the longer-term prospects for the economy or by increasing uncertainty about future tax burdens and government spending – and thus restrain recovery. Concerns about the government's long-run fiscal position may also constrain the flexibility of fiscal policy to respond to current economic conditions.[49]

According to both Bernanke and the CBO, unrestrained fiscal spending and/or declining tax revenues have resulted in an ever-increasing fiscal deficit that is unsustainable.[50] Both acknowledge the need for proper rules, along with careful consideration of the options that are available to return the federal budget to a position of fiscal sustainability.[51]

Moreover, any attempt to make fiscal adjustments designed to improve the underlying structural components of the fiscal deficit will mean that international consequences have to be taken into account. This is because if the United States were to act too aggressively in its pursuit of deficit reduction it may thwart any recovery in the international economy. The opposite is also true, namely, if the United States were to do nothing to address the issue of fiscal sustainability in the longer term, a new crisis could emerge which would undermine financial stability and long-run economic growth in both the United States and the international economy.[52]

---

49 Bernanke 2010a (Fiscal Sustainability and Fiscal Rules. Speech by Ben S. Bernanke, Chairman of the Board of Governors of the Federal Reserve System, delivered at the annual meeting of the Rhode Island Public Expenditure Council, Providence, Rhode Island, 4 October 2010), p. 1. Available at: <http://www.federalreserve.gov/newsevents/speech/bernanke20101004a.htm>.

50 US Government 2011 (Reducing the deficit: Spending and revenue options. The Congress of the United States. Washington, DC: Congressional Budget Office, March 2011).

51 Bernanke makes the valid point that although the options to returning the federal budget to fiscal sustainability will require choices and trade-offs that may well be difficult, "it is better to make these choices deliberately and thoughtfully." Ibid., (n. 49), p. 2.

52 See for example, Yellen 2010. (Fiscal responsibility and global rebalancing. Speech delivered by Janet L. Yellen, Board of Governors of the Federal Reserve System, at the Committee for Economic Development 2010 International Counterparts Conference, New York, 1 December 2010), pp. 3–4. Available at: <http://www.federalreserve.gov/newsevents/speech/yellen20101201a.htm>.

The European Union

Initially viewed as an American problem, the GFC was soon to engulf the entire world, including the member states of the European Union (EU). Unlike the United States, the EU does not have a legal mandate over the fiscal policy of its member states. Instead, the EU adopted a combination of communiqués, monetary policy and bailout packages in responding to the crisis.

The EU's communiqués were designed to provide an effective and coordinated policy response to any emerging issue arising from the crisis. In addition to the EU, some member states also individually responded to the crisis with a number of announcements and policy initiatives designed to address market volatility and investor uncertainty arising from the global crisis.

The EU Banking Communication

The EU Commission issued a communication entitled "The application of State aid rules to measures taken in relation to financial institutions in the context of the current global financial crisis," commonly called the "Banking Communication."[53] The EU issued the communication on 13 October 2008 following the collapse of Lehman Brothers in the United States. The Banking Communication was designed to bring stability to European financial markets, as well as the banking sector. By releasing the communication, the Commission implicitly recognized the importance of providing an effective policy response to the emerging crisis, which had "intensified markedly and now impacted heavily on the EU banking sector."[54]

According to the Commission the problems confronting financial markets in the United States had led to an erosion of investor confidence in the EU banking sector.[55] Investor uncertainty concerning the credit risk and financial viability of financial institutions, which included banks, building societies and credit unions, led to a crisis unfolding in interbank lending, which in turn led to liquidity shortages as lending and credit dried up in financial markets.

The Commission had also been acutely aware that interconnected financial markets increased the risk that a failure of a major financial institution would have systemic ramifications for European banks and financial markets.[56] The Commission felt it necessary to provide a determination regarding the use of state aid for member states to adopt and follow so that the measures "do not generate

---

53   OJ C 270/02, 25 October 2008.

54   European Union Commission 2008a (The application of state aid rules to measures taken in relation to financial institutions in the context of the current global financial crisis. 2008/C 270/02), 13 October 2008, paragraph 1.

55   Ibid., paragraphs 2 and 3.

56   Ibid., paragraph 4.

unnecessary distortions of competitions between financial institutions operating in the market or negative spillover effects on other Member States."[57]

Hence, the central purpose of the Banking Communication was to provide guidance for the development of depositor guarantee schemes for financial institutions, including banks, in each member state of the EU. To avoid any significant distortion of competition, the eligibility criteria for the depositor guarantee were to be objective, transparent, well targeted, proportionate to the challenge faced, and designed to minimize negative spillover.[58]

Under the Banking Communication, member states could provide retail deposit guarantees for their banks and financial institutions.[59] The retail deposit guarantees would give depositors additional security for customer deposits with EU banks. According to the Commission, the retail deposit guarantee would represent a "legitimate component of the public policy response."[60]

The Banking Communication also allowed member states to provide wholesale guarantees for their banks and financial institutions, provided these guarantees were targeted, practical and necessary to overcome the adverse effects of the financial crisis.[61] Provision for a wholesale guarantee was justified on the basis that the interbank lending market had dried up and there had been a systemic erosion of confidence among financial institutions. However, such guarantees were not to be extended to cover subordinate debt or any other associated liability, as this would provide protection to shareholders and other risk capital investors.[62]

In late 2008, EU member states began implementing guarantee schemes for their respective banks and financial institutions. The EU allowed its member states to increase its retail depositor guarantee from €20,000 to €50,000 initially and then up to €100,000.[63] The increase in the retail deposit guarantee by the EU would reduce the risk of bank runs, since the EU would guarantee retail deposits of up

---

57   Ibid., paragraph 5.
58   For criteria relating to the depositor guarantee scheme see paragraph 15 of the Banking Communication. Ibid., (n. 54).
59   Ibid., paragraphs 19–20.
60   Ibid., paragraph 19.
61   Ibid., paragraph 20.
62   Ibid., paragraph 23.
63   According to the Internal Market and Services Commissioner of the EU, the guarantees were required to provide additional stability to European financial markets and bank depositors/investors: "The adoption of today's package marks the Commission's latest endeavour to bring transparency and responsibility to Europe's financial system in order to prevent and manage future crises. European consumers deserve better. They need reassurance that their savings, investments or insurance policies are protected no matter where in Europe they are based. To make this a reality, I now call upon the European Parliament and the Council to make rapid progress in approving today's package." M. Barnier, see European Union Commission 2010a. (Commission proposes package to boost consumer protection and confidence in financial services. Press release, 12 July 2010 (IP/10/918)).

to €100,000. The guarantee and would also be extended to cover the European Economic Area (EEA) member states, Norway, Iceland and Liechtenstein.[64]

Some member states such as Ireland went further then the EU mandate, providing an unlimited guarantee for retail depositors in Irish banks. The unlimited guarantee was designed to promote stability in Ireland's banks and financial institutions and to overcome the risk of runs. During 2008 and 2009 there had been a significant decline in investor confidence in Irish banks and a mounting uncertainty that had been driven largely by Ireland's mounting fiscal deficit and sovereign debt.

During 2010 funding and access in the interbank markets in Europe improved as a result of the wholesale guarantees provided by the member states. The improvement in wholesale funding in Europe's financial, bond and money markets led to discussion that the wholesale guarantee should be gradually wound back.

On 2 December 2009, the European Competition and Finance Council (ECOFIN) concluded that a strategy should be designed and implemented for a gradual phasing out of the wholesale guarantee. The conclusion arrived at by ECOFIN was endorsed by the European Council on 11 December 2009. The European Parliament further resolved on 9 March 2010 that member states should not provide support or assistance indefinitely in the form of wholesale guarantees to its banks and financial institutions.[65] The EU Competition Working Group concluded:

> As a consequence of the general improvement in market conditions, the risks for financial stability at large have subsided, and the distortions of competition between those banks that issue guaranteed bonds but are not currently under restructuring obligations and those that issue strictly under market conditions has become greater.[66]

The proposed gradual phasing out of the wholesale guarantee by member states was also consistent with the overall improvement in market conditions. Market data collected by the EU Competition Working Group in 2010 demonstrated that the use of government guarantees by banks in the member states had declined since the peak of 2009. The improved market conditions in bond, credit and interbank lending markets led to a decline in the reliance of financial institutions

---

64   EU Finance Ministers agreed on 7 October 2008 that all member states would be committed to raising the level of the deposit guarantee to €50,000 and even up to €100,000. See European Union Commission 2008b (Commission sets out proposal to increase minimum protection for bank deposits to 100,000 euros. Press release, 15 October 2008 (IP/08/1508). Brussels).

65   European Union Commission 2010b (DG Competition Staff Working Document, The application of state aid rules to government guarantee schemes covering bank debt to be issued after 30 June 2010, EU Commission: Brussels, 30 April 2010), p. 2.

66   Ibid., p. 3.

on wholesale guarantees issued by the member states, since there had been improvements in both the pricing and availability of bonds.

The EU Recapitalization Communication

The Banking Communication issued by the EU in October 2008 also recognized the importance of providing effective recapitalization schemes to promote stability and confidence in European financial markets. On 12 October 2008 the EU concluded that:

> Governments commit themselves to provide capital when needed in appropriate volume while favouring by all available means the raising of private capital. Financial institutions should be obliged to accept additional restrictions, notably to preclude possible abuse of such arrangements at the expense of non beneficiaries, and legitimate interest of competitors must be protected, in particular through the State aid rules.[67]

The Recapitalization Communication served to provide a number of common objectives, including: restoring financial stability, ensuring lending to the real economy is maintained and ensuring that any systemic risk is effectively dealt with in the event of a major bank insolvency.[68] The Communication provided guidelines for the recapitalization of banks which may require additional capital if they encounter difficulties with sourcing funding requirements from bond markets and from interbank lending.

According to the Communication, member states are not allowed to provide an unfair competitive advantage to any banks to which a state may provide assistance relative to other competitor banks from other member states.[69] Hence, member states would not be permitted to use state aid under the guise of recapitalization to achieve an unfair advantage, nor would they be permitted to use recapitalization to distort competition in the banking sector.[70]

The Communication recognizes that in any recapitalization of banks, a balance needs to be struck between potential competition concerns and the objectives of restoring financial stability with European Banks.[71] Hence, the Communication provides that in the event that a member state is required to provide state aid to a bank or a financial institution, it needs to properly assess any state intervention.

---

67   European Union Commission 2009a (Communication from the Commission – The recapitalization of financial institutions in the current financial crisis: Limitation of aid to the minimum necessary and safeguards against undue distortions of competition. *Official Journal of the European Union*, 15 January 2009 (2009/C 10/03)).

68   Ibid., (n. 67), paragraph 4–6.

69   Ibid., paragraph 8.

70   Ibid., paragraph 8–10.

71   Ibid., paragraph 11.

Accordingly, the intervention should be both proportionate and temporary and "should be designed in a way that provides incentives for banks to redeem the State as soon as market circumstances permit, in order for a competitive and efficient European banking sector to emerge from the crisis."[72]

The EU Treatment of Impaired Assets Communication

In February 2009, the EU Commission issued a further communication on the treatment of impaired assets in the community banking sector.[73] The Communication was designed to provide specific guidance on the application of state aid rules for impaired assets relief. The new Communication would provide guidance on the following issues:

1. Transparency and disclosure requirements.
2. Burden-sharing between all relevant stakeholders, including the state, shareholders and creditors.
3. Aligning incentives for beneficiaries with public policy objectives.
4. Principles for designing asset relief measures in terms of eligibility, valuation and management of impaired assets.
5. The relationship between asset relief, other government support measures and the restructuring of banks.[74]

The EU considered that impaired assets which belonged to financial institutions were a key problem in the banking industry. Considerable uncertainty had been generated because of the valuations attached to impaired assets, including confusion over the precise location of impaired assets within European banks. The uncertainty, in turn, had continued to undermine confidence in the banking sector and had weakened government efforts to promote stability within European financial markets.[75]

Although European banks had recorded significant write-downs of their impaired asset holdings, the problem of toxic assets was still generating considerable uncertainty for investors in European financial markets. According to the IMF and data complied by the EU, there had been a total of over $US1 trillion in write-downs involving toxic assets by banks. Of this, over 70% of the write-downs related to US-based banks and approximately 30% or $US300 billion

---

72   Ibid., paragraph 11.
73   European Union Commission 2009k (State aid: Commission provides guidance for the treatment of impaired assets in the EU banking sector. Press release, 25 February 2009 (IP/09/322), Brussels).
74   Ibid., (n. 73), p. 1.
75   Ibid., paragraph 6.

involved asset write-downs by European banks.[76] The IMF estimated that total write-downs for toxic assets worldwide would be in excess of $US2.2 trillion.[77] The estimate by the IMF was based on total worldwide holdings of mortgage-backed securities and securitized structural financial products.

The EU acknowledged that the type and size of any response by member states to purchasing toxic assets from their respective banks and financial institutions would necessarily involve budgetary considerations. The likely asset relief program would invariably involve billions of dollars and require governments and taxpayers in member states to effectively foot the bill and finance the purchase of impaired assets.

The EU Communication on impaired assets provides a set of guidelines for member states to follow when providing state aid involving the purchase of toxic assets from European banks. According to the EU communication, any asset relief buy-back program should be subject to full and independent transparency and disclose the amount of impaired assets that would be purchased by the member state as part of the impaired asset buy-back.[78] The application of state aid should also follow a full review of the bank's trading activities and balance sheet. The purpose of the review is to assess the bank's capital adequacy and working capital capabilities, and to provide an indication of whether the bank is a going concern.[79]

The EU communications on banking, recapitalization and impaired assets provided a coordinated response to the global crisis confronting European financial markets and financial institutions. Member states made use of the guidance and permissions contained in the communications to seek approval from the Commission on the provision of state aid to distressed financial institutions and banks. It was not uncommon through 2008, 2009 and 2010 for member states to intervene and provide state assistance to financial institutions, banks and bank depositor schemes in order to promote stability and confidence to investors and other market participants.[80] The EU Commission has also given member states

---

76   Ibid.

77   Ibid., paragraph 6.

78   All assets purchased under the asset relief program should be subject to adequate valuation, verified by independent experts. Disclosure of impaired assets should occur before any government aid from the member states and this will ordinarily involve the identification of the aid amount and details of any incurred losses for the bank flowing from the asset transfer. Ibid., (n. 73), 5.1 and paragraphs 19–20.

79   Ibid., paragraph 20.

80   See, for example, European Union Commission 2008l (Commission authorises support package for Greek credit institutions. Press release, 19 November 2008, (IP/08/1742)); European Union Commission 2008g (Commission approves revised Irish support scheme for financial institutions. Press release, 13 October 2008 (IP/08/1497)); European Union Commission 2009e (Commission approves recapitalization of Anglo Irish Bank. Press release, 14 January 2009 (IP/09/50)); European Union Commission 2009f (Commission approves recapitalization of Bank of Ireland. Press release, 26 March 2009 (IP/09/483); European Union Commission 2010e (Commission approves

formal approval to provide assistance to specific financial institutions that have been experiencing financial and liquidity constraints. In some instances the EU Commission was required to provide approval for government intervention with the liquidation process of distressed financial institutions.[81]

---

restructuring plan of Bank of Ireland. Press release, 15 July 2010 (IP/10/954)); European Union Commission 2008m (Commission authorises Italian scheme for refinancing credit institutions. Press release, 14 November 2008 (IP/08/1706)); European Union Commission 2009j (Commission authorises support package for Hungarian financial institutions. Press release, 12 February 2009 (IP/09/253)); European Union Commission 2008f (Commission approves Finnish support scheme for financial institutions. Press release, 14 November 2008 (IP/08/1705)); European Union Commission 2008n (Commission authorises French scheme for refinancing credit institutions. Press release, 31 October 2008 (IP/08/1609)); European Union Commission 2008d (Commission approves Danish state support scheme for banks. Press release, 10 October 2008 (IP/08/1483)); European Union Commission 2008c (Commission approves Cypriot scheme to support credit institutions. Press release, 22 October 2008 (IP/09/1569)); European Union Commission 2008o (Commission authorises support package for Lithuanian financial institutions. Press release, 5 August 2010 (IP/10/1032)); European Union Commission 2008e (Commission approves Dutch guarantee scheme for financial institutions. Press release, 31 October 2008 (IP/08/1610)); European Union Commission 2009c (Commission approves Polish support scheme for financial institutions. Press release, 25 September 2009 (IP/09/1360)); European Union Commission 2009d (Commission approves Portuguese support scheme for financial institutions. Press release, 30 October 2008 (IP/08/1601)); European Union Commission 2009i (Commission approves Slovak bank support scheme. Press release, 8 December 2009 (IP/09/1889)); European Union Commission 2008h (Commission approves Slovenian support scheme for credit institutions. Press release, 12 December 2008 (IP/08/1964)); European Union Commission 2008i (Commission approves Spanish fund for acquisition of financial assets from financial institutions. Press release, 4 November 2008 (IP/08/1630)); European Union Commission 2008j (Commission approves Swedish support schemes for financial institutions. Press release, 30 October 2008 (IP/08/1600)); European Union Commission 2008k (Commission approves UK support scheme for financial institutions. Press release, 13 October 2008 (IP/08/1496)); European Union Commission 2009g (Commission approves restructuring package for Northern Rock. Press release, 28 October 2009 (IP/09/1600)); European Union Commission 2009h (Commission approves restructuring plan of Lloyds Banking Group. Press release, 18 November 2009 (IP/09/1728)); European Union Commission 2009b (State aid: Commission approves impaired asset relief measure and restructuring plan of Royal Bank of Scotland. Press release, 14 November 2009 (IP/09/1915)).

    81   See, for example, European Union Commission 2010d. State aid: Commission approves of liquidation of Bradford & Bingley (a building society in the UK). According to the Communication, the Commission authorized the liquidation measures because they considered the process "appropriate and necessary for an orderly winding down of the bank while taking into account the necessity to preserve the confidence of creditors in the financial system and remedy a serious disturbance of the UK economy." Press release, Brussels, 25 January 2010, IP/10/47.

EU Monetary Policy

The European Central Bank (ECB) is responsible for the coordination of monetary policy in the EU. Some member states have adopted the euro as their currency and the ECB as their central bank. Others, such as the United Kingdom, Sweden, Denmark and Poland, have their own central bank, currency and monetary policy. Like other central banks around the world, the ECB was quick to reduce its key interest rate during 2008 and 2009 to stimulate economic activity and help promote financial stability within European financial markets.

During 2008 and 2009 the ECB moved quickly to cut its main refinancing rate (fixed rate and variable rate), including its marginal lending facility rate. The ECB, through a series of reductions, cut its main refinancing rate from 4.25% in July 2008 to 3.75% in October 2008, 3.25% in November 2008, 2.50% in December 2008, 2.00% in January 2009, 1.50% in March 2009, 1.25% in April 2009 and, finally, to 1.00% in May 2009. The rate had not changed up to late 2011.

In addition to reducing interest rates, the ECB also attempted to improve liquidity within European financial markets. The ECB intervened in money markets through a series of auctions in the form of Term Auction Facilities. The auctions were coordinated with the US Federal Reserve and were designed to improve US dollar liquidity in European money markets.

On 10 January 2008 the ECB carried out term auctions for a total of $US30 billion with terms of maturity of 28 days.[82] This was followed by further terms auctions of US dollar denominated bonds in July 2008, when up to $US50 billion of term auctions took place, with maturities of 28 days and 84 days.[83] The term auction facilities were further supplemented by coordinated reciprocal swap currency arrangements between the US Federal Reserve, the Bank of England, the Swiss National Bank and the Bank of Canada.[84]

In response to the collapse of Lehman Brothers and to the heightened risk confronting European financial markets, the ECB undertook further measures designed to boost liquidity in short-term money markets. On 29 September 2008, the Federal Open Market Committee of the Federal Reserve of the United States and the ECB decided to double their temporary reciprocal currency swap arrangements from $US120 billion to $US240 billion.

---

82 European Central Bank 2008a (European Central Bank again offering US dollar liquidity. Press release, 10 January 2008). Available at: <http://www.ecb.europa.eu/press/pr/date/2008/html/pr080110_2.en.html>.

83 European Central Bank 2008b (Measures to enhance the US dollar term auction facility. Press release, 30 July 2008). Available at: <http://www.ecb.europa.eu/press/pr/date/2008/html/pr080730.en.html>.

84 European Central Bank 2008c (Measures designed to address elevated pressures in the short-term US dollar funding markets. Press release, 26 September 2008). Available at: <http://www.ecb.europa.eu/press/pr/date/2008/html/pr080926.en.html>.

In addition to this arrangement, central banks from other countries, including the Bank of Canada, the Bank of England, the Bank of Japan, the National Bank of Denmark, the Swiss National Bank, the Reserve Bank of Australia and the National Bank of Norway, also entered into reciprocal currency swap arrangements with the US Federal Reserve.[85] The coordinated measures by the ECB and other international central banks were designed to improve liquidity and funding to financial institutions, which were beginning to face serious financial difficulties and access to European and US financial markets.[86]

Despite the policy responses and measures undertaken by the ECB, the Central Bank reported that in December 2008 significant risks and vulnerabilities remained in European financial markets. The ECB in a press release stated:

> Following the bankruptcy of Lehman Brothers, the persistent liquidity stresses eventually gave way to deeper concerns about the creditworthiness of even the largest financial institutions and the adequacy of capital buffers.[87]

According to the ECB, the situation confronting European financial markets was to improve by the end of 2009. In a press release issued in December 2009, the ECB reported that the extraordinary actions undertaken by European authorities including the policy response measures adopted by other central banks and governments had been successful in restoring confidence to fragile financial markets.[88]

The policy responses had not only improved underlying investor confidence in European financial markets but, importantly, also reduced the risk of contagion spreading further to cause damage to the real economy. Expansionary macroeconomic policies in the form of lowering key interest rates, as well as quantitative easing measures designed to boost liquidity in short-term money markets, also proved successful in promoting economic activity and stimulating economic growth.

The EU Sovereign Debt Crisis

Although the policy measures adopted by European authorities helped to stabilize financial markets, new concerns were soon to arise in the form of sovereign debt

---

85   European Central Bank 2008d (Measures designed to address elevated pressures in the short-term US dollar funding markets. Press release, 29 September 2008). Available at: <http://www.ecb.europa.eu/press/pr/date/2008/html/pr080926.en.html>.

86   European Central Bank 2008e (Measures designed to address elevated pressures in the short-term US dollar funding markets. Press release, 13 October 2008). Available at: <http://www.ecb.europa.eu/press/pr/date/2008/html/pr081013.en.html>.

87   European Central Bank 2008f (Financial Stability Review December 2008: Risks and vulnerabilities in financial system persist. Press release, 15 December 2008). Available at: <http://www.ecb.europa.eu/press/pr/date/2008/html/pr081215.en.html>.

88   European Central Bank 2009 (Financial Stability Review December 2009. Press release, 18 December 2009). Available at: <http://www.ecb.europa.eu/press/pr/date/2009/html/pr091218.en.html>.

crisis for a number of European nations. The first signs to emerge from the new crisis were in May 2010, when the ECB reported:

> Outside the financial system, the progressive intensification of market concerns about sovereign credit risk among the industrialized economies in the early months of 2010 opened up a number of hazardous contagion channels and adverse feed back loops between financial systems and public finances, in particular the euro area.[89]

The ongoing sovereign debt crisis was to take a turn for the worse when investors began to lose confidence in Greece's ability to repay its sovereign debt. In 2008 Greece's public debt was among the highest in the world and stood at approximately 110% of GDP.[90] As the GFC took hold to undermine investor confidence in debt-laden firms and financial institutions, investors began to turn their attention to the state of the public finances.

To compensate for the heightened level of risk associated with Greece's sovereign debt, investors demanded higher yields on Greece's government bonds. As the US Congressional Budget Office reported, by 2010 Greece was paying over 4% more in interest on 10-year government bonds compared with Germany.[91]

Greece's plight was to worsen during 2010, as investors continued to push up yields on Greece's 10-year bonds. Yields on Greece's credit default swaps also continued to widen as investors demanded higher returns from the elevated risk of default. Credit default swaps on Greek government bonds continued to rise to an all-time high, signalling the loss of confidence by investors and bondholders in Greece's ability to combat its fiscal crisis.

In response to the crisis that was unfolding in Greece, EU member states and the International Monetary Fund (IMF) established a financial support program to assist Greece with its fiscal crisis. In May 2010 Greece was to receive a total of €80 billion, which would be distributed to Greece's Treasury between May 2010 and June 2013.[92] The IMF was to provide an additional standby facility of €30 billion to Greece over the same period.[93] The EU and IMF Funding program

---

89   European Central Bank 2010 (Financial Stability Review June 2010. Press release, 31 May 2010). Available at: <http://www.ecb.europa.eu/press/pr/date/2010/html/pr100531. en.html>.

90   See US Government 2010 (The Congress of the United States. Federal debt and the risk of a fiscal crisis. Washington, DC: Congressional Budget Office, 27 July 2010), p. 2.

91   Ibid., p. 6.

92   European Union Commission 2011 (The Economic Adjustment Programme for Greece. Third Review, Winter 2011, Directorate-General for Economic and Financial Affairs, Occasional Paper 77, February 2011), p. 4.

93   Ibid.

would allow Greece to maintain its access to short-term funding in European financial markets.[94]

By the beginning of 2011 a total of three instalments, of €20 billion (May 2010), €9.0 billion (September 2010) and €9.0 billion (December 2010 and January 2011) had been provided to Greece for the nation to meet its short-term and medium-term refinancing needs. Ten additional instalments were expected to be paid to Greece over the following three years: €15 billion (March 2011); €12 billion (June 2011); €8 billion (September 2011); €5 billion (December 2011); €10 billion (March 2012); €6.0 billion (June 2012); €6.0 billion (September 2012); €2.0 billion (December 2012); €6.0 billion (March 2013); €2.0 billion (December 2012); €6.0 billion (March 2013) and €2.0 billion (June 2013).[95]

For Greece to receive funds under the financing package that was arranged by the EU and the IMF, the Greek government was required to commit to a strict fiscal deficit reduction program. Greece would have to commit to significant austerity measures in the form of cuts to overall government expenditure and increases in tax collections and tax revenues. The measures were designed to reduce Greece's fiscal deficit below 3% of GDP in 2014, representing a reduction in the fiscal deficit of over 8%.[96]

To achieve the ambitious fiscal stabilization program, Greece would be required to deliver significant cuts and savings in key areas, including health care expenditures, tax collections and taxation revenue, defence spending, public service expenditures and public enterprises and education expenditure.[97] Greece would be committed to making the required improvements to its fiscal deficit, otherwise it would risk losing funding from the joint EU and IMF funding program.

However, the austerity measures proposed for Greece were quite severe and caused a great deal of hardship for a number of households, families, businesses, public sector employees and individuals. Greece resembled a battlefield of rioters prepared to vent their anger and frustration at their country's parliament and politicians. One of the main challenges facing Greece was to somehow juggle its fiscal austerity measures at a time when the world had been plunged into a severe recession. Again, the major losers would be public sector employees, small- and medium-sized businesses and individuals who were required to make sizeable savings and cuts in expenditure and, at the same time, watch unemployment rise.

Despite the implementation of the austerity measures it was reported by the European Union Directorate General for Economic and Financial Affairs, by early 2011, that Greece's fiscal imbalances had not shown significant improvement. According to the Directorate General, the country had been held back because of an "unsuccessful fight against tax evasion and incomplete expenditure control."[98]

---

94   Ibid.
95   Ibid., (n. 92), p. 5.
96   Ibid., (n. 92), p. 2.
97   Ibid.
98   Ibid., p. 17.

The reasons for Greece's less than successful attempt to address its fiscal imbalances were many and varied. One of the main problems confronting Greece was the fierce resistance led by Greece's public servants to the structural reforms that would be required to achieve fiscal sustainability.

Resistance was strong because many of the austerity measures, which were designed to reduce Greece's fiscal deficit, fell heavily on Greece's public servants, small businesses and individuals. The Directorate General also found that there were significant shortfalls in tax collection by Greece's taxation authorities.[99] During 2010, tax collections were continually revised downwards due to weaker than expected domestic demand, economic growth and corporate activity.[100]

During 2010 and 2011, the Greek government initiated structural reforms to public administration and tax policy. One of the key features of the joint EU and IMF funding program required the Greek government to implement reforms to fight tax evasion, simplify its taxation framework and improve its taxation audit services. The reforms were designed to improve overall tax collections and implement a sustainable fiscal deficit reduction strategy.

To implement the fiscal reforms, in 2011 the Greek government introduced a draft bill which included measures designed to strengthen the government's ability to prosecute tax evaders.[101] The reforms included the creation of a new office of economic crime and the criminal prosecution of new tax offences, including fraud, tax evasion, tax avoidance and VAT avoidance.[102] The range of penalties for economic crimes would also increase in line with the tougher stance on tax fraud. In addition to these measures, the draft bill also intended to reduce corporate taxes from the current 24% to 20% in line with the EU average. The reduction in the corporate tax rate was designed to remove current distortions in Greece's taxation framework, as well as stimulate corporate and entrepreneurial activity.[103]

In line with the structural reforms to Greece's taxation policy, new initiatives have also been undertaken in the areas of health care and pensions. The pension reforms have been particularly controversial since they implement a new national retirement age of 65 years of age, up from the previous retirement age of 61 years and in some cases 53 years. The new retirement age in Greece would bring the country into line with the EU average retirement age and was designed to save the state billions of euros in welfare payments.

All of the austerity measures were designed to allow Greece time to implement its taxation, welfare and expenditure reforms before the country was required to source additional funding from international financial markets. With a stronger fiscal position, it was anticipated that Greece's reputation in European markets

---

99 Ibid., p. 19.
100 Ibid.
101 Ibid., p. 27.
102 Ibid.
103 Ibid.

would improve and allow investors to gain confidence in Greece's ability to repay its outstanding loans.

Greece was not the only European country to encounter fiscal constraints. Ireland's fiscal crisis was highly correlated with the onset of the GFC. As the global housing bubble started to unwind, Ireland experienced a hard landing as the nation's obsession with property speculation in the boom time was turned upside down. Ireland was particularly vulnerable to any downturn in residential house prices since its economic activity relied heavily on booming real estate construction and investment.

As in the United States, as the housing bubble popped and house prices began to spiral downwards, Ireland's financial institutions were exposed to massive write-down of residential mortgage securities. The same banks and financial institutions which rode the housing bubble and provided benefits to Ireland's GDP during 2002–2007 were now experiencing severe financial difficulties because of their over-leveraged positions.[104]

In response to the build-up in risk of Ireland's banks and financial institutions, the Irish government was forced to adopt extensive bailout measures. Among these measures was the purchase of toxic mortgage-backed securities, including the provision of additional capital so as to avoid any major collapse. The damage to Ireland's real economy from the fallout from the housing bubble was also significant. Tax revenues declined substantially as economic activity in Ireland stalled and welfare payments increased as unemployment rose.

The overall downturn in housing construction and economic activity along with declining tax revenues and costly bailouts resulted in a fiscal imbalance for Ireland that ultimately proved fatal. With the crisis in fiscal sustainability flowing from Greece and on to Ireland, concern arose that sovereign default could spread to other fiscally vulnerable nations, including Spain, Portugal and Italy.

In November 2010, the Irish government was forced to ask for assistance from the EU and the IMF. Whilst both welcomed the request for assistance, many in Ireland felt humiliated and let down by their government for the failure in managing the economy and the country's finances.[105]

Following Ireland's request in December 2010, the EU and the IMF, together with other European nations agreed to provide up to €85 billion in funding. The funding package consisted of €22.5 billion from the Emergency Financing Mechanism of the IMF, €45 billion from the EU and €17.5 billion from Ireland's

---

104   Organization for Economic Co-operation and Development (OECD) 2009 Economic Survey of Ireland 2009. OECD Economics Department, November 2009, Paris: OECD, pp. 3–4.

105   The Managing Director of the IMF, Dominique Strauss-Kahn stated: "I welcome the response from the European Union and euro-area Member States to the Irish Government's request for financial assistance to safeguard financial stability." International Monetary Fund 2010e (Statement by IMF Managing Director Dominique Strauss-Kahn on Ireland. Press release 10/452, 21 November 2010, Washington, DC: IMF).

cash reserve and liquid assets, with the remainder coming from bilateral loans with other member states of the EU.[106]

The funding program between the IMF and the EU requires Ireland to undertake a number of reforms, which are designed to strengthen Ireland's banks and financial institutions and reduce the sovereign debt risk associated with Ireland's fiscal position. To achieve these objectives, the Irish government introduced legislation in early 2011 to enhance the Central Bank of Ireland's supervisory and oversight powers over Irish banks and financial institutions. The draft Bill contained provisions requiring the appointment of a special manager to oversee Ireland's troubled banks and to provide the Central Bank with the legal authority to transfer assets and liabilities of troubled banks to other financial institutions in an orderly manner.[107]

In addition to these banking reforms, Irish banks must complete a series of stress tests, which are designed to determine whether the banks require additional capital. The stress tests must include providing appropriate valuations of bank assets and verifying whether sufficient capital provision has been made to achieve a core tier 1 capital ratio of 10.5% in the bank's balance sheet.[108] Ireland's banks must also submit plans to provide effective deleveraging to Irish authorities.[109] The main objective of the banking reforms is to "achieve a leaner, more robust banking system with a stable funding base not dependent on government support."[110]

The Irish government must also take active steps to reduce its fiscal deficit so as to achieve fiscal sustainability within a reasonable timeframe. The draft Finance Bill that was introduced into Ireland's parliament by the Irish government in January 2011 aims to introduce significant taxation and welfare reforms designed to reduce Ireland's fiscal deficit.[111] These reforms include cuts to government expenditure, including health care and the universal social charge.[112]

In February 2011, the IMF conducted an interim review of Ireland under its Emergency Financing Mechanism.[113] The aim of the review was to assess whether Ireland had been in compliance with the intended reforms that were agreed to by the IMF and the EU. The IMF reported that Ireland's reform implementation program

---

106   The bilateral loans between Ireland and the UK, Sweden and Denmark provided the remainder of the funding from the €85 billion funding package. See International Monetary Fund 2010a (IMF Executive Board Approves €22. 5 billion extended arrangement for Ireland. Press release, 16 December 2010, Washington, DC: IMF), p. 1.

107   International Monetary Fund 2011. Ireland: Extended Arrangement – Interim Review Under the Emergency Financing Mechanism. IMF Country Report 11/47, 2 February 2011, Washington, DC: IMF), p. 5.

108   Ibid.

109   Ibid.

110   Ibid.

111   Ibid., (n. 107), p. 6.

112   Under the recently introduced budget, the universal social charge will be reduced from its current rate of 7% to 4% for medical card holders. Ibid., (n. 107), p. 6.

113   Ibid.

120 The Global Financial Crisis

had remained on track. However, recent political developments concerning the dissolving of Parliament on 1 February 2011 and the announcement of Irish elections scheduled for 25 February had introduced turbulence and uncertainty into the political landscape of Ireland.[114]

The IMF further reported that the banking sector remained under stress, with bank asset quality and real estate prices in Ireland continuing to deteriorate. The continued decline in prices and asset quality warranted greater provisioning and write-downs, which kept Ireland's banks from reporting a profit in 2010–2011.[115] Since Ireland's short-term money markets and wholesale markets remained fragile, interbank lending for Irish banks was almost non-existent. This, in turn, made Irish banks become wholly reliant on liquidity from the Eurosystem and the Emergency Liquidity Assistance program.[116]

Another important observation from the IMF was the mixed response from investors regarding Ireland's reform implementation program and the joint funding mechanism between the IMF and the EU.[117] The IMF reported that although there had been some reduction of credit default swaps on Ireland's bonds, the spreads remained historically elevated.[118] This was despite the interventions by the European Central Bank in purchasing Irish sovereign paper in European money markets.

The continued uncertainty regarding Ireland's political landscape provides one possible explanation for the high spreads that currently exist on Ireland's bonds. This view is supported by the IMF, which reported that the change in government in Ireland was abrupt, notwithstanding that the change had been largely anticipated.[119] This is because the uncertainty stemmed not so much from the fact of the change in government, but instead related to the uncertainty that persisted regarding the new government's reform program. Further, doubts lingered as to whether a new government would be committed to implement politically unpopular austerity measures aimed at reducing Ireland's fiscal deficit.

The Greek and Irish sovereign debt crises also served to highlight the perceived vulnerability of other member states in the EU that had high fiscal deficits and large underlying sovereign debt. Countries such as Spain, Portugal and Italy were often cited as potential new candidates for a fiscal crisis given their elevated sovereign debt levels. Recent downgrades by rating agencies Moody's and Fitch of the sovereign debt of Spain and Portugal continued to unnerve investors.[120] The

---

114 Ibid., (n. 107), p. 3.
115 Ibid.
116 Ibid.
117 Ibid., (n. 107), p. 4.
118 Ibid.
119 Ibid.
120 Moody's and Fitch both downgraded sovereign debt ratings for Spain and Portugal in March 2011, reflecting the higher level of risk associated with the fiscal position of the two countries.

ratings downgrades reflected investor anxiety over the relatively high sovereign debt of the two countries. Investors continued to maintain elevated positions for their credit default swaps, as was evidenced by the heightened 5- and 10-year spreads on Spanish and Portuguese bonds relative to Germany's government bonds.

The continued volatility was not only apparent in credit default swaps and sovereign spreads but also in the underlying value of the euro. After witnessing currency volatility with the United States dollar in 2008 and 2009, the relative stability of the euro was also threatened in 2010. Investors began questioning the stability of European financial markets in light of sovereign debt concerns in a number of member states of the EU. There were also concerns about the sustainability of the euro, with some commentators predicting that it would not survive as the common currency for EU member states for much longer.

At the centre of investor concern for the euro was the issue of the EU's effective control of the common currency, when the EU had a legal mandate over EU monetary policy but no effective authority over the fiscal policy of its member states. With European monetary policy controlled by the ECB, fiscal policy had been decoupled from any centralized control because it remained vested with each individual member state at the time the Union was formed.

Despite these misgivings, the euro celebrated its tenth anniversary on 1 January 2009, and until the outbreak of the sovereign debt crisis with Greece and Ireland, it had been a source of strength and stability in an otherwise troubled world. With improvements in financial markets generally, along with stabilization measures that were announced in Greece and Ireland, the euro had become less susceptible to market volatility. However, it remains to be seen whether the relative stability of the euro will continue.

Looking at the longer term, there may well be a need for member states to transfer their fiscal powers to the EU. The transfer of taxation and expenditure powers remains a highly controversial issue that requires analysis and understanding of not only economic matters but also cultural, historical, social and environmental considerations of each member state in the Union. Divisions continue to exist over whether a member state should give up its fiscal powers to the EU. Hence, it remains to be seen whether monetary policy will continue to be decoupled from fiscal policy in the Union or whether there will indeed be a push for greater fiscal consolidation across the member states.

The United Kingdom

Like other countries that had been confronted with dislocated and dysfunctional financial markets, authorities in the UK were also required to implement effective policy responses to stabilize UK banks and the financial sector. Following the collapse of Lehman Brothers, the Bank of England responded immediately by reducing its key benchmark rate from 5% to 4.5%.[121] The Bank of England noted the risks to the downside of a sharp slowdown in economic activity due to disruptions in financial markets and continued decline in house prices.

With continued weakness in economic activity, the Bank of England again reduced its key benchmark rate in November 2008 by 150 basis points to 3.0%.[122] The Bank justified its aggressive move to reduce interest rates on the basis that since Lehman's collapse in September 2008, "the global banking system has experienced its most serious disruption for almost a century."[123]

While acknowledging that it had been proactive by providing accommodative settings with monetary policy, the Central Bank also noted that the availability of credit to households and businesses remained restricted.[124] With continued disruption experienced by international and UK financial markets, the Bank again reduced its official bank interest rate by a further 1.0% to 2.0% in December 2008.[125] The expansionary monetary policy was aimed at countering the continued decline in consumer spending and business investment, along with the severe downturn experienced in residential housing construction. The Central Bank also noted that whilst the accommodative policy settings were taken to raise bank capital and ease funding constraints, liquidity remained tight in short-term money markets. Credit markets also remained under significant stress, which further restricted the availability of credit to consumers and businesses.[126]

The situation continued to deteriorate in early 2009. The Bank of England again revised the official bank rate to the downside, reducing it by 0.5% to 1.5% in January.[127] The Bank expressed concern that the international economy was experiencing an unprecedented "sharp and synchronised downturn [...] measures of business and consumer confidence [had] fallen markedly. World trade growth this year is likely to be the weakest for some considerable time."[128]

---

121   Bank of England 2008a (Bank of England reduces Bank Rate by 0.5 percentage points to 4.5%. Press release, 8 October 2008. London: BoE). Available at: <http://www.bankofengland.co.uk/publications/news/2008/index.htm>.

122   Bank of England 2008b (Bank of England reduces Bank Rate by 1.5% to 3.0%. Press release, 6 November 2008). Available at: <http://www.bankofengland.co.uk/publications/news/2008/index.htm>.

123   Ibid.

124   Ibid.

125   Bank of England 2008c (Bank of England reduces Bank Rate by 1.0 percentage point to 2.0%. Press release, 4 December 2008, London: BoE). Available at: <http://www.bankofengland.co.uk/publications/news/2008/index.htm>.

126   Ibid.

127   Bank of England 2009c (Bank of England reduces Bank Rate by 0.5 percentage points to 1.5%. Press release, 8 January 2009, London: BoE). Available at: <http://www.bankofengland.co.uk/publications/news/2009/index.htm>.

128   Ibid.

With economic events not improving, the Bank of England again reduced the official bank rate, to 1.0% in February 2009[129] and to 0.5% in March.[130] In addition to reducing interest rates, the Bank also decided to boost liquidity by undertaking a program of asset purchases. In March 2009 it announced asset purchases of £75 billion sterling, which was to be financed out of central bank reserves.[131] The quantitative easing program was designed to boost liquidity in UK financial markets and help restore stability in credit and bond markets. The quantitative easing measures adopted by the Bank were in response to continued deterioration in world economic growth, excessive market volatility and persistent problems in international credit markets.[132]

The size of the Bank of England's quantitative easing program increased again in May 2009 when the Monetary Policy Committee voted to increase the asset purchase program to £125 billion sterling.[133] The Bank of England justified its increased liquidity measures on the basis that economic activity and output had continued to decline and international trade had "fallen precipitously."[134] Since the world's economy remained in recession throughout 2009, the Bank of England urged on the side of caution and decided to increase its quantitative easing program with a further £50 billion asset purchase. This brought the total assets purchased by the Bank of England to £200 billion.[135]

The Bank of England responded to the GFC with expansionary monetary policy settings, which included quantitative easing in the form of a £200 billion sterling asset purchase program. However, the fallout from the financial crisis was now hurting the real economy. Economic output had fallen by almost 6% since the beginning of 2008.[136] Consumer spending remained constrained as house prices

---

129   Bank of England 2009d (Bank of England reduces Bank Rate by 0.5 percentage points to 1.0%. Press release, 5 February 2009, London: BoE). Available at: <http://www.bankofengland.co.uk/publications/news/2009/index.htm>.

130   Bank of England 2009e. Bank of England reduces Bank Rate by 0.5 percentage points to 0.5% and announces £75 billion Asset Purchase Programme. Press release, 5 March 2009, London: BoE). Available at: <http://www.bankofengland.co.uk/publications/news/2009/index.htm>.

131   Ibid.

132   Ibid.

133   Bank of England 2009a. (Bank of England maintains Bank Rate at 0.5% and increases size of Asset Purchase Programme by £50 billion to £125 billion. Press release, 7 May 2009, London: BoE). Available at: <http://www.bankofengland.co.uk/publications/news/2009/index.htm>.

134   Ibid.

135   Bank of England 2009b (Bank of England maintains Bank Rate at 0.5% and increases size of Asset Purchase Programme by £25 billion to £200 billion. Press release, 5 November 2009, London: BoE). Available at: <http://www.bankofengland.co.uk/publications/news/2009/index.htm>.

136   Ibid.

continued to decline. Evidence was also emerging that the UK economy might be experiencing deflationary pressures, particularly with falling asset prices.

Faced with mounting unemployment, low economic activity and declining growth, the Gordon Brown government adopted fiscal stimulus measures designed to stimulate demand and output. The Chancellor of the Exchequer, Alastair Darling, announced that the government would provide up to £20 billion sterling in loan funding for small businesses. In addition to the loans, the government also reduced rates of personal tax on low incomes and temporarily reduced the rate on Value Added Tax (VAT).[137]

The fiscal stimulus packages announced by Gordon Brown were not without controversy. Some commentators, including members of the Conservative Party, argued that the Labour government had not gone far enough and called for even larger assistance to UK businesses. However, others argued that the Labour government had already provided significant assistance in the form of expensive bailouts for financial institutions such as Northern Rock. Some had even expressed concern at the ever-increasing fiscal deficit and mounting public debt that was forecast to increase significantly following the global economic recession.

The Russian Federation

The Russian Federation was not immune from the GFC. Despite Russia being a major commodity exporter, the crisis had a significant impact on Russia's ability to export, since international demand for commodities collapsed in 2008 and 2009. The significant falls in commodity prices also led to considerable decline in income and expenditure for the Russian Federation.

The decline in industrial production, activity and output, along with the consequential rise in unemployment, also led to further consumer and investor pessimism. Investors became increasingly risk-averse, which led to a sell-off of stocks and significant falls on Russian equity markets. The adverse reaction to the GFC was not limited to Russia's financial sector. Russia's real economy was also severely impacted by the global crisis. Real GDP declined in 2009 by almost 8% year on year and unemployment rose to over 8% in 2009.[138]

With the decline in household income came the inevitable downturn in consumer expenditure and overall economic activity. The Russian government and the Bank of Russia designed policies that were aimed at stimulating growth, which at the same time provided much-needed liquidity to financial markets. The Bank of Russia provided over 300 billion roubles to Russian banks to improve liquidity in Russian financial markets. The central bank also relaxed capital reserve ratios,

137   BBC Today 2009 (Small business loan plan unveiled. BBC News, London: 14 January 2009). Available at: <http://news.bbc.co.uk/go/pr/fr-/2/hi/business/7827273.stm>.

138   Bank of Russia 2010 (Financial Stability Review 2009. Moscow: Research and Information Department of the Bank of Russia), p. 5.

which allowed Russian banks to lend to consumers and businesses.[139] To stimulate economic activity in the midst of the downturn, the Bank of Russia also cut its key benchmark overnight rate throughout 2009.

To protect the integrity of Russia's banking and financial sector, the Bank of Russia and the Russian government undertook bank bailouts for vulnerable financial institutions.[140] The measures included providing additional financial assistance to improve bank capital ratios in an attempt to prevent further bank failures. The bailout measures also extended to Russia's vulnerable non-bank financial institutions. The interest rate reductions, enhanced liquidity and bank capital measures along with the bailout packages all helped to stabilize Russia's banking and financial sector.

However, improvements in economic output and activity in the Russian Federation proved more difficult to achieve. Unemployment remained stubbornly high throughout 2010 and in early 2011 the rate of unemployment remained higher than the average rate before the onset of the GFC. Russia's real GDP also remained sluggish in 2010 following the steep decline in 2009. It was not until early 2011 that economic activity in Russia began to improve, following rises in commodity prices as the international recovery began to take hold.

Canada

The Canadian economy remained relatively resilient in the lead-up to the GFC. It was not until the collapse of Lehman Brothers in September 2008 that regulatory authorities expressed any real concern for the Canadian economy or the Canadian financial sector.[141] After monitoring international developments and ongoing market turbulence, the Bank of Canada announced that it would reduce its overnight lending rate by 0.55% to 2.5% in a coordinated effort with other central banks around the world.[142] In the same month, the Bank of Canada again reduced its key overnight rate by a further 0.25% as the GFC intensified

---

139 Ibid., pp. 23–25.

140 Ibid., p. 25.

141 See for example the Bank of Canada, which reported in early September 2008 that domestic demand in Canada had slowed but remained strong. However, international developments in financial markets and ongoing turbulence in the United States increased the risk of a "more pronounced interplay between the weakness in the US economy and tightness in credit conditions." Bank of Canada 2008a (Bank of Canada keeps overnight rate target at 3 percent. Press release, 3 September 2008, Ottawa: Bank of Canada).

142 Bank of Canada 2008d (Central banks announce coordinated interest rate reductions. Press release, 8 October 2008, Ottawa: Bank of Canada). The move was supported by other central banks including: the Bank of England; the European Central Bank; the US Federal Reserve; the Swiss National Bank; the Bank of Japan and the Central Bank of Sweden.

in late 2008 and early 2009.[143] Bank lending had been affected and Canada's financial sector was beginning to feel the pain of dislocated international financial markets.

Commodity prices were also beginning to decline, reflecting lower levels of economic activity in the US, Japan and Europe, which led to an uncertain outlook for economic growth in Canada.[144] In response to declining economic activity, the Bank of Canada again reduced its overnight rate target in December 2008, this time by 0.75% to 1.5%.[145] The central bank expressed concern that world economic conditions had "deteriorated significantly and the global recession [would] be broader and deeper than previously anticipated."[146]

In response to the growing international crisis, the Bank of Canada again reduced its overnight target rate in January 2009,[147] March 2009[148] and April 2009.[149] By April the overnight rate stood at 0.25%, the lowest on record. The central bank also reaffirmed its commitment to keep the overnight target rate at 0.25% until the end of the second quarter of 2010.

Like other central banks around the world, the Bank of Canada responded in an active manner by reducing its overnight target rate in late 2008 and throughout 2009. The policy response was consistent with the desire of the central bank and the Canadian government to provide an environment that was conducive to stimulating consumer demand and hence promoting economic activity and economic growth in the Canadian economy. By late 2009, signs began to emerge that the Canadian economy was in a preliminary phase of recovery, following a decline in real GDP of 2.4% in 2009.[150]

By the end of the first quarter in 2010 the Canadian economy had enjoyed strong economic growth, recording a 6.1% rise in real GDP by the end of March 2010. In response to the better than expected recovery, the Bank of Canada increased its

---

143   Bank of Canada 2008b (Bank of Canada lowers overnight rate target by ¼ percentage point to 2¼ percent. Press release, 21 October 2008, Ottawa: Bank of Canada).
144   Ibid.
145   Bank of Canada 2008c (Bank of Canada lowers overnight rate target by ¾ percentage point to 1½ percent. Press release, 9 December 2008, Ottawa: Bank of Canada).
146   Ibid.
147   Bank of Canada 2009a (Bank of Canada lowers overnight rate target by ½ percentage point to 1 percent. Press release, 20 January 2009, Ottawa: Bank of Canada).
148   Bank of Canada 2009b (Bank of Canada lowers overnight rate target by ½ percentage point to ½ percent. Press release, 3 March 2009, Ottawa: Bank of Canada).
149   Bank of Canada 2009c (Bank of Canada lowers overnight rate target by ¼ percentage point to ¼ percent and, conditional on the inflation outlook, commits to hold current policy rate until the end of the second quarter of 2010. Press release, 21 April 2009. Ottawa: Bank of Canada).
150   Bank of Canada 2009d (Bank of Canada maintains overnight rate target at ¼ percent and reiterates conditional commitment to hold current policy rate until the end of the second quarter of 2010. Press release, 20 October 2009, Ottawa: Bank of Canada).

overnight rate to 0.5% in June 2010, the first rise in almost two years.[151] With an improved economic outlook the central bank again increased its overnight target rate in late 2010 and early 2011.[152]

Australia and New Zealand

Australia and New Zealand were also not immune from the crisis that had its genesis in the United States and soon spread to engulf the world's financial markets. Australia and New Zealand were similar to other commodity-producing countries, in that both remained relatively resilient in the lead-up to the GFC. It was not until the collapse of Lehman Brothers that volatile and dysfunctional conditions in international markets began to spill over into Australia and New Zealand.

In September 2008 the Reserve Bank of Australia (RBA) reduced its cash rate by 0.25% to 7.0%.[153] The RBA Governor noted that "conditions in international financial markets remain difficult, with heightened concerns over credit persisting."[154] The situation was to take a dramatic turn for the worse after Lehman's collapse. In October 2008, the RBA lowered the cash rate by 1.0% to 6.0% because of a worsening of conditions, large-scale financial failures and dislocation in short-term money markets.[155]

In response to the serious distortions being played out in international money and equity markets, the RBA again reduced its key interest rate, the cash rate, by 0.75% to 5.25% in November 2008.[156] The RBA not only noted the deterioration in major industrialized countries but also observed further signs of weakness in China and other emerging economies, including South East Asia and India.[157] In December 2008, the RBA again reduced its key cash rate by a further 1.0% to 4.25%,[158] followed by another 1.0% reduction in February 2009.[159]

---

151   Bank of Canada 2010a (Bank of Canada increases overnight rate target to ½ percent and re-establishes normal functioning of the overnight market. Press release, 1 June 2010, Ottawa: Bank of Canada).

152   Bank of Canada 2010b Bank of Canada increases overnight rate target to 1 percent. Press release, 8 September 2010, Ottawa: Bank of Canada).

153   Reserve Bank of Australia 2008a (Statement by Glenn Stevens, Governor: Monetary policy. Press release, 2 September 2008, Sydney: RBA).

154   Ibid.

155   Reserve Bank of Australia 2008b (Statement by Glenn Stevens, Governor: Monetary Policy. Press release, 7 October 2008, Sydney: RBA).

156   Reserve Bank of Australia 2008c (Statement by Glenn Stevens, Governor: Monetary Policy. Press release, 4 November 2008, Sydney: RBA).

157   Ibid.

158   Reserve Bank of Australia 2008d (Statement by Glenn Stevens, Governor: Monetary Policy. Press release, 2 December 2008, Sydney: RBA).

159   Reserve Bank of Australia 2009 (Statement by Glenn Stevens, Governor: Monetary Policy. Press release, 3 February 2009, Sydney: RBA).

The expansionary policy measures undertaken by Australia's central bank were all designed to provide an effective policy response to the growing and alarming deterioration in the world's financial markets and economic conditions. The dislocated short-term money markets and interbank lending markets, along with major financial and corporate collapses were now having an adverse impact on developed and developing economies. Australia was not immune, since the nation's economy was highly dependent upon international trade and elevated commodity prices.

The Australian government under Prime Minister Kevin Rudd also announced short-term stimulus measures designed to boost consumer demand and expenditure. The stimulus package comprised an initial $A10 billion measure that would provide low-income earners with a cash bonus. The initial stimulus measure was then followed by a much larger package, which amounted to $A42 billion in the form of a Nation Building Economic Stimulus Plan.[160]

The effectiveness of the announced economic stimulus measures was viewed as a mixed success. The Rudd Labor government considered that the stimulus policy played an important role in keeping Australia out of recession. However, other commentators, including members of the Liberal National Party Coalition, viewed the policy response as ineffectual.

In addition to the Reserve Bank of Australia's reductions in interest rates and the government's announced stimulus measures, the Rudd government also introduced government guarantees for retail deposits and wholesale funding. The Prime Minister of Australia, Kevin Rudd, announced the guarantee scheme on 12 October 2008.[161] Under the scheme the Australian government would provide a guarantee for all retail deposits with Australian banks, building societies and credit unions. The scheme also provided eligible institutions with a government guarantee for wholesale term funding. The Australian government would essentially lend for hire its AAA sovereign credit rating to eligible financial institutions to enable the institutions to borrow from international wholesale money markets in return for the payment of a fee to the Treasury.

A further initiative to deal with the GFC was announced by the Australian Treasurer, Wayne Swan. The Treasurer announced in September 2008 that the Australian Office of Financial Management would conduct purchases of an additional $A4 billion in Residential Backed Mortgage Securities.[162] The asset purchases by the Australian government were designed to provide much-needed

---

160 Australian Government 2010 (Nation Building Economic Stimulus Plan, Commonwealth Coordinator-General's Progress Report to 31 December 2009, Canberra: Commonwealth of Australia, December 2010). Available at: <http://www. economicstimulusplan.gov.au/documents/pdf/YearinfocusWEB4.pdf>.

161 Prime Minister of Australia 2008 (Global Financial Crisis, statement by P.M. Kevin Rudd. Press release, 12 October 2008, Canberra: Australian Government).

162 Ibid., p. 1.

liquidity in the mortgage market and avoid many of the problems that had plagued residential lending and construction in the United States and Europe.

Australia was one of only a few countries to avoid a recession. Unemployment also peaked at much less than had originally been thought, with the rate hovering between 5.0% and 6.0% during the height of the global crisis. Government debt levels also remained relatively low at approximately 10% of GDP. Economic growth in Australia quickly rebounded as the world economy improved and commodity prices regained their strength as demand for iron ore, coal, oil and gas gained momentum with the upswing in international trade.

With the improved economic outlook, the RBA was one of the first central banks to announce an increase in interest rates in March 2010. Justifying the 0.25% increase in the cash rate, Australia's central bank noted "economic conditions in 2009 were stronger than expected, after mild downturn a year ago. The rate of unemployment appears to have peaked at a much lower level than earlier expected."[163] The RBA again increase its key benchmark rate in April,[164] May[165] and November 2010.[166]

The interest rate rises reflected a much-improved economic outlook for Australia. With the downturn being less severe than was anticipated, regulatory authorities such as the RBA were able to reverse the accommodative settings in monetary policy and resume a more appropriate interest rate policy than was consistent with underlying economic activity.

New Zealand was in similar position to Australia when the GFC erupted in the United States. The first signs of any downturn began to emerge in August and September 2008. The Reserve Bank of New Zealand (RBNZ) responded by reducing the official cash rate in July and again in September 2008.[167] With the global outlook deteriorating further following the collapse of Lehman Brothers, New Zealand's central bank again lowered the official cash rate by 1.0% from 7.5% to 6.5% in October 2008.[168]

---

163 Reserve Bank of Australia 2010a. Statement by Glenn Stevens, Governor: Monetary Policy. Press release, 2 March 2010, Sydney: RBA).

164 The RBA increased its cash rate in April 2010 by 0.25% to 4.25%: Reserve Bank of Australia 2010b (Statement by Glenn Stevens, Governor: Monetary Policy. Press release, 6 April 2010, Sydney: RBA).

165 The RBA announced a further 0.25% increase in the cash rate to 4.50% in April 2010. See Reserve Bank of Australia 2010c (Statement by Glenn Stevens, Governor: Monetary Policy. Press release, 4 May 2010, Sydney: RBA).

166 Reserve Bank of Australia 2010d (Statement by Glenn Stevens, Governor: Monetary Policy Decision. Press release, 9 November 2010, Sydney: RBA).

167 The Reserve Bank of New Zealand reduced its cash rate from 8.25% to 8.0% in July 2008 and again in September by 0.5% to 7.5%. Reserve Bank of New Zealand 2008c (Press release, 24 July 2008, Wellington: RBNZ); Reserve Bank of New Zealand 2008d (Press release, 11 September 2008, Wellington: RBNZ).

168 Reserve Bank of New Zealand 2008e (Press release, 23 October 2008 Wellington: RBNZ).

With the ongoing turmoil in international markets, along with further deterioration in international trade and economic activity, the RBNZ lowered the official cash rate by 1.5% from 6.5% to 5.0%.[169] The RBNZ was to continue reducing its cash rate in January 2009,[170] March 2009[171] and April 2009.[172]

Like other central banks in the world, the RBNZ responded to the global crisis with expansionary monetary policy. This was not the only measure that was adopted by New Zealand policy authorities. On 12 October 2008 the Minister of Finance announced that the New Zealand government would guarantee all retail deposits with New Zealand banks and building societies.[173] The deposit scheme, like other schemes announced by governments all over the world, was designed to provide additional certainty and security to depositors and maintain the integrity of New Zealand banks. The guarantee scheme proved successful in preventing a run on the banks and providing further protection from any fallout impacting on the New Zealand economy.

In addition to the expansionary monetary policy settings and the government guarantee, the central bank of New Zealand announced in November 2008 two new facilities designed to support bank liquidity. The two facilities included a term auction facility[174] and a treasury bill tender.[175] Both measures were aimed at providing up to $NZ4 billion in liquidity to New Zealand's banks and financial markets. The structured facilities came in addition to the earlier announced purchases of Residential Mortgage Backed Securities.[176]

The New Zealand regulatory authorities continued their accommodative policy settings throughout 2009. By early 2010 the New Zealand economy enjoyed a

---

169   Reserve Bank of New Zealand 2008f (Press release, 4 December 2008, Wellington: RBNZ).

170   The Reserve Bank of New Zealand reduced its official cash rate from 5.0% to 3.5% in January 2009. See Reserve Bank of New Zealand 2009a (Press release, 29 January 2009, Wellington: RBNZ).

171   The Reserve Bank of New Zealand reduced the official cash rate in March 2009 by 0.5% to 3.0%. See Reserve Bank of New Zealand 2009b Press release, 12 March 2009, Wellington: RBNZ).

172   The Reserve Bank of New Zealand lowered the official cash rate in April by 0.5% to 2.5%. See Reserve Bank of New Zealand 2009c (Press release, 30 April 2009, Wellington: RBNZ).

173   Reserve Bank of New Zealand 2008a (Press release, 12 October 2008, Wellington: RBNZ, 15 October 2008).

174   For terms and guidelines on the term auction facility (TAF) see Reserve Bank of New Zealand 2008b Domestic Markets Operations. Available at: <http://www.rbnz.govt.nz/news/2008/3483444.html>.

175   For details regarding the Reserve Bank bill tenders. Available at: <http://www.rbnz.govt.nz/news/2008/3483444.html>.

176   Reserve Bank of New Zealand 2008g. Press release, 7 November 2008 (Wellington: RBNZ).

strong upswing in activity and a simultaneous rise in the terms of trade.[177] Despite the improved economic outlook, concerns and challenges remained.[178] This was particularly evident with the 2010 European sovereign debt crisis that threatened to unleash a new global crisis onto the world stage.

Japan

The Japanese economy was not in good shape when the GFC erupted. For almost two decades, the economy struggled with deflation, high levels of government debt, low economic output and higher than normal unemployment. Throughout the 1990s and into the new millennium successive governments attempted to pump-prime the economy with the aim of stimulating growth and generating sustainable economic activity. The policies implemented by the Japanese government involved a zero interest rate policy and large fiscal deficits. Japan's fiscal deficits were of concern because they led to Japan recording one of the largest public debt-to-GDP ratios in the world, which amounted to over 200% by 2010.[179]

Since the Japanese key overnight rate was set at almost 0%, Japanese regulatory authorities were required to implement alternative policy responses to address the challenges posed by the GFC.[180] In October 2008, in a coordinated move with other central banks, the Bank of Japan announced measures to improve liquidity in short-term US dollar denominated credit markets.[181] The Bank of Japan also announced additional measures in October 2008 designed to improve liquidity and stability in Japanese financial markets. These measures included providing additional liquidity in Japan's repo and commercial paper

---

177   Reserve Bank of New Zealand 2010d. Financial system outlook improved but fragile. Press release, 19 May 2010 (Wellington: RBNZ).

178   In June 2010 the Reserve Bank of New Zealand announced that it would increase the official cash rate by 0.25% to 2.75%. This was the first rise in nearly two years. See Reserve Bank of New Zealand 2010e (Reserve Bank raises Official Cash Rate to 2.75%. Press release 10 June 2010, Wellington: RBNZ). The Reserve Bank of New Zealand again increased the official cash rate in July 2010 by a further 0.25% to 3.0%, reflecting a stronger New Zealand economy and improved economic conditions. See Reserve Bank of New Zealand 2010f. (Reserve Bank of New Zealand raises official cash rate to 3.0%. Press release, 29 July 2010, Wellington: RBNZ).

179   Japan's public debt to GDP stood at 225% of GDP in 2010. See CIA World Factbook (Central Intelligence Agency 2010. Online. Available at: <https://www.cia.gov/library/publications/the-world-factbook/fields/2186.html>).

180   Japan's uncollateralized overnight market rate remained in the range of 0.1%–0.3% throughout 2008 and 2009.

181   The Bank of Japan acted in a coordinated move with other central banks, including the Bank of England, the European Central Bank, the US Federal Reserve and the Swiss National Bank. See Bank of Japan 2008a.(Further Measures to Improve Liquidity in Short-Term US Dollar Funding Markets. Press release, 13 October 2008, Tokyo: Bank of Japan).

markets. The Bank of Japan also introduced measures to improve liquidity and facilitate funding with corporate and business lending by lowering the criteria for credit ratings from A- to BBB.[182]

As the GFC deteriorated at the end of 2008, the Bank of Japan noted that the central bank had limited capacity to influence global events: "The Bank, while strains in global financial markets have mounted, has undertaken various prompt and decisive measures in providing liquidity, bearing in mind that the most important contribution a central bank can make in this situation is to ensure stability in financial markets."[183]

At the beginning of 2009, the Bank of Japan lowered its uncollateralized overnight rate to 0.1%, down from 0.3%.[184] The Bank of Japan also announced further measures to boost corporate financing by providing a government guarantee on commercial paper. The policy responses announced by the Bank of Japan were designed to provide additional stability to Japanese financial markets and to boost liquidity to finance bank and corporate lending.[185]

The Bank of Japan also undertook additional quantitative measures, including the purchase of Japanese government bonds in early 2009. In March 2009, the Bank of Japan purchased Japanese government bonds to the value of 21.6 trillion yen per year, an increase from 16.8 trillion yen a year earlier.[186] The purchases of government bonds were designed to improve liquidity in Japanese financial markets.

Despite the policy announcements, the Japanese economy continued to deteriorate throughout 2008 and the first half of 2009 as exports and private domestic demand weakened following higher levels of unemployment and lower levels of economic activity.[187] The first signs of stabilization occurred in August

---

182   Bank of Japan 2008b (Introduction of Money Market Operation Measures to Facilitate Corporate Financing. Press release, 2 December 2008, Tokyo: Bank of Japan).

183   Bank of Japan 2008c (On Monetary Policy Decisions. Press release, 31 October 2008. Tokyo: Bank of Japan).

184   Bank of Japan 2009a (Statement of Monetary Policy. Press release, 19 February 2009, Tokyo: Bank of Japan).

185   The policy measures announced by the Bank of Japan included:
    (1) Expanding special funds – supplying operations to assist in corporate lending;
    (2) Purchases of corporate bonds;
    (3) Provision of additional liquidity for the commercial paper market;
    (4) Expansion in the range of corporate debt facilities;
    (5) US dollar funding operations;
    (6) Provision of government guarantees for commercial paper markets;
    (7) Purchases of Japanese government bonds. See attachment to Bank of Japan 2009a.

186   Bank of Japan 2009b (Statement on Monetary Policy. Press release, 18 March, 2009, Tokyo: Bank of Japan).

187   Bank of Japan 2009c (Statement on Monetary Policy. Press release, 16 June 2009, Tokyo: Bank of Japan).

2009, when exports began to pick up following the government's expansionary policies which provided a much-needed boost to expenditure and income.[188]

By October 2009, the recovery in Japan was under way as exports continued to rise, business sentiment rose and the decline in household income and expenditure slowed. Despite the improvements, consumer sentiment remained subdued due to the high levels of unemployment.[189] The Bank of Japan noted the risks to the downside following the instability and uncertainty that continued to confront the world's financial markets and the international economy.[190]

Throughout 2010 and early 2011, the Bank of Japan maintained its overnight call rate at between 0.0% and 0.1%. In addition to the ultra-low interest rate for borrowings, the Bank of Japan also undertook further quantitative easing through purchases of exchange-traded funds, treasury bills, asset-backed commercial paper, corporate bonds and Japanese real estate investment trusts. The Japanese government would purchase approximately 40 trillion yen in assets during this time.[191]

By the end of 2010 and the beginning of 2011 the recovery in the Japanese economy continued to take shape.[192] The Bank of Japan noted in January and February 2011 that due to the continued improvement in the international economic outlook, along with the policy responses of the Bank of Japan and the Japanese government, Japan's economy showed signs of a modest recovery.[193] Real GDP for 2010 came in at a solid 3.3%.

Despite the improved economic outlook, there continued to be lingering doubt as to whether the recovery would be self-sustaining.[194] Concerns remained as to whether the Japanese economy would overcome the debilitating effects of deflation and whether the economy would return to sustainable long-term growth. With this in mind, the Bank of Japan continued its accommodative policy measures, which were designed to stimulate economic activity and growth, and provide a sustainable platform for higher levels of employment, productivity and national income.

---

188   Bank of Japan 2009d (Statement on Monetary Policy. Press release, 11 August 2009, Tokyo: Bank of Japan).

189   Bank of Japan 2009e (Statement on Monetary Policy. Press release, 14 October 2009, Tokyo: Bank of Japan).

190   Ibid.

191   Bank of Japan 2010d (Statement on Monetary Policy. Press release, 28 October 2010, Tokyo: Bank of Japan).

192   Bank of Japan 2010b (Statement on Monetary Policy. Press release, 30 April 2010, Tokyo: Bank of Japan). See also Bank of Japan 2010c (Statement on Monetary Policy. Press release, 21 May 2010, Tokyo: Bank of Japan).

193   Bank of Japan 2011 (Statement on Monetary Policy. Press release, 25 January 2011, Tokyo: Bank of Japan).

194   Bank of Japan 2010a (Statement on Monetary Policy. Press release, 26 January 2010, Tokyo: Bank of Japan).

India

The Indian economy enjoyed strong economic growth from the 1990s and throughout 2000–2008. Average GDP was in the range of 8%–10%, as Indian exports to developed countries gathered pace. However, the Indian economy was also not immune from the adverse consequences of the GFC. The volatility in international financial markets led to liquidity restrictions which adversely affected Indian banks and financial institutions.

Concerned with the overall stability of Indian financial markets, the central bank of India lowered its key repo rate from 9% to 8% in October 2008.[195] The repo rate was lowered again to 7.5% in November 2008.[196] To enhance liquidity in Indian banks, the Reserve Bank of India (RBI) lowered the cash reserve ratio from 7.5% to 6.5% on 11 October 2008.[197] The RBI again lowered the cash reserve ratio for Indian banks to 5.5% on 25 October with a further reduction to 5.0% in November 2008.[198] The RBI also approved of temporary facilities designed to allow Indian banks the flexibility to manage their short-term funding needs.

As the financial crisis continued to unfold, the Reserve Bank of India reduced the cash reserve ratio from 5.5% to 5.0% in January 2009.[199] India's key benchmark rate, the fixed rate repo, was also reduced from 6.5% to 5.5% in January 2009.[200] The measures were designed to stimulate consumer demand and borrowings, as well as provide additional liquidity to India's financial markets. In March 2009, the Reserve Bank of India again reduced the repo rate from 5.5% to 5.0% due to concerns that an international slowdown in economic activity would have an adverse effect on India's industrial production and economic growth.[201]

The measures appeared to have had a positive effect on India's growth. GDP growth for 2009–2010 remained at 6.0% and inflation for the year stood at 4.0%.[202] Despite the modest improvement the Reserve Bank decided to again lower its repo rate from 5.0% to 4.75%.[203] However, by the end of 2009, inflation began

---

195   Reserve Bank of India 2008 (RBI Measures for improving Domestic and Foreign Currency Liquidity. Monetary and Credit Information Review, Vol. V, Issue 6, December 2008), p. 4.

196   Ibid.

197   The cash reserve ratio is the minimum amount of liquid assets a bank needs to keep in its reserves. See Ibid., p. 4 (Important Banking and Financial Developments in 2008).

198   Ibid.

199   Reserve Bank of India. 2009a (Monetary and Credit Information Review, Important Banking and Financial Developments in 2008. Vol. V, Issue 7, January 2009), p. 4.

200   Ibid.

201   Reserve Bank of India 2009b (Policy. Monetary and Credit Information Review, Vol. V, Issue 9, March 2009), p. 4.

202   Reserve Bank of India. 2009c.(Annual Policy Statement for 2009–10. Monetary and Credit Information Review, Vol. V, Issue 10, April 2009), p. 4.

203   Ibid.

to re-emerge as growth and industrial production picked up. By November 2009 inflation stood at 6.5%, a rise from the previous reading of 4.0%.[204]

The Reserve Bank acknowledged the rise in inflation and would closely monitor any further increases in consumer prices.[205] In March 2010, with the improved international outlook, the Reserve Bank of India revised India's GDP from 6.0% to 7.5%.[206] At the same time wholesale inflation was projected to rise from the previous estimate of 6.5% to 8.5%.[207]

With growth returning towards trend and inflation rising, the central bank decided to increase the repo rate from 5.25% to 5.50% in July 2010.[208] This was the first time for over two years that there had been an increase in interest rates. The interest rate rise reflected the improved outlook for economic growth and income in India since the onset of the GFC. The Reserve Bank of India again increased the repo rate in August 2010 from 5.50% to 5.75%, with growth again revised to 8.5% with an upward bias. The main concern for the central bank now was not how to stimulate economic activity but rather to contain a build-up of inflationary pressures: "On the basis of the overall assessment, the stance of monetary policy in 2010–2011 will broadly be to contain inflation and anchor inflationary expectations, while being prepared to respond to any further build-up of inflationary pressures."[209]

The expansionary policy responses by the Reserve Bank helped to steer the Indian economy through the worst of the crisis. India already had a strongly performing economy before the GFC took hold. Nevertheless, the economy was not immune from volatile and disruptive international financial markets. The Reserve Bank of India played an important role through its various responses to facilitate corporate lending and maintain stability and liquidity for Indian banks and financial institutions. Without these measures the Indian economy would have slowed further, as the international economy remained weak and fragile during the height of the crisis.

China

The Chinese economy was widely regarded as the powerhouse economy throughout the GFC. Unlike other developed economies which relied heavily upon consumer expenditure and housing for economic growth, China derived much of its wealth

204   Reserve Bank of India. 2009d (Second Quarter Review of Monetary Policy 2009–10. Monetary and Credit Information Review, Vol. VI, Issue 5, November 2009), p. 4.

205   Ibid.

206   Reserve Bank of India 2010e (Policy. Monetary and Credit Information Review, Volume VI, Issue 9, March 2010), p. 1.

207   Ibid.

208   Reserve Bank of India 2010f (Policy. Monetary and Credit Information Review, Vol. VII, Issue 1, July 2010), p. 1.

209   Reserve Bank of India 2010g (First Quarter Review of Monetary Policy for the year 2010–11. Monetary and Credit Information Review, Vol. VII, Issue 2, August 2010), p. 4.

from value-added manufactured exports. Some commentators had even gone as far as to suggest that the Chinese economy had effectively "decoupled" itself from the US economy.

The decoupling argument was not completely accurate, as it failed to take proper account of the interlinkages that existed between China and the international economy, particularly through trade. As the IMF reported in 2010, "China was hit hard by the global financial crisis, predominately through trade channels."[210] China's growth relied heavily on international trade and a growing international economy which allowed China to export low-cost manufactured goods.

The GFC had disrupted trade in international markets. First, the GFC led to significant distortion and dislocation in international financial markets. The dislocation adversely affected the ability of buyers to purchase China's manufactured goods. Purchasers found it increasingly difficult to access sufficient credit to pay for China's exports. Second, the distortions in international financial markets triggered a crisis in confidence and uncertainty in both consumer and business sentiment. Uncertainty was then replaced by panic, corporate collapses and bank closures in the United States and Europe, which adversely affected consumer and business expenditure and overall economic activity.

The combination of collapsing consumer demand and dysfunctional financial and credit markets led to the largest economic downturn since World War II and the Great Depression. The global recession was felt particularly hard in the United States and Europe, which were at that stage the largest consumers of China's manufactured exports. As millions of workers lost their jobs, consumers reduced their purchases of manufactured goods. China had now also become a victim of the global crisis, as its exports fell in line with the decline in consumer and business expenditure in the United States and Europe.

As the IMF reported, the policy response by Chinese authorities was "quick, determined and effective."[211] Like other countries that were confronted with the adverse effects of the crisis, China's policy response consisted of implementing expansionary fiscal and monetary policy and making currency adjustments to the currency, the renminbi.[212] The expansionary fiscal stimulus largely consisted of bringing forward government expenditures on the country's infrastructure, including new roads, bridges, schools, universities, hospitals, highways, tunnels, nuclear plants and dams. Some stimulus measures were also aimed at providing a boost to consumer expenditure through the provision of tax cuts for workers.

China's central bank also attempted to boost business lending for investment purposes by removing limits on credit growth. The People's Bank of China reduced the capital reserve requirements for China's banks, and at the same time reduced

---

210 International Monetary Fund 2010d (People's Republic of China: 2010 Article IV Consultation – Staff Report; 10/238, July 2010. Washington, DC: IMF), p. 4.
211 Ibid.
212 Ibid.

China's key benchmark rate for business and consumer borrowings.[213] In addition to the expansionary measures undertaken by both the Chinese government and the Bank of China, the central bank also re-pegged the renminbi, to the US dollar.

The measures helped China overcome the adverse effects the crisis had on its exports and trade income. By the middle of 2009, China's GDP averaged 9%, an increase from the 2008 estimate of 6%.[214] China's financial markets also stabilized quickly, as lending and business investment continued to gain traction with the initiatives implemented by the Bank of China. The IMF reported that by the middle of 2010 the economic recovery was well under way in China, with export volumes returning above their pre-crisis levels.[215] Forward indicators had also revealed that China's industrial production and output would be self-sustaining. According to the IMF, the main issue now for policymakers in China would be to carefully calibrate an exit strategy from expansionary monetary and fiscal policy that had been provided to the economy during the GFC.[216]

The unprecedented policy responses undertaken by the Chinese authorities in responding to the GFC helped the Chinese economy to recover more quickly than would otherwise have been the case. The fiscal stimulus measures that were implemented by the Chinese government not only gave an additional short-term boost to economic activity but would also furnish the economy with the long-term benefits of improved infrastructure. These important improvements to China's infrastructure would increase the nation's industrial and productive capacity in the future. China would now be in a position to boost its exports and lead in the next phase of the international recovery.

Latin America

Latin American countries including Brazil, Argentina and Chile were also not immune from the crisis engulfing the world's most powerful economies. Following the volatile conditions on international financial markets, the G20 finance ministers met in November 2008 in São Paulo, Brazil, to develop a coordinated approach to deal with the crisis. The São Paulo meeting was attended by representatives from all G20 member states, including the United States, Japan, Germany, China, India, Australia, Brazil, Argentina, South Africa, Indonesia, Mexico, Russia, Saudi Arabia, France, Italy, South Korea, Turkey, Canada, Britain and the EU.

The G20 meeting in Brazil was timely because it provided recognition that the GFC had not only affected developed nations but had also adversely affected emerging countries. In 2009 the IMF endorsed a proposed framework which would allow emerging countries such as Brazil to purchase up to US$10 billion in

---

213   Ibid.
214   Ibid.
215   Ibid., p. 6.
216   Ibid., pp. 7–8.

IMF notes over a two-year horizon.[217] The funding program would assist Brazilian banks and financial institutions to overcome the worst of the GFC by providing liquidity to banks and the financial sector.

Similar programs were also in place for other Latin American countries, including Mexico and Columbia. The IMF provided a new Flexible Line of Credit to emerging countries to assist them with access to additional funding, which would allow Latin American banks to draw upon funds when needed.[218] The policy responses and the underlying strength of Latin American economies allowed the region to handle the crisis more effectively compared with other, developed nations. The region's economies contracted on average by only 1.8% in 2009 and the region was well on the way to recovery by 2010. [219]

Commenting on the relative strength of emerging countries such as Peru and Brazil, the IMF concluded that significant social investment had been made in a number of Latin American countries, including policies to combat poverty and unemployment. The progress in social welfare along with strong industrial output and employment growth allowed the region to emerge from the crisis much more quickly and stage a robust recovery in 2010 and 2011.

Conclusion

The world's leading central banks, monetary authorities and governments responded quickly to the GFC. Their responses included a combination of fiscal stimulus and expansionary monetary policy designed to stimulate economic activity, growth and employment. Conventional policy responses were coordinated with non-conventional measures that included the establishment of temporary credit lines and quantitative easing measures designed to boost liquidity in fragile financial markets.

The United States, Europe and the IMF led the way with policy responses that would assist the international economy to overcome the difficulties and challenges posed by the crisis. In some instances the policy responses that were adopted were innovative and non-conventional measures. Driving much of the policy response was the fear that the world's major industrialized economies would collapse, leading to a repeat of the Great Depression of the 1930s. Acutely aware of the dangers that the global crisis posed, authorities all over the world were keen to develop a coordinated approach.

The policy responses by and large proved successful, providing much-needed liquidity to volatile financial markets. The fiscal stimulus measures adopted by a

---

217   International Monetary Fund 2010b (IMF signs US$10 billion note purchase agreement with Brazil. Press release 10/14, 22 January 2010, Washington, DC: IMF).

218   International Monetary Fund 2010c (Latin America helps shape global economic recovery. *IMF Survey Magazine*, 24 May 2010, In the News, Washington, DC: IMF).

219   Ibid., p. 2.

number of countries helped provide additional public expenditure at a time when household expenditure and business investment had fallen dramatically. Countries that were dependent upon export demand and income were also required to adopt expansionary measures to offset steep declines in international trade. With the policy responses in place throughout 2009 and 2010, the international outlook began to improve, as is evidenced by a return to growth in the United States and Europe.

Despite these improvements, headwinds, which included stubbornly high levels of unemployment and lacklustre growth, remained for policymakers. The recovery to date has been described as a "jobless recovery," since growth has not been sufficiently high to reduce unemployment, particularly in the United States and parts of Europe. Concerns also continue to mount with the sovereign debt crisis confronting Greece, Ireland and Portugal, which remains a live issue requiring further attention from the EU and the international authorities.

Chapter 6
Inquiries and Proposals for Reform

Introduction

In the aftermath of the global financial crisis, a number of regulatory authorities and government agencies proposed wide-ranging reforms to the regulatory frameworks of the world's financial markets. These bodies undertook and proposed extensive reforms to the way financial markets would be regulated, including proposing reforms aimed at improving international coordination.

Reform proposals that were put forward included enhanced regulation of deposit banks, investment banks, non-bank financial institutions, brokers and financial intermediaries. Some commentators had argued that the crisis revealed much deeper structural weaknesses and vulnerabilities with the entire system of market capitalism. There had also been widespread criticism from investors, businesses and the unemployed over the handling of the crisis, particularly with the large-scale bailouts that had been proposed and implemented for Wall Street investment firms. Many had expressed concern that bailouts would contribute to a moral hazard, where the firms that had contributed to the crisis would be favoured with generous taxpayer-funded assistance, by contrast with the treatment of the unemployed.

The ideologies of Karl Marx and modern-day socialist revisionists found much favour in the concerns of the unemployed during the height of the crisis. One unforgettable consequence of the recent financial crisis was the spillover of financial mayhem from financial markets into the wider community when the Great Recession emerged to devastate both developed and emerging economies. Millions of workers would lose their jobs, factories and business would be forced to close, and the long-term unemployed would become the norm in previously booming industrial economies.

Governments and policymakers around the world sought to overcome the worst of the crisis and to avoid a repeat of a global depression by putting forward proposals for regulatory reform. Many of the suggested reforms called for international coordination, expressing the realization that without a global solution to a global problem any suggested reforms would be largely ineffective. Other proposals relied on domestic intervention aimed at strengthening national regulatory frameworks. It was now clear that the status quo in terms of regulation could no longer be maintained, and the world's banking and financial systems would be required to undergo considerable change to make them more robust and less susceptible to global imbalances.

Group of Thirty: Financial Reform a Framework for Financial Stability

The Group of Thirty (G30), a private think tank made up of 30 participating members, undertook an investigation of the causes of the global financial crisis. The G30 members focused their attention specifically on how the financial system might be organized once the current crisis has passed. In January 2009, the G30 released its report on the causes of the current crisis and the impact the crisis has had on the international financial system.[1]

The G30 Report on the GFC attempted to address the following issues: policy issues related to redefining the scope and the boundaries of prudential regulation; reforming the structure of prudential regulation, including the role of central banks, the workings of the "lender of last resort," the provision of a "safety net," the need for greater international coordination, improving governance, risk management, regulatory policies, accounting practices and standards, and improvements in transparency and financial infrastructure arrangements.[2]

In addressing the above policy and related issues, the G30 made a number of recommendations designed to overcome perceived weaknesses in the global financial system. These suggestions included making improvements in supervisory and prudential regulation of financial markets. One of the key recommendations to emerge from the G30 report was the need to enhance and improve prudential regulation and supervision of global banking institutions. According to the G30, a single regulator should have the responsibility to prudentially regulate all banks and government-insured deposit-taking institutions. A single regulator would achieve more efficient regulation of banking institutions with the largest and most complex institutions subject to greater scrutiny and supervision.[3]

By targeting the largest banking institutions, the G30 recognizes not only the economic importance of banks and lending institutions but also the increased likelihood of systemic problems flowing from a big bank collapse. The G30 further recommended placing nationwide limits on deposit concentration for banks and other government-insured deposit-taking institutions. Avoiding excessive concentration in national banking systems would reduce systemic risk and improve overall systemic stability because there would be greater diversification of bank activity. With reduced concentration among banks as well as other financial institutions, risk would be diversified within the global banking system. Through diversification the likelihood of systemic risk or contagion would be reduced as default risk is spread more broadly through the financial system.

---

1 G30 Working Group on Financial Stability 2009. Financial reform: A framework for financial stability. Washington, DC: Group of Thirty, 15 January 2009.
2 See G30 Recommendation 1, Ibid., pp. 3–4.
3 Ibid., p. 8.

Enhanced prudential regulation of financial institutions was not to be limited to banks. In its report the G30 further recommended that consolidation should occur with the supervisory practices of prudential regulators over non-bank financial institutions.[4] The regulation of non-bank financial institutions recognized the growing importance of investment banks, broker–dealers and other financial intermediaries which were active in global financial markets.

Money market mutual funds and private equity providers should also be made subject to prudential regulation. Scrutiny of private fund managers should extend to periodic regulatory reporting as well as public disclosure of material information: "the size, investment style, borrowing, and performance of the funds under management."[5] According to the G30, a prudential regulator should also have the authority and mandate to "establish appropriate standards for capital, liquidity, and risk management."[6]

Another key recommendation made by the G30 was the need to develop and further enhance international regulatory and supervisory coordination.[7] The GFC has been a truly international crisis, which has exposed the weaknesses in the global financial architecture. The G30 recommendation to improve international coordination is consistent with focusing regulatory and prudential attention on cross-border transactions and offshore banking institutions, and monitoring global systemic risk. Minimizing gaps and overcoming weaknesses in international regulation by enforcing international standards represents a pragmatic approach to dealing with any future global crisis.

Recognizing the importance of increasing collaboration and supervisory oversight of international banking organizations,[8] the G30 concludes that through greater collaboration with international agencies and information exchanges, leverage and liquidity mismatches could be minimized.[9] The G30 further recommends that institutional policies and standards be enhanced and strengthened,

---

4 Ibid., pp. 8–9.

5 See G30 Recommendation 4, Ibid., p. 9.

6 Ibid.

7 See G30 Recommendation 8, Ibid., p. 11.

8 See G30 Recommendation 8, Ibid., p. 11. According to the G30, the focus of enhanced international coordination should be to: "(i) better coordinate oversight of the largest international banking organizations, with more timely and open information sharing, and greater clarity on home and host responsibilities, including in crisis management; (ii) move beyond coordinated rule making and standard setting to the identification and modification of material national differences in the application and enforcement of such standards; (iii) close regulatory gaps and raise standards, where needed, with respect to offshore banking centres; and (iv) develop the means for joint consideration of systemic risk concerns and the cyclicality implications of regulatory and supervisory policies." Ibid., (n. 1), p. 11.

9 Ibid., p. 12.

especially in the areas of corporate governance and risk management,[10] regulatory capital standards,[11] and liquidity risk management.[12]

To minimize the potential for any future financial crisis, the G30 made a number of important recommendations regarding the regulation of financial markets and financial products.[13] Importantly, the G30 recognizes the challenges posed by off-balance sheet financial arrangements which can have a material effect on a firm's risk profile and vulnerability. With off-balance sheet liabilities, a firm's overall indebtedness can be understated. One major consequence of understating an entity's leverage position is that the entity's risk profile can be adversely affected. A firm can appear to be in a strong financial position but in reality can be exposed to high levels of debt. The G30 proposed that all forms of off-balance sheet financing should be disclosed to investors and lenders, which, in turn, would improve the overall level of transparency.

Similarly, the G30 were of the view that the regulation of rating agencies should also be reformed to achieve improved transparency, particularly at the international level.[14] Improving international collaboration between rating agencies would enhance the investor's ability to monitor, evaluate and review a firm's overall risk profile.[15]

In a related theme, the G30 were also cognisant of the need to improve the regulation and supervisory oversight of Over-the-Counter (OTC) derivatives markets.[16] OTC markets have traditionally been the domains of sophisticated

---

10   The G30 was of the view that regulatory standards relating to corporate governance practices should be strengthened through greater reliance on and employment of independent directors on corporate boards. Compensation arrangements should also be scrutinized and reviewed in light of risk management practices, along with the balancing of risk with the long-term interests of shareholders. Corporate governance practices should be regularly reviewed in light of the need to balance risk with shareholder returns. Further, a firm's risk profile should be regularly reviewed in light of the entity's risk-return parameters. See G30 Recommendation 9, Ibid., (n. 1), p. 12.

11   The G30 recommended that international global capital and liquidity standards should be strengthened and possibly redefined to provide greater transparency. See G30 Recommendation 10, Ibid., (n. 1), p. 13.

12   According to the G30, liquidity risk management policies need to be continually reviewed in order to remain relevant. Liquidity disclosure standards should also be continually enhanced along Basel principles. See G30 Recommendation 11, Ibid., (n. 1), p. 13.

13   The G30 recommends that there should be greater transparency within financial markets and financial products. See Recommendation 13, Ibid. (n. 1), pp. 14–15.

14   The G30 recommended that risk ratings issued by ratings agency should be periodically reviewed and revised for their intended use by investors as well as other end-users. See Recommendation 14, Ibid., (n. 1), p. 15.

15   The G30 was also of the view that market regulators should improve the regulation of directors' remuneration so as to achieve greater alignment between incentives among providers of risk ratings and their clients and users.

16   See Recommendation 15, Ibid., (n. 1), pp. 15–16.

investors, as opposed to retail investors. Hence, OTC markets have been exposed to lower levels of regulation and supervisory oversight. The regulatory position of OTC markets is to be contrasted with exchange-traded markets, which typically have a higher level of regulatory and supervisory oversight. This is because exchange-traded markets have more involvement from retail end-users. Consumer-type protections are more relevant for exchange-traded derivatives markets. Market regulators have also vigorously enforced disclosure rules for retail end-users of exchange-traded derivatives products.

Since OTC derivatives markets have been subject to lower regulatory burden, product issuers of financial derivatives products have incentives to engage in regulatory arbitrage. The regulatory game- playing behaviour was not limited to the differences that existed between the regulatory burdens for futures markets and OTC markets.[17] There was some evidence to suggest that product issuers may have also been attempting to circumvent rigid securities laws when developing new OTC financial products.[18]

Securities market regulators such as the United States Securities and Exchange Commission (SEC) and the Commodities Futures Trading Commission (CFTC) had adopted aggressive enforcement practices when policing issuers of OTC financial products. Hence, it was not uncommon for financial market regulators in the form of the SEC and CFTC to prosecute product issuers of OTC financial products with alleged breaches of securities laws or futures market regulation. Indeed, the practice was not limited to financial market regulators in the United States.

Since the GFC there have been a number of proposals put forward for further reform of financial derivatives markets regulation. Much of the regulatory focus has fallen on OTC derivatives markets. One such proposal, which has attracted the attention of US regulators as well as market participants, has involved proposing to transfer OTC derivatives activity to an exchange-based system of settlement and clearing. Financial market regulators in the United States proposed that OTC derivatives markets in the form of swaps, forwards and other OTC derivatives should be centrally cleared by certified and regulated derivatives clearing organizations (DCOs).[19]

17　Ciro. T. 2005. Game theory in financial markets litigation, *Journal of International Banking Law and Regulation*, 20(7) (2005), p. 315.

18　Ibid., pp. 319–20.

19　Central clearing of OTC derivatives was a key reform proposal which was contained in H.R. 3795 *Over-the-Counter Derivatives Markets Act 2009*, 111th US Congress 2009–10. The Act proposed making amendments to the *Commodity Exchange Act 1936* requiring a number of OTC derivatives products and markets as well as financial market intermediaries (including swap dealers, swap participants and swap brokers) to be placed under the jurisdiction of a federal prudential regulator. The prudential regulatory could be either by the US Federal Reserve, the Office of the Comptroller of the Currency or the Federal Deposit Insurance Corporation. The Act also proposed making a number of amendments to the *Securities Exchange Act 1934* to allow for a centralized settlement

The basic premise for proposing centralized clearing of OTC derivatives is that OTC derivatives markets lacked transparency. With financial market regulators not knowing what was being bilaterally negotiated and settled between OTC counterparties, it was argued that OTC market practices could contribute to increased systemic risk and contribute to financial instability. Hence, it was proposed that one way of improving transparency and reducing the potential for systemic or contagion risk for financial markets was to have a centralized and regulated clearing system for OTC derivatives markets.

As is discussed in Chapter 2, debates concerning the regulation of financial derivatives have not been without controversy. OTC derivatives were often complex instruments which had not been well understood by all. Market regulators, including the SEC and CFTC, had been calling for wholesale changes to the regulatory landscape for years. Greenspan was of the view that derivatives by themselves posed little actual risk; however there was insufficient understanding of how OTC derivatives could contribute to systemic risk:

> Yet beneath all of the evidence of the value of derivatives to a market economy, there remains a deep-seated fear that while individual risks seem clearly to have been reduced through derivative facilitated diversification, systemic risk has become enlarged, as a consequence. Without question, derivatives facilitate the implementation of leveraged trading strategies, though the very technology that has made derivatives feasible has also improved the ability to leverage without derivatives. Nonetheless, the possibility of increased systemic risk does appear to be an issue that requires fuller understanding.[20]

Derivatives markets had been considered to be at least a contributory factor to the current crisis, a point that was reinforced by the Financial Crisis Inquiry Commission, which concluded that OTC derivatives "contributed significantly to the crisis."[21] The Financial Crisis Inquiry Commission formed the view that OTC derivatives and, in particular, credit default swaps were at the centre of the

---

and clearing facility for securities-based swaps. H.R. 3795 *Over-the-Counter Derivatives Markets Act 2009* was not passed by the 111th Congress. However, other financial reforms which included reforms to swap markets were approved in the form of *H.R. 4173 Dodd-Frank Wall Street Reform and Consumer Protection Act 2010*. H.R. 4173 was passed by the House of Representatives (US) and the Senate on 30 June and 15 July 2010 respectively. H.R. 4173 was signed into law on 21 July 2010.

20   Greenspan 1999 (Financial derivatives. Remarks by Chairman Alan Greenspan before the Futures Industry Association, Boca Raton, Florida, 19 March 1999. The Federal Reserve Board).

21   Financial Crisis Inquiry Commission 2011. Final report of the National Commission on the causes of the financial and economic crisis in the United States, January 2011 (Washington, DC: G.P.O.), pp. xxiv–xxv.

financial storm that engulfed the entire financial landscape when the US housing bubble burst.[22]

United States Financial Crisis Inquiry Report

The Financial Crisis Inquiry Commission in the United States was established soon after the emergence of the global crisis. Charged with providing a detailed examination of the causes of the financial crisis, the Inquiry conducted a number of hearings with witnesses that were at centre stage of the financial meltdown.[23] The Commission's legal authority to conduct the enquiry was given legislative backing in the form of the *Fraud Enforcement and Recovery Act 2009*.[24] The Commission concluded its enquiry into the causes of the global financial crisis in January 2011.

After obtaining all of the submissions and evidence from the witnesses, the Financial Crisis Commission arrived at nine conclusions regarding the causes of the current global financial crisis. The overall finding from the Commission was that the current crisis was avoidable. According to the Commission there had been systemic failure in the supervision and regulation of financial markets and financial products.[25] The Commission was also of the view that the US government and regulatory authorities were under-prepared for the crisis and there had been a widespread failure in professional ethics and standards regarding financial markets, including financial intermediaries.[26]

Armed with the findings from the public hearings and the conclusions from the majority of the members of the Commission, the Financial Inquiry Commission's Final Report also began laying the groundwork for reform. The Commission was critical of what it considered to be an outdated and outmoded system of regulation and supervisory oversight of US financial markets.[27] The Commission was also critical of the role ratings agency played in the financial crisis and the fact that credit-rating agencies had been largely unregulated by the SEC as well as other market regulators.[28]

---

22 Ibid., p. xxv.

23 The Commission interviewed over 700 witnesses and conducted public hearings through 2010 in New York, Washington and a number of regional cities and towns. Ibid., (n. 21), p. xi.

24 Public Law 111-21 US 2009.

25 Financial Crisis Inquiry Commission Final report Ibid., (n. 21), pp. xv–xxv.

26 Ibid.

27 The Financial Inquiry Commission was particularly critical of the role of the Securities and Exchange Commission in not providing adequate supervisory oversight of investment banks. The Commission criticized the role of the market regulator in not monitoring adequately investment bank activities, especially capital and liquidity activities. Ibid., (n. 21), p. 155.

28 Ibid., (n. 21), pp. 125–6.

The parallel banking system and its participants also came under criticism for allowing shadow financial institutions to operate largely unchecked within the United States.[29] According to the Commission, the shadow banking system had contributed significantly to the global financial crisis because of the large build-up of risk. The unregulated nature of the shadow banking sector meant that market regulators were either not aware of, or failed to fully appreciate, the level of risk that was posed by the parallel system to conventional banks and financial markets.[30]

The Commission also noted that banking and market regulators had not properly regulated traditional banks and investment banks. The inadequacies of the regulatory and supervisory framework led to structural weaknesses and flaws in lending and risk management practices. This, in turn, contributed to a further build-up of risk at the time when the US housing bubble had begun to unwind. The widespread use of credit default swaps and CDOs further led to a build-up of risk because the derivatives were complex instruments, opaque and not properly understood by investors.

The conclusions from the Commission were consistent with the premise that the regulatory and supervisory oversight framework of US financial markets had failed to achieve its stated aims. The Commission was of the view that further reforms of financial markets regulation would be required to improve market integrity and promote overall financial stability. Enhanced regulation and supervisor oversight would provide improved monitoring of bank and investment bank trading activities. Providing greater legislative powers and authority to the SEC, the CFTC and the US Federal Reserve would also allow for an improved legal mandate for the monitoring and supervision of trading activity within US financial markets.[31]

Regulation would also extend to covering perceived weaknesses and gaps in the current regulatory and supervisory framework. OTC derivatives such as credit default swaps, synthetic derivatives, structured products and collateralized debt obligations would all now be regulated by the SEC or the CFTC.[32] OTC

---

29   Ibid., (n. 21), p. 255.

30   Ibid.

31   According to the Commission, the SEC as well as other market regulators failed to provide adequate supervision of large investment banks and insurance companies such as American Insurance Group, Citigroup, Lehman Brothers, Bear Stearns and Merrill Lynch. The failure to provide adequate supervision and monitoring meant that sub-prime mortgage-lending practices as well as related investment and trading activity went largely unchecked and rewarded short-term risk-taking at the expense of long-term financial stability. Ibid., (n. 21), p. 279.

32   The Commission was critical of the use of OTC derivatives such as credit default swaps, synthetic derivatives and CDOs in the period leading up to the GFC. The unregulated nature of these instruments meant that there had been inadequate supervision of trading activities and open positions which, in turn, contributed to a build-up of risk in the US financial sector. Market and banking regulators realized too late the potential

derivatives markets would be regulated in a similar way to the way securities and futures contracts are currently regulated under the *Securities Exchange Act 1934* and the *Commodity and Futures Trading Act 1974*.

US Senate Report: Wall Street and the Financial Crisis

In April 2011, the US Senate Permanent Subcommittee investigating the origins of the 2008 financial crisis released its report.[33] In conducting its investigation the Permanent Subcommittee issued numerous subpoenas, conducted over 150 interviews and consulted with government departments, and academic and private sector experts.[34] The Subcommittee also reviewed and analysed millions of pages of transcripts and documents held by the SEC, as well as other regulatory and banking authorities.[35]

The US Senate Subcommittee found that a number of failures existed which had contributed to the GFC. These failings included regulatory failures on the part of the Office of Thrift Supervision, the issuing of inflated ratings by rating agencies Moody's and Standard & Poor's, and investment bank abuses involving Goldman Sachs and Deutsche Bank.

The findings from the US Subcommittee prompted the Subcommittee to make a number of recommendations for reforms to the Office of Thrift Supervision, investment banks, high-risk lending practices and credit-rating agencies. In relation to high-risk lending, the Subcommittee recommended that the practice should be curtailed and all mortgages which are deemed to be "qualified residential mortgages" have a low risk of delinquency or default.[36]

The Subcommittee was critical of the role of credit-rating agencies in issuing credit ratings "for tens of thousands of US residential mortgage-backed securities (RMBSs) and collateralized debt obligations (CDOs)."[37] By issuing the AAA highest rating for a large proportion of residential mortgages and structured financial products, the credit-rating agencies effectively deemed the securities "safe investments."[38] The Subcommittee found that the issuing of AAA and other investment-grade ratings for the mortgage securities and other related financial

---

systemic threat posed by unregulated financial instruments and markets and exposed an added structural weakness in the regulatory and supervisory framework within the United States. Ibid., (n. 21), p. 308.

33   United States Senate Permanent Subcommittee on Investigations 2011 (Wall Street and the financial crisis: anatomy of a financial collapse, Majority and Minority Staff Report, Permanent Subcommittee on Investigations, Committee on Homeland Security and Governmental Affairs, US Senate, 13 April 2011).

34   Ibid., p. 1.
35   Ibid., p. 1.
36   Ibid., p. 12.
37   Ibid., p. 6.
38   Ibid.

instruments was inaccurate and "introduced risk into the US financial system and constituted a key cause of the financial crisis."[39]

The Subcommittee revealed that typically, AAA-rated investments have less than 1% probability of default. This is because AAA credit rating provides investors with reassurance that the investment is safe and prudent. However, by 2010 the Subcommittee found that over 90% of the AAA credit ratings that were given to sub-prime mortgage-backed securities and CDOs had been downgraded to junk status.[40]

The downgrading of the mortgage-backed securities and CDOs led to significant losses for investors. The losses were shared broadly among the financial community to include large-scale investment houses, investors both large and small, pension funds, trustees, local authorities, government authorities and private investors. The losses flowing from sub-prime mortgages and CDOs undermined investor confidence and increased instability and volatility in financial markets generally.

The Subcommittee reported that its investigations discovered a number of factors that were responsible for the inaccurate credit ratings that were issued on sub-prime mortgage debt and structured financial instruments. According to the Subcommittee, the factors included conflicts of interest, inaccurate credit-rating models, inadequate surveillance and rating resources, market share gains and pressure from investment banks.[41]

Product issuers that required a credit rating for the products they intended to market and sell to the public provided remuneration to the ratings agencies.[42] According to the Subcommittee's investigation, since rating agencies were required to rate an issuer's financial product, the issuer would often "shop around" for the highest obtainable rating. This process was called "ratings shopping" and the practice had been reported to the SEC as early as 2003: "the potential conflicts of interest faced by credit rating agencies have increased in recent years, particularly given the expansion of large credit rating agencies into ancillary advisory and other businesses, and the continued rise in importance of rating agencies in the US securities markets."[43]

The perceived conflict of interest between credit-rating agencies and issuers of financial products was of particular concern to the Subcommittee. In its

---

39   Ibid.

40   Ibid., p. 31.

41   Ibid., p. 267.

42   Ibid., p. 31 and n. 51. According to the Subcommittee, S&P's gross revenues from rating tranches of RMBSs and CDOs increased from over $US64 million in 2002 to over $US265 million in 2006. Ibid., (n. 33), pp. 30–31.

43   See also US Securities and Exchange Commission. 2003 (Report on the role and function of credit rating agencies in the operation of the securities markets. Washington D.C.: SEC). According to the SEC report, "concerns had been expressed that a rating agency might be tempted to give a more favorable rating to a large issue because of the large fee, and to encourage the issuer to submit future large issues to the rating agency." Ibid., p. 40.

recommendations for reform, the Subcommittee proposed that regulation be introduced to authorize the SEC to enhance its powers and authority for inspection, examination and regulatory authority so as to ensure that credit-rating agencies incorporate effective internal control procedures.[44] The internal control procedures would also extend to covering credit-rating methodologies and employee conflicts-of-interest safeguards designed to improve the overall accuracy of ratings.[45]

The Subcommittee also recommended further reforms to the regulation of credit-rating agencies, including providing the SEC with further regulatory authority to rank rating agencies in terms of their overall performance and to make the ranking available to investors and the public.[46] Accountability of credit-rating agencies was also high on the agenda of the Subcommittee.[47] According to the Subcommittee, the SEC should assist investors in filing civil law suits for any inflated credit ratings that are issued by credit-rating agencies, where the agency "knowingly or recklessly fails to conduct a reasonable investigation of the rated security."[48]

At one level the accountability measures proposed by the Subcommittee in relation to inaccurate credit ratings may be seen as a muted response, since no new laws are proposed by the Subcommittee. However, on another level the Subcommittee was also foreshadowing a strong signal that market regulators, including the SEC, would take seriously inaccurate credit ratings issued by a credit-rating agency if the agency knowingly or recklessly failed to conduct a proper investigation into the rated security. In other words, if circumstances exist to demonstrate that a credit-rating agency knowingly or recklessly issued an inaccurate credit rating, the SEC could take action against the agency.

The Subcommittee's recommendation was squarely aimed at improving accountability of credit-rating agencies, particularly when investors have relied upon a possibly inaccurate credit rating to make their investment choices. The Subcommittee was also of the view that the US federal government's reliance on private credit ratings should also be reduced.[49] Although the Subcommittee has made this recommendation, it is unclear what federal government authorities would use in their place when evaluating alternative investments. After all,

---

44 Ibid., (n. 43), p. 14.

45 Ibid.

46 Ibid., p. 13.

47 During the Subcommittee's investigation of the activities of Moody's and Standard & Poor's during the GFC, the Subcommittee concluded that credit-rating agencies had become increasingly reliant on the fees that were generated by issuing a large volume of ratings on structured financial products: "In the end, Moody's and S&P provided AAA ratings to tens of thousands of high-risk RMBS and CDO securities and then, when those products began to incur losses, issued mass downgrades that shocked the financial markets, hammered the value of the mortgage-related securities, and helped trigger the financial crisis." US Senate Subcommittee Report 2011. Ibid., (n. 33), p. 7.

48 Ibid., (n. 33), p. 13.

49 Ibid., (n. 33), p. 14.

credit ratings do serve a useful purpose in providing information concerning the risk profile and risk assessment of alternative financial investments. Moreover, the recommendation does not extend to state governmental agencies or local authorities, which often have mandated requirements to invest surplus funds or pension funds into AAA-rated financial products.

Many institutions and investors, both public and private, rely on credit ratings to assess the creditworthiness and risk profile of financial products that are issued and sold into the market.[50] The requirement to only consider AAA-rated financial instruments by these state and local authorities is usually enshrined in law or in constitutions. The same investment rules generally apply to private trustees, superannuation, and pension funds which have governing documents in the form of constitutions that lay down requirements for the trustee to invest surplus funds into prudent AAA-rated financial products.

The Subcommittee was also highly critical of the role of investment banks in contributing to the global financial crisis through risky lending practices. The Subcommittee investigated the practices of Goldman Sachs and Deutsche Bank, two investment banks active in the marketing of high-risk RMBSs and CDOs. Both Goldman Sachs and Deutsche Bank were underwriters and market-makers of various structured financial products, increasing liquidity for willing market participants to buy and sell financial instruments.

The Subcommittee concluded that after examining the practices of Goldman Sachs and Deutsche Bank, "a variety of troubling practices that raise conflicts of interest and other concerns involving RMBS, CDO, CDS and ABX related financial instruments that contributed to the financial crisis."[51] In particular, the Subcommittee's investigation of Goldman Sachs focused on how the firm "used net short positions to benefit from the downturn in the mortgage market, and designed, marketed and sold CDOs in ways that created conflicts of interest with the firm's clients and at times led to the bank's profiting from the same products that caused substantial losses for its clients."[52]

The investigations by the Subcommittee regarding the activities of Goldman Sachs and Deutsche Bank in the lead-up to the global financial crisis revealed a number of questionable practices. According to the Subcommittee, both investment banks issued "high risk, poor quality mortgages, and sold risky securities to investors across the United States and around the world."[53] The practices that investment banks engaged in, in the sale and marketing of RMBSs, CDOs

---

50   The US Subcommittee reported that in the lead-up to the GFC during the period 2004–2007 Moody's and S&P issued a record number of ratings and in return received fees for rating RMBS and CDOs. The US Subcommittee reported that S&P generally charged between $US40,000 and $US135,000 to rate bundles of RMBS and from $US30,000 to $US750,000 to rate the CDOs. Ibid., (n. 33), p. 30.

51   Ibid., (n. 33), p. 8.

52   Ibid.

53   Ibid., (n. 33), p. 11.

and other related structured financial products were not isolated practices. The Subcommittee's investigation revealed that both Goldman Sachs and Deutsche Bank:

> sold CDO securities without full disclosure of the negative views of some of their employees regarding the underlying assets and, in the case of Goldman, without full disclosure that it was shorting the very CDO securities it was marketing, raising questions about whether Goldman complied with its obligations to issue suitable investment recommendations and disclose material adverse interests.[54]

The activities of Goldman Sachs and Deutsche Bank were also questioned by the Subcommittee, as both investment banks continued to market new CDOs in 2007, at the time when US mortgage defaults began to intensify.[55] According to the Subcommittee "both kept producing and selling high risk, poor quality structured finance products in a negative market."[56] In arriving at its conclusion, the Subcommittee was particularly critical of the role of investment banks in the lead-up to the global financial crisis. The Subcommittee concluded that "the investment banks that engineered, sold, traded and profited from mortgage related structured finance products were a major cause of the financial crisis."[57]

In proposing recommendations to reform the practices of investment banks, the Subcommittee recommended that federal regulators review the activities of Wall Street banks, including their role in issuing securitized and structured financial products. The purpose of any review would be "to identify any violations of law and to examine ways to strengthen existing regulatory prohibitions against abusive practices involving structured finance products."[58] The Subcommittee further recommended that federal regulators should design and implement stronger conflict-of-interest prohibitions.[59]

The recommendations proposed by the Subcommittee in relation to credit-rating agencies and investment banks were designed to overcome some of the existing deficiencies in the current supervisory and regulatory framework of financial markets. The Subcommittee attributed much of the causes of the financial crisis to the role and practices of credit-rating agencies and investment banks. According to the Subcommittee, an inescapable conclusion of the current crisis was that a culture of greed existed on Wall Street that was founded upon fundamental conflicts of interest.[60]

---

54 Ibid., (n. 33), p. 11.
55 Ibid.
56 Ibid.
57 Ibid.
58 Ibid., (n. 33), p. 14.
59 Ibid.
60 According to the Subcommittee, investment banks built up large proprietary positions to short the mortgage market. This was the case in 2006 with Goldman Sachs,

The lack of proper safeguards, inaccurate and misleading credit ratings and insufficient regulatory and supervisory oversight, along with dubious and questionable market practices, undermined investor confidence and trust in financial markets. The Subcommittee also concluded that there existed a number of regulatory failures which further contributed to the crisis and allowed risky lending practices to continue unabated.

The Subcommittee recommended that federal banking regulators should undertake a comprehensive review of ratings systems used by federal banking regulators to evaluate asset quality, capital adequacy, management, earnings, liquidity and sensitivity to market risk for financial institutions.[61] The Subcommittee's enquiry also revealed a number of shortcomings in the regulatory and supervisory framework in the United States. This was particularly relevant to credit default swaps, since swaps had been expressly excluded from the jurisdiction of federal regulators through the enactment of the *Commodity Futures Modernization Act 2000*.[62]

The exclusion of credit default swaps from the *Securities Act 1933*, as well as the *Commodity Exchange Act 1936*, effectively meant that credit default swaps and other OTC derivatives were largely unregulated and unsupervised by the federal authorities. As the Subcommittee revealed in its report, this meant that there effectively existed a multi-trillion dollar swaps market in the United States with little or "no disclosure requirements, no restrictions, and no oversight by any federal agency, including the market for credit default swaps which played a prominent role in the financial crisis."[63]

As is discussed in Chapter 4, the unregulated nature of OTC derivatives markets, including credit default swaps, had been controversial, with some market regulators in favour of deregulation and others arguing for greater regulation of OTC financial derivatives.[64] As was noted by the Subcommittee, the recent enactment

---

which had accumulated a large portfolio in mortgage-related products. "In late 2006, Goldman Sachs decided to reverse course, using a variety of means to bet against the mortgage market. In some cases, Goldman Sachs took proprietary positions that paid off only when some of its clients lost money on the very securities that Goldman Sachs had sold to them and then shorted" Ibid., (n. 33), p. 36.

61 Ibid., (n. 33), p. 37.

62 The *CFMA* expressly excluded the regulation of swaps as securities and, hence, excluded the operation of the *Securities Act 1933* from regulating swaps, including credit default swaps. See *Commodity Futures Modernization Act 2000* H.R. 4577 (P.L. 106-554).

63 Ibid., (n. 33), p. 40.

64 See, for example, former SEC Chairman Christopher Cox, who testified before the Senate Committee on Banking, Housing and Urban Affairs and stated in relation to the credit default swap market that it "is completely lacking in transparency," "is regulated by no one," and "is ripe for fraud and manipulation." See Cox 2008 (Turmoil in US credit markets: Recent actions regarding government sponsored entities, investment banks and other financial institutions. Statement of SEC Chairman Christopher Cox before the US Senate Committee on Banking, Housing and Urban Affairs, Senate

of the *Dodd-Frank Act 2010* removed the *Commodity Futures Modernization Act 2000* prohibition on the regulation of OTC credit default swaps.[65] The prohibition had been removed because of the perception that deregulation of OTC derivatives markets had not worked, and had in fact contributed significantly to the build-up of risk in both the shadow banking system and the conventional banking sector in the United States.

Another problem identified by the Subcommittee concerned the patchwork nature of federal and state laws regulating mortgage lending, mortgage brokers and consumer protection.[66] Misleading and deceptive practices involving numerous mortgage applications led to consumers being signed up to loans that they could not afford. It was not until well after the financial crisis took hold that deceptive practices involving sub-prime mortgage consumers had been revealed.

The abusive practices involving millions of sub-prime mortgages resulted in many consumers of residential mortgages being misled as to the true value and nature of their loans. Many consumers of sub-prime residential mortgages were first-time borrowers who had been lulled into taking out long-term loans with low introductory interest rates commonly referred to as "honeymoon rates." At the end of the honeymoon period, interest rates would be reset at a higher rate, causing sub-prime borrowers to be exposed to higher repayments and the prospect of defaulting on their loans.

As the housing bubble began to unwind in the United States, the value of the sub-prime mortgage loan would typically be larger than the value of the residential home. Since a number of residential mortgages in the United States involved non-recourse loans, borrowers could simply refuse to pay any more of their mortgage and hand back the home to the lender. The lender would have no choice but to foreclose on the loan. The borrower would have an incentive to simply walk away from the home and the related mortgage, where the loan was greater then the value of the underlying residence. This is typically referred to as "negative equity," since the borrower no longer has any equity in the property to either use as collateral or to sell and realize.

The non-recourse nature of mortgage loans was a common feature of residential home loans in many US state jurisdictions. Some have argued that non-recourse mortgage loans in fact made the crisis in the United States worse, since sub-prime borrowers left their homes and forced lenders to foreclose on millions of vacated homes. The additional supply of foreclosed property led to continued price declines, which in turn led to more homes being foreclosed as residential house values plummeted. As house prices continued to dramatically fall, more and more borrowers simply refused to make any further payments on their mortgage, which led to a feedback loop for lenders.

Hearing Washington, DC, 23 September 2008). See also US Senate Subcommittee Report 2011 (Ibid., (n. 33), p. 40.

   65   Ibid., (n. 33), p. 40.

   66   Ibid.

The problem with residential sub-prime mortgage lending was aggravated because of the abusive and aggressive marketing practices of mortgage lenders. As the Subcommittee reported, there was inadequate regulation of mortgage-lending practices and ineffective protection for vulnerable consumers. The patchwork nature of state laws in the United States meant that state regulators had been unable to effectively enforce state laws against federal US banks.

Added to this was the US Supreme Court decision in *Cuomo v Clearing House Association*,[67] which held that the Office of Comptroller of the Currency (OCC) did not have the legal authority to enforce state consumer protection laws against US federal national banks.[68] The Supreme Court decision was in response to a challenge to the OCC's attempt to pre-empt the application of state laws, including the New York fair-lending laws, to US National Banks. In a majority judgment, the US Supreme Court held that state laws could be enforced by state regulators against National Banks and the OCC could not stand in the way of state regulators.[69]

The *Dodd-Frank Wall Street Reform Act 2010* has now introduced widespread sweeping changes to the regulation of lending practices in the mortgage industry. The reforms are discussed in more detail in Chapter 7. Congress recognized the failings and inadequacies of the current regulation of mortgage-lending practices which led to the inadequate protection and redress of consumers against abusive practices.

The Subcommittee's investigation into the financial crisis revealed that no single regulator was charged with the responsibility or mandate for "identifying, preventing, or managing risks that threatened the safety and soundness of the overall US financial system."[70] Hence, there was no regulator specifically tasked with the responsibility of overseeing the build-up of systemic risk which would eventually engulf the entire US financial system. As the Subcommittee concluded, there was effectively "no regulatory agency focused on what would happen when poor quality mortgages were allowed to saturate US financial markets and contaminate RMBS and CDO securities with high risk loans."[71]

The Subcommittee's investigation revealed serious issues regarding the role of credit-rating agencies, investment banks and high-risk lending practices in the lead-up to the GFC. The Subcommittee's report also revealed gaps in the regulatory and supervisory framework regulating financial markets. This was

67   Case No 08-453, 129 S.Ct. 2710 (2009).
68   See also US Senate Subcommittee report 2011. Ibid., (n. 33), p. 41.
69   In *Cuomo v Clearing House Association*, in the majority judgment 5:4 the majority consisted of Scalia, Ginsburg, Souter, Beyer, Stevens JJ, who opined that state regulators do have preemptive rights to enforce state laws, including consumer protection laws over Federal National Banks.
70   US Senate Subcommittee report 2011. Ibid., (n. 33), p. 41.
71   Ibid., (n. 33), p. 41.

particularly the case with the regulation of mortgage lending and the inadequate protection provided to consumers of sub-prime mortgages.

Importantly, the Subcommittee not only highlighted the problems that existed and contributed to the crisis but also put forward recommendations for reform. The recommendations were designed to overcome the deficiencies in the current regulatory framework governing financial markets and the banking and mortgage sectors. Further, the recommendations for reform also provided additional redress to consumers of residential mortgages. One of the central objectives of the proposed consumer protection measures was to prevent abuses from recurring in the future.

The United States Department of the Treasury

In June 2009, the US Treasury Department released its report into financial markets regulatory reform.[72] The report was commissioned by the US Treasury Secretary and involved wide-ranging consultations with the President's Working Group on Financial Markets, members of Congress, market participants and the broader community. The Department of the Treasury concluded that any new proposal for financial markets regulation in the United States should satisfy five key objectives:

1. To promote robust supervision and regulation of financial firms.
2. To establish comprehensive supervision of financial markets.
3. To protect consumers and investors from financial abuse.
4. To provide the government with the tools it needs to manage financial crisis.
5. To raise international regulatory standards and improve international cooperation.[73]

The US Treasury proposed strengthening regulatory and supervisory oversight of financial markets, financial services and financial products. To achieve the five stated objectives, Treasury proposed establishing the Financial Stability Oversight Council (FSOC) with the responsibility of identifying emerging systemic risks originating either in the United States or overseas.[74]

In addition to the FSOC, Treasury also proposed to provide the Federal Reserve with new authority to supervise all financial firms that pose a threat to systemic

---

72 US Department of the Treasury 2009 (Financial regulatory reform: a new foundation, rebuilding financial supervision and regulation, 17 June 2009, Washington, DC).

73 Ibid., pp. 3–4.

74 As is discussed in Chapter Seven, the *Dodd-Frank Wall Street Reform Act 2010* established the Financial Services Oversight Council in July 2010.

stability, including large interconnected firms capable of causing widespread disruption.[75] The US Treasury proposed comprehensive supervision of financial markets by key federal regulators. The proposed enhanced supervisory oversight was to extend to cover all OTC derivatives markets and to give new authority to the Federal Reserve to oversee payment, clearing and settlement processes with OTC markets.[76]

The proposed new rules regulating OTC derivatives, including credit default swaps markets, were taken up by the *Dodd-Frank Act 2010*. Regulating OTC derivatives was now a priority, since it emerged that unregulated derivatives exposed the US regulatory framework to gaps and structural weaknesses. Since OTC derivatives in the form of credit default swaps played a significant role in the crisis, it would be inevitable that regulators and federal authorities would focus their attention on derivatives markets.

The inadequate protection that existed for consumers who were victims of abusive mortgage- lending practices would also be the subject of further reform. Treasury proposed that a new Consumer Financial Protection Agency be established that would be designed to protect consumers across the financial sector from "unfair, deceptive, and abusive practices."[77] The Consumer Agency would be charged with the responsibility of overseeing stronger regulation designed to "improve the transparency, fairness, and appropriateness of consumer and investor products and services."[78]

One of the main objectives with establishing the new Consumer Agency was to rebuild trust and confidence with consumers of financial services and investors in financial products. The crisis saw a dramatic loss of trust and confidence by investors in US and international financial markets. At the height of the crisis, many financial markets witnessed a collapse in investor confidence and negative market sentiment. Treasury's proposal to bolster regulation and supervision of financial services and financial products would signal that US regulators would no longer tolerate the abuses that had occurred with sub-prime mortgage-lending during the financial crisis.

Importantly, Treasury's proposals also included recommendations for a "level playing field and higher standards for providers of consumer financial products and services, whether or not they are part of a bank."[79] The proposal recognizes the growing importance of non-bank mortgage originators, brokers and financial intermediaries, and government-sponsored mortgage originators such as Fannie Mae and Freddie Mac. A number of non-bank financial operators also operated within the shadow banking system, which led to a significant build-up of risk that subsequently contaminated conventional banks and financial markets.

---

75   Ibid., (n. 72), p. 3.
76   Ibid.
77   Ibid.
78   Ibid.
79   Ibid.

The interconnected nature of international financial markets led Treasury to call for further improvements to be made in the regulatory tools and authority of market and banking regulators. To assist key market regulators in providing effective regulatory and supervisory oversight, Treasury proposed a new resolution regime that was designed to resolve non-bank financial institutions which fail and have significant systemic effects on the wider US financial system.[80]

The so-called "too big to fail" dilemma was also of considerable concern to the US Treasury. The global financial crisis highlighted the importance of developing strong, robust and coordinated policy responses at an international level. Treasury recognized the need to develop greater international cooperation to minimize the recurrence of global crises in the future. To assist US regulators in providing effective regulation, Treasury proposed improvements to the oversight of global financial markets and coordination of the supervision of globally active financial firms.[81]

The leadership role that the United States would play in any future international cooperative would be inevitable, given the size and importance of its economy. Treasury recognized that the US already played a strong leadership role in international financial markets forums, including the G20 Leaders and Finance Ministers conferences, the Financial Stability Board and the Basel Committee on Banking Supervision.[82] Treasury's suggested reforms would allow the United States to continue to provide leadership in international forums established to discuss future regulatory reforms of financial markets.

UK Financial Services Authority Turner Review

In late 2008, following a request by the Chancellor of the Exchequer, the Financial Services Authority (FSA) reviewed the causes of the global financial crisis and made a number of recommendations for the reform of financial markets in the UK. The FSA released its report, the Turner Review, in March 2009.[83] The Turner Review reported that in the lead-up to the global financial crisis there had been a considerable build-up of leverage and financial innovation, which in turn led to a build-up of financial risk in financial markets, the UK economy and the international economy.

In its report the Turner Review presented a timeline of stages of the crisis that had elapsed between 2006 and 2009.[84] According to the FSA, the crisis began in the United States with the sub-prime mortgage defaults, which quickly spread to

80 Ibid., (n. 72), p. 4.
81 Ibid.
82 Ibid., (n. 72), p. 8.
83 Financial Services Authority 2009, The Turner Review: A regulatory response to the global financial crisis, March 2009 (London: FSA).
84 Ibid., p. 27.

other financial markets by early 2008. Funding concerns began to intensify during 2008 and by September there had been a catastrophic loss of confidence following the collapse of Lehman Brothers. The collapse of Lehman Brothers witnessed panic runs by depositors on other deposit-taking institutions, which led to the collapse of Bradford & Bingley and Washington Mutual, and the public buyout of Northern Rock.[85]

The Turner Review in the United Kingdom also revealed that, as in the United States, there had been a considerable run-up of household debt in the United Kingdom in the decade preceding the crisis. The Turner Review reported that between 1997 and 2007 total residential mortgage debt had increased from 50% to over 80% of GDP.[86] Over the same period, residential house prices also increased dramatically, fuelled by low interest rates and foreign capital inflows. As in the US, the UK had low interest rates which resulted in rapid credit expansion, rising household debt and large current account deficits.[87]

In response to the perceived structural weaknesses in the UK banking and financial sector, the Turner Review made a number of recommendations designed to improve the resilience of the UK authorities in responding to the crisis. One such recommendation involved UK banks and retail deposit institutions providing higher capital adequacy and liquidity standards to cover bank deposits.[88] To achieve this objective the Turner Review proposed working with the Basel Committee on Bank Supervision. The Turner Review also proposed that the FSA would undertake a domestic review of minimum regulatory capital requirements for UK banks and deposit-taking financial institutions.[89]

As is discussed below, the Basel Committee on Banking Supervision has also proposed new guidelines for the phasing in of revised capital adequacy and liquidity standards. The proposal by Basel, commonly called "Basel III," is intended to replace Basel II, the current capital adequacy and liquidity standards for international banks and deposit-taking institutions.

The Turner Review's recommendation to revise the minimum capital requirements for UK banks and deposit institutions was a response to the public and political perceptions that during the financial crisis some banks had been undercapitalized and were at risk of collapse. This was certainly the case with Bradford & Bingley and Northern Rock, which required government assistance at the height of the crisis. The panic runs by depositors revealed structural weakness in both institutions, which resulted in their collapse and subsequent bailout.

---

85   Ibid. The Turner Review also commented on the state of Icelandic Banks, which had been the forerunner of problems that would soon beset the UK banking sector, the US financial system and the international economy.

86   Ibid., p. 29.

87   Ibid., pp. 31–32.

88   Ibid., p. 118.

89   Ibid.

Whether holding more capital in a liquid state would have resolved the problems encountered in Bradford & Bingley and Northern Rock is purely hypothetical. As history has shown, when panic runs begin it becomes difficult to stem the tide, particularly when sentiment has turned negative towards a specific financial institution.[90] Certainly, the requirement of financial institutions to hold more of their assets in liquid form would help in ensuring that banks have a greater ability to service deposit withdrawals. However, it is not clear whether simply varying the liquidity ratio by a small margin would alleviate panic runs by investors that target individual banks.

At the height of the crisis, panic runs had emerged as a reason for the collapse in confidence by investors and depositors. The dramatic decline in sentiment did affect the serviceability of some banks and deposit-taking institutions in the UK, the US and elsewhere to service bank withdrawals by retail depositors. Improving both the quality and quantity of liquid assets to be held by deposit-taking institutions should help in minimizing the risk of a default and reducing any further erosion of public confidence in the banking sector.

Another important benefit of increasing liquid assets in financial institutions is that they would effectively be forced to "recapitalize," so that they are less vulnerable to any sudden change in investor sentiment. Hence, banks and deposit-taking institutions become less risky as higher capital and liquidity ratios help to minimize the risk of default from sudden changes in market sentiment.

The Turner Review made additional recommendations designed to improve liquidity in the UK financial sector.[91] The FSA foreshadowed that the proposals put forward to strengthen liquidity standards for UK banks would lead to financial institutions reshaping their business models over the next few years.[92] The FSA even went further, to suggest that the "current agreements and practices will have to be reviewed and the status quo may no longer be acceptable [...]. We make no apology for tough prudential standards."[93]

According to the FSA proposal and endorsed by the Turner Review, UK financial institutions that are regulated by the FSA should aim to have adequate liquidity and become self-sufficient for their funding needs.[94] The self-sufficiency requirement essentially requires that all financial institutions must not rely on

---

90   See Chapter 2 in this volume and, in particular, the discussion of the Great Depression in the 1930s, when bank runs were common, making an already bad situation dire and resulting in many financial institutions and ordinary banks collapsing.

91   The FSA released a consultation paper earlier in the year which put forward proposals for improving liquidity standards for UK banks and retail deposit institutions. See Financial Services Authority 2008. Strengthening liquidity standards, Consultation Paper 08/22, December 2008 (London: FSA: December).

92   Ibid., p. 3.

93   Ibid.

94   Ibid., p. 4.

other segmented parts of their group to ensure that the institution has sufficient liquid assets to survive bouts of market stress.[95]

The FSA also proposed implementation of new prudential regulation requirements for UK financial institutions which would require firms to undergo ongoing stress tests. The stress tests would be designed to assess whether UK institutions could survive liquidity stress arising from adverse changes in market sentiment. UK institutions would be required to analyse their liquidity positions across alternative risk drivers, including: wholesale funding, intra-group liquidity, cross-currency liquidity, retail funding, off-balance sheet liquidity, franchise-viability risk, marketable assets, non-marketable assets and funding diversification.[96]

Ongoing monitoring and reporting of stress test results by UK financial institutions to the FSA would represent a significant change to current and existing arrangements for financial institutions that report to the FSA. The FSA's liquidity proposals are designed not only to enhance reporting processes but also to improve and strengthen the liquidity position of financial institutions.

To achieve enhanced liquidity it is anticipated that financial institutions in the UK will be required to diversify their funding sources so that there is less reliance on short-term wholesale funding. The GFC showed that if banks and financial institutions become overly dependent on short-term wholesale funding to service their day-to-day lending operations, institutions could become vulnerable to any adverse changes in credit conditions and investor sentiment.

During the lead-up to the global crisis, US and UK banks had become dependent upon wholesale funding from overseas money markets to service customer loans. The reliance on wholesale short-term funding for UK financial institutions made UK banks vulnerable to external shocks and credit squeezes in international credit markets. At the height of the crisis, when Lehman Brothers collapsed, commercial paper markets froze, leading to a credit crisis all over the world. The volatile credit conditions in international markets caused disruptions for UK banks which had become dependent upon wholesale funding for their lending needs.

The situation was made worse when international bondholders demanded higher risk premiums for banks that did not have the highest credit ratings. Since a number of UK financial institutions did not have high credit ratings, the institutions were forced to pay significantly higher funding costs to rollover their loans. The higher funding costs were, in turn, passed on to borrowers who had entered into loans with UK banks at much lower rates when there had been easier credit conditions. All of this made an already challenging situation dire, as US, UK and European banks found it difficult to obtain sufficient wholesale funding from international credit markets, and businesses and customers could not obtain loan approvals for their day-to-day operations.

---

95   Ibid.
96   Ibid., p. 5.

As is discussed in Chapter 5, governments all over the world responded to the impending liquidity crisis in wholesale markets by providing sovereign guarantees to domestic banks and financial institutions. The provision of sovereign guarantees to financial institutions allowed UK, European and Australian banks access to wholesale international credit markets and at borrowing costs that were much lower than would otherwise have been the case.

To avoid a repeat of the reliance and dependence on international wholesale credit markets, the FSA has also recommended that UK financial institutions limit the source of funds flowing from foreign counterparties. To achieve this rebalance in wholesale term funding, UK banks and financial institutions would be required to attract a higher proportion of retail deposits from domestic depositors, and at the same time improve the "amount and quality of stocks of liquid assets, including a greater proportion of those assets held in the form of government debt."[97]

Report on Financial Supervision in the European Union

In February 2009, the European Union released its report on the current state of financial supervision in the European Union.[98] Like other enquiries, the European Union's de Larosière Report considered the current financial crisis a global problem requiring a coordinated global solution. The report recommended that there should be greater international coordination with other international regulatory and policy authorities, including the International Monetary Fund, the Financial Stability Forum, the Basel Committee and the G20 Leaders and Finance Minister meetings.[99]

The de Larosière Report laid down three principles for the development of a new regulatory and supervisory framework for the member states of the European Union:

1. A new regulatory agenda designed to reduce the build-up of risk in financial institutions, strengthen transparency and improve the EU financial system's ability to deal with systemic risk.
2. Enhanced supervisory prudential coordination throughout the European Union, including both micro and macro prudential structures.

---

97   Ibid.
98   See de Larosière 2009 (The High-Level Group on Financial Supervision in the European Union. Report, 25 February 2009, Brussels: European Union Commission). The mandate and terms of reference for the enquiry chaired by Jacques de Larosière was provided by the President of the European Commission, José Manuel Barroso, in October 2008.
99   Ibid., p. 3.

3. The development of effective crisis management procedures and structures designed to enhance confidence among regulators, investors and depositors in the European Union.[100]

In its enquiry into the causes of the global financial crisis, the de Larosière Report concluded that there had been a systemic failure in regulatory, supervisory and crisis management procedures and systems.[101] According to the EU report, insufficient attention had been paid by key market regulators and supervisors to the liquidity of markets.[102] Market regulators in the European Union had spent too much time focusing on individual firms without considering properly wider systemic issues.[103]

Similarly, derivatives markets in the European Union had expanded rapidly and there had been insufficient regulatory and supervisory attention. The lack of regulatory and supervisory oversight led to significant deficiencies in the ability of EU regulators to properly assess the build-up of risk associated with the use of sub-prime RMBSs, CDOs and synthetic derivatives.[104]

The lack of transparency and opaqueness in derivatives markets, including other financial markets, also created challenges for market regulators in the EU. The EU report concluded that "EU supervisors had a more difficult task in assessing the extent to which exposure to subprime risk had seeped into EU-based financial institutions."[105] The report was critical of EU supervisors who had failed to adequately assess the build-up of risk in EU financial institutions which had purchased exposure to US sub-prime residential mortgage assets. As is described in Chapter 2, the sub-prime mortgage assets later turned toxic as credit-rating agencies downgraded their value. The toxic mortgage securities were often hidden from EU regulators, as they were usually not reported on financial institutions' balance sheets.

According to the de Larosière Report, the regulatory response to the crisis by EU regulators had been made worse because of the inadequate crisis management structure that currently existed in the EU.[106] The report was generally supportive of the actions taken by the European Central Bank, discussed in Chapter 5, in responding to the crisis by injecting large amounts of capital, a policy designed to improve liquidity in EU financial markets and the banking sector.[107]

However, despite the best efforts of the European Central Bank there had been insufficient coordination and cooperation between national supervisors and

---

100   Ibid., p. 4.
101   Ibid., p. 10.
102   Ibid.
103   Ibid.
104   Ibid.
105   Ibid.
106   Ibid., p. 12.
107   Ibid.

national public authorities in the member states of the European Union.[108] The inadequate cooperation at the national level of EU member states compromised an otherwise effective policy response by EU authorities to the crisis. National supervisors and policymakers in each of the member states had failed to properly assess the build-up of risk in their nations' banks and financial institutions. The member states had also failed to properly put into place effective crisis management plans to deal with the ongoing situation.

To overcome the deficiencies, the de Larosière Report made a number of recommendations designed to improve market transparency, rectify gaps in regulation and supervision, and improve coordination and cooperation within the EU.[109] Among its key recommendations the de Larosière Report recommended that financial stability should be promoted at the international level.[110] The Report argued that it was in the EU's interest to "try to shape the reform of the international financial architecture."[111] If the EU adopted a leadership role in pursuing international regulatory reform, it would have much greater input in setting new regulatory standards.

The de Larosière Report also recommended that there should be greater regulatory consistency in the regulation of financial markets, credit-rating agencies, derivatives markets and corporate governance standards. Enhanced coordination and consistency would also help to avoid regulatory arbitrage and minimize regulatory turf wars between different jurisdictions.[112] Regulatory arbitrage would only be possible if differences in regulatory rules existed, so as to produce incentives for firms to exploit. Reducing differences in the way financial markets are regulated between member-state jurisdictions through greater coordination, cooperation and consistency would minimize the potential for regulatory arbitrage.

To achieve the objective of regulatory consistency and minimize the incidence of regulatory arbitrage, the de Larosière Report recommended that the Financial Stability Forum (FSF) should be the lead coordinator working in conjunction with other international authorities, including the Basel Committee and the IMF. Not surprisingly, the report also recommended that the FSF and the IMF should work together to ensure greater cooperation for macroeconomic surveillance and crisis prevention.[113]

Interestingly, the de Larosière Report proposed as part of the strengthening of international coordination and cooperation that the IMF should implement an international early-warning mechanism.[114] The warning system would build on the

---

108 Ibid.
109 Ibid., pp. 23–5.
110 Ibid., pp. 59–61.
111 Ibid., p. 59.
112 Ibid., p. 60.
113 Ibid., pp. 63–6.
114 Ibid., p. 63.

identification of systemic vulnerabilities that currently exist in the international financial architecture.[115]

The report proposed that the IMF would work with the FSF to create a comprehensive international risk map and international credit register.[116] The purpose of developing an international risk map and credit register would be to provide up-to-date information to regulators regarding emerging areas of risk. Risk-mapping would close the information gap that currently exists between market and government regulators on the one hand and market participants and intermediaries on the other.[117] Consistent with the proposal of mapping financial risk areas, the de Larosière Report goes one step further to recommend that measures should be implemented to intensify international coordination to encourage "poorly regulated or uncooperative jurisdictions to adhere to the highest level international standards and to exchange information among supervisors."[118]

The report made no mention of which jurisdictions have weak regulatory frameworks or are uncooperative. Nor was it particularly clear as to whether risk-mapping or an international early warning system would be effective if financial markets continues to remain under stress or operate in a less than transparent manner. One of the challenges exposed by the current crisis was that financial innovation had been given too much latitude and regulation had fallen behind. However, applying too much regulation might stifle financial innovation, which in turn could lead to less than optimal results for consumers of financial products and financial services.

As is discussed in Chapter 8, achieving the correct balance between financial innovation and regulation will always be challenging. If one attempts to create a global financial architecture that is risk-averse, and to impose greater regulatory and supervisory oversight, the outcome might be less than optimal. This is because inventors of financial instruments might find that there are insufficient returns for innovative financial products.

Conversely, if regulation and supervision are set too low, risk might build up if financial innovation is not sufficiently understood, is overly complex or is the instrument of abuse. Indeed, the current financial crisis probably witnessed too much financial innovation that was largely unregulated and unsupervised. In that sense, many of the financial products that had been created to take advantage of the US and global housing bubble were the ideal candidates for manipulation and abuse. The abuse did not, of course, stop at financial markets in the United States but spilled over to contaminate markets in Europe, the UK, Asia and Latin America.

---

115   Ibid.
116   Ibid., p. 63.
117   Ibid., p. 64.
118   Ibid., p. 66.

Basel III Basel Committee on Banking Supervision

In 2010 the Basel Committee on Banking Supervision proposed new global liquidity and capital adequacy standards for the world's banks and financial institutions.[119] The new proposals, commonly known as "Basel III," are intended to replace the current liquidity and capital adequacy minimum ratios for banks and financial institutions known as "Basel II."[120] The new guidelines on liquidity and capital adequacy proposed by Basel III were the most concrete response from the Basel Committee on the global financial crisis. Unsurprisingly, Basel III proposed increasing the liquidity and minimum capital adequacy ratios for international banks and retail deposit institutions.

Under Basel III, the minimum requirement for capital adequacy would be raised from the current requirement of 2% of banks' net assets to 4.5%. In addition to the minimum capital equity ratio of 4.5%, banks would be required to provide a capital buffer of up to 2.5% by 2019.[121] The capital conservation buffer is to allow for build-up during good times and a countercyclical measure during market stress. Hence, under the Basel III proposal, the minimum common equity capital ratio for all banks and retail deposit institutions would be 7.0%, representing a significant increase from Basel II.[122]

Under the proposed Basel III guidelines there would also be an increase in 2013 in the minimum Tier 1 capital liquidity ratio of 4.5% of a bank's net assets; this would rise steadily to 6.0% by 2015.[123] The minimum total capital ratio would be set at 8.0% of total bank net assets and the minimum total capital including the conservation buffer would increase from 8.0% in 2013 and be phased in to 10.5% in 2019.[124] According to the Basel Committee, "strong capital requirements are a necessary condition for banking sector stability but by themselves are not sufficient. Equally important is the introduction of stronger bank liquidity as inadequate standards were a source of both firm level and system wide stress."[125]

The Basel III proposals are deliberately aimed at improving the capital adequacy and liquidity of international banks. The Basel Committee considered

---

119 Basel Committee on Banking Supervision 2010 (The Basel Committee's response to the financial crisis: Report to the G20, October 2010, Basel: Bank for International Settlements).

120 The Basel Committee on Banking Supervision is based at the Bank of International Settlements in Basel, Switzerland, and is made up of a number of central bank representatives, including: the United States, the United Kingdom, Australia, Spain, China, Germany, France, Italy, Japan, Russia, Sweden and The Netherlands.

121 Basel Committee Report. Ibid., (n. 119), p. 16.

122 Ibid., (n. 119, p. 16.

123 Ibid., (n. 119), p. 16.

124 Under Basel III the minimum total capital including the conservation buffer will be 8% in 2013, 8.0% in 2014, 8.0% in 2015, 8.625% in 2016, 9.25% in 2017, 9.875% in 2018 and 10.5% in 2019.

125 Ibid., (n. 119), p. 6.

that one important lesson to be learnt from the current financial crisis was that a number of financial institutions, including banks, did not respond well to the liquidity crisis confronting the international financial system. The post-GFC world would require new minimum benchmarks for liquidity and capital adequacy that would better position banks for external shocks and bouts of market stress.

Conclusion

The proposals for reform that have been discussed in this chapter have demonstrated a clear commitment from domestic and international regulators and policymakers to reform and overhaul the current regulatory framework. There is an undeniable sense that the regulatory and supervisory framework that existed in the lead-up to the crisis was inadequate and was prone to failure. Regulatory gaps, a lack of coordination and cooperation, regulatory arbitrage and failure to properly regulate financial innovation all contributed to make the financial crisis much worse than would otherwise have been the case.

Systemic failure in regulation coupled with widespread market failure combined to create the perfect financial storm. The storm that is now known as the global financial crisis emerged to engulf and undermine the world's financial system and place in peril the entire international economy. Given the deficiencies and failings in international regulation it is not surprising that many of the proposals of reform make recommendations for enhanced regulation of financial markets, financial intermediaries, banks, investment banks, and consumer protection.

There may well have been insufficient or inadequate regulation of financial markets, which contributed to a lack of market discipline. However, it remains unclear why state regulation on its own would be the panacea for the perceived failings of a market-based financial system. The build-up of risk in financial institutions and financial markets had not been properly understood by anyone. Regulators, policymakers, government and sophisticated market participants were unaware of the impending meltdown, yet many benefited from the financial innovation and global housing bubble during the boom times.

Many of the proposed reforms are indeed sensible and would make improvements to the way financial markets are regulated and supervised. However, there may also be a risk that the reforms would go too far and impose too high a burden on market participants and market intermediaries, which could lead to less financial innovation. A proper balance is needed to ensure that financial markets are properly and adequately regulated so that they are safe, reliable and sound. At the same time, financial innovation should be encouraged so long as the instruments and markets that are developed in the future serve a useful purpose, are properly understood and are not the subject of abuse.

Chapter 7
New Financial Markets Regulation

Introduction

The reform proposals discussed in Chapter 6 led to the development of new regulatory initiatives in the United States, the United Kingdom and other jurisdictions. The financial markets regulatory reforms in the US and the UK represented a comprehensive response to the financial crisis. The introduction of the *Dodd-Frank Wall Street Reform and Consumer Protection Act 2010*[1] in the US heralded a new era for the comprehensive regulation of financial markets, financial products and financial intermediaries. The *Dodd-Frank Act 2010* also introduced groundbreaking reforms for consumers of financial services and residential mortgages.

The *Dodd-Frank Act 2010* implemented many of the reforms that were proposed by a number of regulators, including the US Federal Reserve, the US Securities Exchange Commission, the Commodities and Futures Trading Commission, the US Department of the Treasury and the Office of the Comptroller of the Currency. The reforms were designed to provide enhanced regulation and supervision of financial markets and financial intermediaries in the US. Most notably, the Act provides for comprehensive regulation of credit default swaps and centralized clearing of OTC derivatives contracts.

The *Dodd-Frank Act 2010* established the Financial Stability Oversight Council (FSOC) to provide supervision and regulation of non-bank financial institutions. The Financial Stability Council will also be responsible for providing up-to-date research and information concerning the activities and financial condition of banks, including non-bank financial entities that have total consolidated assets of $US50 million. In addition to these new initiatives the Act also introduced new measures designed to regulate the activities of advisers to hedge funds, including private equity fund managers and investment banks.

Significantly, the *Dodd-Frank Act 2010* also introduced comprehensive measures to provide greater investor protection. One of these reforms included establishing a new Office of the Investor Advocate, which has the responsibility of representing and promoting the interests of aggrieved retail investors. The Act introduced comprehensive reforms designed to improve financial protection

---

1   Pub L 111-203 H.R. 4173. The Act was passed by Congress "to promote the financial stability of the United States by improving accountability and transparency in the financial system, to end 'too big to fail,' to protect the American taxpayer by ending bailouts, to protect consumers from abusive financial services practices, and for other purposes."

to consumers of financial products, financial services and financial markets. To achieve the stated aim of improving consumer protection, the Act established the Bureau of Consumer Financial Protection, providing the Bureau with a legal mandate to investigate allegations of consumer abuse.

New legislation similar to the *Dodd-Frank Act 2010* has also been introduced in the UK in the form of the *Financial Services Act 2010* (UK).[2] The *FSA 2010* introduces new measures aimed at protecting consumers, including providing them with compensation and redress if they have suffered loss or damage. Importantly, the *FSA 2010* also introduces the new objective of promoting the financial stability of the UK financial system.

Both Acts are consistent with the overall objective of improving the way financial markets, financial products and financial intermediaries are regulated and supervised in the US and the UK. At the centre of both legislative initiatives are the twin objectives of promoting financial stability and providing adequate protection to consumers and investors in financial markets.

The *Dodd-Frank Wall Street Reform and Consumer Protection Act* 2010

President Barack Obama signed into law the *Dodd-Frank Wall Street Reform and Consumer Protection Act* in July 2010. The Act was a joint effort of Congressmen Barney Frank and Senator Chris Dodd. The legislation represented the responses of the House and Senate to the global financial crisis. The Act introduced sweeping reforms to the US financial architecture, including new regulation for OTC derivatives.

Regulation of OTC Swaps Markets

As is discussed in Chapter 2, OTC derivatives, including credit default swaps, synthetic derivatives and structured financial products, played a significant role in the current crisis. Credit default swaps had previously been largely unregulated and not subject to supervisory oversight by the Security Exchange Commission (SEC) or the Commodity Futures Trading Commission (CFTC). The use of financial instruments such as credit default swaps also introduced potential conflicts of interest for hedge fund advisers and investment bankers.

The conflicts of interest were the subject of much enquiry and investigation by the US Senate Subcommittee into Wall Street and the Financial Crisis.[3] It was alleged by the US Senate enquiry that conflicts of interest existed because

---

2 Hereinafter referred to as "*FSA 2010*."

3 US Government 2011. United States Senate (Wall Street and the financial crisis: anatomy of a financial collapse Majority and Minority Staff Report, April 13, 2011, Washington, DC: US Senate Permanent Subcommittee on Investigations). See also Chapter 6 in this volume.

investment banks would often take opposite positions to the clients they had been advising. The use of structured financial products, including credit default swaps, was often used to alter the risk profile of residential mortgage-backed securities so that the security would attract a higher investment rating.

The *Dodd-Frank Act 2010* considered that the time had come to regulate all OTC swaps markets and all financial intermediaries dealing in OTC derivatives. The definition of "swap,"[4] and "swap dealer" under the *Dodd-Frank Act 2010* had the same definition as under the *Commodity Exchange Act 1936*.[5] Congress and the US Senate were also clearly of the view that before any rule-making would take place, the SEC and the CFTC would consult with each other and with any other regulator so as to achieve regulatory consistency and comparability.[6]

The issue of regulatory consistency was important given the previous history of disagreements and turf wars between the two regulators. Regulatory consistency was to be achieved as far as possible in relation to any new rule or order that was issued by the SEC or CFTC in relation to "swaps, swap dealers, derivative clearing organizations with regard to swap, eligible contract participants,"[7] including "security-based swap dealers, security-based swap participants, major security-based swap participants, eligible contract participants with regard to security-based swaps, or security-based swap execution facilities,"[8] and "mixed" swaps.[9]

The *Dodd-Frank Act 2010* also confirmed existing limitations on the jurisdiction and authority of the CFTC to makes rules or orders for: security-based

---

4   The term "swap" was defined to include "an interest rate swap, a rate floor, a rate cap, a rate collar, a cross-currency rate swap, a basis swap, a currency swap, a foreign exchange swap, a total return swap, an equity index swap, an equity swap, a debt index swap, a debt swap, a credit spread, a credit default swap, a credit swap, a weather swap, an energy swap, a metal swap, an agricultural swap, an emissions swap, and a commodity swap." *Dodd-Frank Act 2010*, Section 721.

5   See Section 1a of the *Commodity Exchange Act 1936* (7 U.S.C.). See also section 711 of the *Dodd-Frank Act 2010*: "the terms 'prudential regulator,' 'swap,' 'swap dealer,' 'major swap participant,' 'swap data repository,' 'associated person of a swap dealer or major swap participant,' 'eligible contract participant,' 'swap execution facility,' 'security-based swap,' 'security-based swap dealer,' 'major security-based swap participant,' and 'associated person of a security-based swap dealer or major security-based swap participant' have the same meanings given the terms in section 1a of the Commodity Exchange Act (7 U.S.C. 1a), including any modification of the meanings under section 721(b) of this Act."

6   *Dodd-Frank Act 2010*, Section 712(a)(1) and (2).

7   See Ibid., Section 712(a)(1).

8   See Ibid., Section 712(a)(2).

9   See Ibid., Section 712(8), which provides that for "mixed swaps" "The Commodity Futures Trading Commission and the Securities and Exchange Commission, after consultation with the Board of Governors shall jointly prescribe such regulations regarding mixed swaps, as described in section 1a(47)(D) of the Commodity Exchange Act (7 U.S.C. 1a(47)(D)) and in section 3(a)(68)(D) of the Securities Exchange Act of 1934 (15 U.S.C. 78c(a)(68)(D)), as may be necessary to carry out the purposes of this title."

swaps,[10] activities or functions concerning security-based swaps,[11] security-based swap dealers,[12] major security-based swap participants,[13] security-based swap data repositories,[14] associated persons of a security-based swap dealer or major security-based swap participant,[15] eligible contract participants with respect to security-based swaps[16] and swap execution facilities with respect to security-based swaps.[17]

The Act also confirmed existing limitations on the jurisdiction of the SEC to regulate and make rules or impose orders with respect to: swaps,[18] rules and orders in relation to activities or functions concerning swap dealers,[19] major swap participants,[20] swap data repositories,[21] persons associated with a swap dealer or major swap participant,[22] eligible contract participants with respect to swaps[23] and swap execution facilities with respect to swaps.[24]

The limitations imposed on the SEC and CFTC jurisdictions were to ensure that there would be no confusion over the roles and responsibilities of each regulator. In effect, exclusive jurisdiction would be conferred on the CFTC over the regulation of OTC swaps markets except in the case of securities-based swaps, which would remain under the scope and ambit of the SEC. In relation to "mixed swaps,"[25] the SEC and the CFTC would be required to consult with each other and the Board of Governors to ensure that any rules or orders were jointly issued.[26]

---

10   Section 712(b)(1)(A).
11   Section 712(b)(1)(B).
12   Section 712(b)(1)(B)(i).
13   Section 712(b)(1)(B)(ii).
14   Section 712(b)(1)(B)(iii).
15   Section 712(b)(1)(B)(iv).
16   Section 712(b)(1)(B)(v).
17   Section 712(b)(1)(B)(vi).
18   Section 712(b)(2)(A).
19   Section 712(b)(2)(B)(i).
20   Section 712(b)(2)(B)(ii).
21   Section 712(b)(2)(B)(iii).
22   Section 712(b)(2)(B)(iv).
23   Section 712(b)(2)(B)(v).
24   Section 712(b)(2)(B)(vi).
25   The term "mixed swap" is defined to include a "security-based swap [which] includes any agreement, contract, or transition that is as described in section 3(a)(68) (A) of the Securities Exchange Act of 1934 (15 U.S.C. 78c(a)(68)(A)) and also is based on the value of 1 or more interest or other rates, currencies, commodities, instruments of indebtedness, indices, quantitative measures, other financial or economic interest or property of any kind (other than a single security or a narrow-based security index) or the occurrence of an event or contingency associated with a potential financial, economic, or commercial consequence (other than an event described in subparagraph (A)(iii))." *Dodd-Frank Act 2010*, Section 721.
26   Ibid., Section 712(a)(8).

The *Dodd-Frank Act 2010* also made provision for the possibility that agreement could not be reached by the CFTC and the SEC to jointly prescribe rules and regulations in a timely manner in relation to their joint rule-making authority. The Act provided that the FSOC would have authority to resolve any dispute involving joint rule-making within a reasonable time of a request being made.[27]

Importantly, the *Dodd-Frank Act 2010* arms the CFTC and the SEC with legal authority to deal with any "abusive swaps." The term "abusive swaps" is defined in Section 714 to include any types of swaps or security-based swaps that the Commodity Futures Trading Commission or the Security Exchange Commission considers "detrimental to – (A) the stability of a financial market; or (B) participants in a financial market." Section 714 provides legal authority to either the CFTC or the SEC to collect all relevant information as may be necessary and to issue a report with respect to the abusive swaps.

The Act goes further to give authority to the CFTC and the SEC to undertake a joint study in relation to OTC swap regulation in the United States, Asia and Europe. The joint report aims to provide detailed information on clearing house and clearing agency regulation in the United States, Asia and Europe. The report must also contain information which identifies areas of regulation around the world that are similar in the United States, Asia and Europe, including other areas of regulation that can be harmonized.[28]

The purpose of the joint report is to evaluate the costs and benefits of harmonizing US regulation of OTC swaps with swaps regulation from other jurisdictions. By harmonizing regulation, not only is the objective of regulatory consistency achieved but the problem of regulatory arbitrage is also overcome. In essence, if all of the world's OTC swaps markets are harmonized from a regulatory perspective there is little or no incentive for financial intermediaries to engage in "regulatory window shopping." This is because regulation would be the same in all jurisdictions, thereby curtailing the incentive for financial intermediaries to transact in lower-cost jurisdictions.

Systemic Risk Swaps

The *Dodd-Frank Act 2010* also introduced heightened regulation for institutions that pose systemic risk. All swap entities that pose systemic risk to the US financial sector will be subject to heightened prudential supervision.[29] Not only will entities which pose a systemic risk to the United States be subject to heightened prudential supervision and regulation but also any firm that is placed into receivership or declared insolvent as a result of swap or security-based swap activity will not receive taxpayer funds.[30]

---

27   See Section 712(3).
28   See Section 719(4)(c)(1).
29   Section 716(c).
30   Ibid.

The prohibition of the use of taxpayer funds for any potential bailout is an obvious change in US government policy, which had previously allowed the use of taxpayer funds to prevent a liquidation or for government-sponsored bailouts. Section 716 of the Act makes the prohibition clear and goes further, prohibiting any "federal assistance"[31] for government-sponsored bailouts of any swap entity or security-based swap entity or activity.[32] The prohibition of any bailout of swap entities follows the widespread public outcry over the bailouts of Wall Street investment banks and hedge funds at the height of the crisis.

In addition to the prohibition on government-sponsored bailouts of swap entities and security-based swap entities, a ban on proprietary trading in derivatives has also been imposed by Section 716(m) of the *Dodd-Frank Act 2010*.[33] The ban on proprietary trading in derivatives puts into place the so-called Volcker Rule.[34] Section 619 of the *Dodd-Frank Act 2010* implements the Volcker Rule to prohibit "banking entities from engaging in proprietary trading or from investing in, sponsoring, or having certain relationships with a hedge fund or private equity fund."[35]

Standardized Algorithmic Models

Another important initiative of the *Dodd-Frank Act 2010* was the proposal to commission a joint study by the SEC and the CFTC to investigate the use of standardized computer-readable algorithmic descriptions.[36] The objective of the proposed study is to assess whether standardized computer-readable algorithms can be used to describe both complex and standardized financial derivatives.[37] The

---

31 The term "federal assistance" is broadly defined to include "the use of any advances from any Federal Reserve credit facility or discount window that is not part of a program or facility with broad-based eligibility under section 13(3)(A) of the Federal Reserve Act, Federal Deposit Insurance Corporation insurance or guarantees [...]." Section 716(b).

32 The *Dodd-Frank Act 2010*, Section 716(a) provides for the general prohibition on federal assistance to be made to any swap entity: "Notwithstanding any other provision of law (including regulations), no Federal assistance may be provided to any swaps entity with respect to any swap, security-based swap, or other activity of the swaps entity."

33 Section 716(m) provides that "an insured depository institution shall comply with the prohibition on proprietary trading in derivatives as required by section 619 of the *Dodd-Frank Wall Street Reform and Consumer Protection Act*."

34 The Volcker Rule derives its name from former Chairman of the US Federal Reserve, Paul Volcker. The Volcker Rule and its implementation are discussed in more detail below.

35 US Federal Reserve System, Rules and Regulations, Federal Register, Volume 76, No. 30, Monday February 14, 2011 pp. 8265–78 at p. 8265.

36 Section 719(b).

37 According to Section 719(2) the "algorithmic descriptions shall be optimized for simultaneous use by – (A) commercial users and traders of derivatives; (B) derivative clearing houses, exchanges and electronic trading platforms; (C) trade repositories and regulator investigations of market activities; and (D) systemic risk regulators."

study will also examine the extent to which the algorithmic descriptions, along with standardized legal definitions, may be used as binding legal definitions for derivatives contracts.[38]

The use of standardized and computer-readable algorithms for complex and standardized financial derivatives is an attempt to improve the understandability and transparency of valuations and payment obligations. During the height of the financial crisis, questions were asked as to whether certain financial derivatives had become overly complex, causing confusion and uncertainty among end-users.

The former Federal Reserve Chairman, Alan Greenspan, noted the complexities and non-transparent nature of complex financial derivatives. According to his testimony, the mathematical and algorithmic models used to value and construct payment obligations for financial derivatives may not have been sufficiently accurate to properly quantify risk:

> It was the failure to properly price such risky assets that precipitated the crisis. In recent decades, a vast risk management and pricing system has evolved, combining the best insights of mathematicians and finance experts, supported by major advances in computer and communications technology. A Nobel Prize was awarded for the discovery of the pricing model that underpins much of the advance in derivatives markets. This modern risk management paradigm held sway for decades. The whole intellectual edifice, however, collapsed in the summer of last year because the data inputted into the risk management models generally covered only the past two decades, a period of euphoria. Had instead the models been fitted more appropriately to historic periods of stress, capital requirements would have been much higher and the financial world would be in far better shape today, in my judgment.[39]

A detailed examination of whether algorithms failed to properly take into account the risks involved with the use of complex financial derivatives during the global financial crisis may provide important new directions. Hence, a study that investigates their use as provided by the *Dodd-Frank Act 2010* should provide greater clarity for valuation models used to price financial derivatives.

If it is the case that mathematical models have incorrectly priced risk with complex financial derivatives, then the error or omission may represent an important factor in explaining why synthetic derivatives, collateralized debt obligations and credit default swaps had such an adverse impact during the global financial crisis.[40] The underpricing of risk would certainly be of concern, particularly if

---

38   See Section 719(2).

39   Greenspan 2008 (Testimony of Dr Alan Greenspan to the Senate Committee of Government Oversight and Reform, US House of Representatives, 23 October 2008).

40   Ciro, T. and Longo, M. The global financial crisis. Part 1: Causes and implications for future regulation, *Journal of International Banking Law and Regulation*, 24(12) (2009), p. 599 at p. 602.

Greenspan's view is correct. If the mathematical formulas used to price risk and value financial derivatives led to underpricing, then serious ramifications could follow for ill-informed end-users. Not only would end-users and purchasers of these instruments potentially overpay for the financial derivative, there may in fact be insufficient capital provided to absorb any shortfall in the case of loss or default.

Insufficient capital requirement for losses that flow from mispriced financial instruments would present an important system-wide weakness. If Greenspan is correct, then capital requirements would need to be much higher to take into account heightened levels of financial risk. Capital adequacy and liquidity ratios would need to be modified for banks and investment firms that hold financial derivatives as part of their net assets.[41]

Greenspan raises an interesting point worthy of further investigation. Hopefully, the study proposed by the *Dodd-Frank Act 2010* will properly investigate the issue, since it potentially has widespread ramifications not only for the pricing of risk but also for the adequacy of capital and liquidity requirements.

Derivatives Clearing Organizations

The *Dodd-Frank Act 2010* also introduced amendments to the way derivatives would be now cleared and settled. The amendments included establishing derivatives clearing organizations to provide for centralized clearing and settlement of OTC financial derivatives.[42] Centralized clearing and settlement of forwards, options, swaps and commodity options can now take place through a registered derivatives clearing organization.[43] The *Dodd-Frank Act 2010* amended the *Commodity Exchange Act 1936* to make it mandatory for commodity swaps to be cleared through a centralized exchange unless an exemption applies.[44] The *Dodd-Frank Act 2010* also amended the *Securities Act 1933* to provide for the clearance of security-based swaps through a centralized derivatives exchange and their regulation by the SEC. The *Dodd-Frank Act 2010* also provides for voluntary

---

41   As is discussed in Chapter 6, higher capital adequacy and improved liquidity ratios have been at the forefront of the Basel Committee in its development of the new Basel III capital adequacy and liquidity requirements.

42   See *Dodd-Frank Act 2010*, Section 725.

43   See Section 725(1) and (2).

44   Section 2(h)(1) of the *Commodity Exchange Act 1936* provides that it is unlawful for a swap transaction to occur unless that swap transaction is submitted for clearing with a registered derivatives clearing organization, if the swap is required to be cleared under the Act. One of the allowable exemptions to centralized clearing is provided under section 2(h)(7) of the *Commodity Exchange Act 1936*. Under section 2(h)(7), if a counterparty to the swap transaction is a non-financial entity and is using the swap to hedge against risk and properly notifies the Commodity Futures Trading Commission, the counterparty can elect not to have the swap cleared through a centralized derivatives exchange.

registration for centralized clearing. An entity which is not required to clear agreements, contracts or transactions under the *Commodity Exchange Act 1936* can voluntarily register as a derivatives-clearing organization with the CFTC.[45]

The *Dodd-Frank Act 2010* also amended the *Commodity Exchange Act 1936* to provide for a set of comprehensive core principles for derivatives clearing organizations which ordinarily should include:

i.   adequate financial, operational, and managerial resources as determined by the Commission to discharge each responsibility of the derivatives clearing organization;[46]

ii.   adequate financial commitments to enable the members and participants to cover the largest financial exposure for that organization in extreme but plausible conditions;[47]

iii.   sufficient capital to cover operating costs of the derivatives clearing organization for a period of 1 year;[48]

iv.   procedures to verify, on an ongoing basis, the compliance of each participation and member;[49]

v.   appropriate standards for determining eligibility of agreements, contracts, or transactions submitted to derivatives clearing organizations for clearing;[50]

vi.   membership and participation requirements which shall be objective, publicly disclosed and permit fair and open access;[51]

vii.   management of the risks associated with discharging the responsibilities of the derivatives clearing organization through the use of appropriate tools and procedures;[52]

viii. measurement of credit risk exposures of the derivatives clearing house organization to each member and participant;[53]

ix.   provision of ongoing monitoring of credit exposures to each member and participant;[54]

x.   appropriate margin requirements and other risk control mechanisms designed to limit potential losses from defaults by members and participants;[55]

---

45 *Dodd-Frank Act 2010*, Section 725(b).
46 Section 725(B)(i).
47 Section 725(B)(ii).
48 Section 725(B)(II).
49 Section 725(C)(i)(I).
50 Section 725(C)(i)(II).
51 Section 725(C)(iii).
52 Section 725(D)(i).
53 Section 725(D)(ii).
54 Section 725(D)(ii).
55 Section 725(D)(iii);

xi.   margin requirements shall be sufficient to cover potential exposures in normal market conditions and shall be risk-based and reviewed on a regular basis;[56]

xii.   effective settlement procedures, including completing money settlements on a timely basis,[57] limiting settlement risk,[58] ensuring that money settlements are final and effected,[59] maintaining an accurate record of the flow of funds associated with each money settlement,[60] establishing rules with respect to physical deliveries[61] and managing settlement risk;[62]

xiii.   standards and procedures designed to protect the safety of member and participant funds and assets;[63]

xiv.   rules and procedures designed to allow for the efficient, fair and safe management of events during times when members or participants become insolvent or default on their obligations;[64]

xv.   putting in place clearly stated default procedures and default rules for members and participants and ensuring that the derivatives clearing organization takes timely action to contain losses and liquidity pressures and to continue to meet each obligation;[65]

xvi.   adequate arrangements to ensure effective monitoring and enforce compliance with the rules of the organization, including the resolution of disputes;[66]

xvii.   the design and enforcement of rules with the authority and ability to discipline, limit, suspend, or terminate the activities of a member or participant, including rule enforcement and penalties;[67]

xviii.   the maintenance and establishment of a program of risk analysis and oversight designed to identify and minimize operational risk;[68]

xix.   the maintenance of emergency procedures, including backup facilities, and a plan for disaster recovery, and the provision of the periodic testing of such procedures;[69]

---

56   Section 725(D)(iv) and (v).
57   Section 725(E)(i).
58   Section 725(E)(ii).
59   Section 725(E)(iii).
60   Section 725(E)(iv).
61   Section 725(E)(vi).
62   Section 725(E)(vii).
63   Section 725(F)(i).
64   Section 725(G)(i).
65   Section 725(G)(ii) and (iii).
66   Section 725(H)(i).
67   Section 725(H)(ii) and (iii).
68   Section 725(I)(i).
69   Section 725(I)(ii) and (iii).

xx.   the provision of ongoing monitoring and reporting to the CFTC;[70]

xxi.   the maintenance of records of all activities relating to the business of the organization;[71]

xxii.   the provision of market participants with sufficient public information to enable participants to properly evaluate accurately risks and costs associated with using the services of the derivatives clearing organization;[72]

xxiii.   the disclosure to the public and to the CFTC all information regarding each contract of sale, agreement and transaction cleared and settled by the organization, margin-setting methodology, daily settlement prices, volume and open positions, and any other matter which is relevant to settlement procedures;[73]

xxiv.   appropriate domestic and international information-sharing agreements and the use of the information for proper risk management purposes;[74]

xxv.   proper rules to avoid conflict with anti-trust rules;[75]

xxvi.   governance arrangements that are transparent, including rules that ensure proper enforcement of appropriate fitness standards;[76]

xxvii.   the enforcement of rules to minimize conflicts of interest involving the derivatives clearing organization and the establishment of a process for resolving conflicts of interest;[77]

xxviii.   the inclusion of market participants on the governing board of the derivatives clearing organization;[78]

xxix.   the minimization of legal risk by making sure that the derivatives clearing organization has a well-founded, transparent, and enforceable legal framework for each activity undertaken under the organization.[79]

Transparency is improved if OTC derivatives are centrally cleared through a derivatives exchange. OTC derivatives that are bilaterally negotiated and settled tend to have little, if any, disclosure. OTC derivatives exposures are also not publicly known and are usually the subject of confidentiality agreements. Hence, market regulators including the SEC and the CFTC have inadequate information to provide effective and proper supervisory oversight.

---

70   Section 725(J).
71   Section 725(K).
72   Section 725(L).
73   Section 725(L)(iii).
74   Section 725(M).
75   Section 725(N).
76   Section 725(O)(i) and (ii).
77   Section 725(P).
78   Section 725(Q).
79   Section 725(R).

Although there is some evidence to suggest that OTC derivatives did in fact contribute to the global financial crisis by increasing exposure to leverage and volatility, it remains unclear whether providing centralized clearing will lead to much improvement. This is because almost all markets (exchange-traded and OTC) became highly volatile at the height of the global crisis. At the time Lehman Brothers collapsed, credit markets effectively froze, which led to worldwide restrictions on the availability and supply of credit. The problems encountered in credit markets soon spilled over to other financial markets, including exchange-traded equity markets, futures markets and OTC derivatives markets.

A further point worth mentioning is that supporters of centralized exchanges usually also suggest that transparency equates with improved safety and allows for enhanced regulation and supervisory oversight. Although this assertion may have some truth to it, the global financial crisis also demonstrated that regulatory failure coexisted with market failure. Having more markets heavily regulated may improve transparency, but that may be insufficient to prevent another financial crisis from occurring.

As is discussed in Chapter 6, a number of enquiries have recommended that improvements be made to the current regulatory framework in the United States and in Europe. The *Dodd-Frank Act 2010* recognizes that regulatory failure was as much to blame for the global financial crisis as was market failure. Regulatory gaps, poor oversight and supervision, insufficient and ineffective regulatory action, all existed side by side with market failure. The policy responses by regulators and central banks were largely reactionary, responding to the crisis rather than pre-empting the meltdown.

Public Reporting of Swap Transaction Data

In a bid to improve market transparency in swaps markets, the *Dodd-Frank Act 2010* introduced a new provision requiring the "real-time public reporting" of swap transactions.[80] Under Section 727, the *Dodd-Frank Act 2010* provides that swaps which are subject to mandatory clearing[81] must provide real-time public reporting of such transactions.[82] In relation to swaps that are not subject to mandatory clearing but are nevertheless cleared at a registered derivatives organization, the Commission will also have authority to require real-time public reporting.[83]

Swaps that are not subject to mandatory clearing and are not voluntarily cleared at a centralized derivatives organization can opt for real-time reporting of such transactions.[84] The requirement for real-time reporting ensures that such

---

80 Section 727.
81 The Commodity Futures Trading Commission will determine which swaps require mandatory clearing under Section 2(h)(1) of the *Commodity Exchange Act 1936*.
82 Section 727(C)(i).
83 Section 727(C)(ii).
84 Section 727(C)(iii).

transactions will be disclosed in a manner that does not disclose the business transaction and market positions of any person.[85] The requirement for public reporting of swap transactions data will also apply to swaps which are required to be cleared under a centralized derivatives organization but are not in fact centrally cleared.[86]

The main purpose for the disclosure requirement under section 2(a) of the *Commodity Exchange Act 1936* as amended by Section 727 of the *Dodd-Frank Act 2010* is to "make swap transactions and pricing data available to the public in such form and at such times as the Commission determines appropriate to enhance price discovery."[87] In terms of improving market transparency, enhancing price discovery of swaps is considered to be an important objective, since it provides market participants with important information to make informed decisions.

Importantly, the amendments introduced by the *Dodd-Frank Act 2010* that provide for the public disclosure of swap transactions data are comprehensive. As is discussed above, the amendments cover not only all swaps that are subject to the mandatory clearing requirement but also swaps that are voluntarily cleared through centralized derivatives organizations. Swaps transactions data will also have to be reported for swaps that are not cleared centrally. The comprehensive nature of the disclosure requirement is aimed at removing incentives to circumvent reporting requirements. Whether a swap is centrally cleared or not is irrelevant, all market participants engaged in swap transactions will be required to disclose and report transactions data.

Legal Certainty for Swaps

The *Dodd-Frank Act 2010* also makes provision for minimizing the legal risk for swaps that are transacted in the United States.[88] Section 739 of the *Dodd-Frank Act 2010* amends section 22(a) of the *Commodity Exchange Act* to provide that:

> no agreement, contract or transaction between eligible contract participants [...] shall be void, voidable, or unenforceable, and no party to such agreement, contract, or transaction shall be entitled to rescind, or recover any payment made with respect to, the agreement, contract, or transaction under this section or any other provision of Federal or State law, based solely on the failure of the agreement, contract or transaction.[89]

---

85   Ibid.
86   Section 727(C)(iv).
87   Section 2(a)(13) (B) *Commodity Exchange Act* 7 U.S.C. 2(a) as amended by Section 727 of the *Dodd-Frank Act 2010*.
88   Section 739.
89   Section 22(a)(4) of the *Commodity Exchange Act 1936* 7 U.S.C. 25(a) as amended by section 739 of the *Dodd-Frank Act 2010*.

Many OTC derivatives participants had been adversely affected by legal risk and legal uncertainty.[90] In the past, OTC derivatives have been challenged on the basis that they amounted to unlawful gambling and bucket shops.[91] Some contracts have been held to be void and unenforceable by the courts;[92] and in some disputes, losing counterparties have been allowed to walk away from loss-making derivatives agreements.[93]

To overcome the legal risk posed by gaming statutes and state bucket shop laws, the US and UK legislatures have introduced comprehensive reforms. In the US, the *Commodity Exchange Act 1936*[94] was amended with the passing of the *Commodity Futures Modernization Act 2000* and the *Bank Products Legal Certainty Act 2000*. The amendments removed the legal risk posed by state gaming and bucket shop laws to OTC financial derivatives transacted in the US. In the UK, the *Financial Services Act* 1986 introduced amendments to provide for greater legal certainty for financial investments, including OTC derivatives.[95]

The amendments introduced by the *Dodd-Frank Act 2010* build on these earlier reforms and are designed to further minimize legal risk for swaps. The recent amendments to the *Commodity Exchange Act 1936* introduced by the *Dodd-Frank Act 2010* provide for greater legal certainty for all swaps transactions carried out in the US. The *Dodd-Frank Act 2010* amendments provide for greater legal certainty

---

90   Ciro, T. *Derivatives Regulation and Legal Risk: Managing Uncertainty in Derivatives Transactions* (London: Euromoney Books, 2004).

91   See, for example, the decision in *re Thrifty Oil Co* 212 B.R. 147, 153 (Bank Reports S.D. Cal. 1997).

92   Ciro, T. Gaming law and derivatives, *Company and Securities Law Journal* (1999) 17(3), pp. 171–86.

93   See, for example, the US Supreme Court decision in *Irwin v Williar* 110 US 499 (1884). See the UK decision of *Grizewood v Blane* 138 ER 578, where the court upheld the losing counterparty's claim that forward transaction involving the future sale of shares was unenforceable under Section 18 of the *Gaming Act* 1845 (UK). In *Grizewood v Blane*, Jervis CJ described the agreement as "a colourable contract for the sale and purchase of railway shares, where neither party intended to deliver or to accept the shares, but merely to pay differences according to the rise and fall of the market [...] the transaction was clearly gambling, and a practice which everyone must condemn." (138 ER 578 at 584).

94   7 U.S.C.

95   See Section 63 of the *Financial Services Act 1986* (UK). This section was later superseded by amendments to the *Gambling Act 2005* (UK) which repealed a number of old UK Gaming Statutes: Section 334 of the *Gambling Act 2005* (UK) provides that (1) The following shall cease to have effect – (a) section 1 of the *Gaming Act 1710* (c. 19) (voiding of security for winnings or for repayment of gaming loan, &c.), (b) remaining provisions of the *Gaming Act 1835* (c. 41) (security deemed given for illegal consideration), (c) section 18 of the *Gaming Act 1845* (c. 109) (voiding of gaming contracts), (d) section 1 of the *Gaming Act 1892* (c. 9) (voiding of promise to repay), and (e) in section 412 of the *Financial Services and Markets Act 2000* (c. 8) (gaming contracts).

for hybrid instruments[96] and long-dated swaps transacted before the enactment of the *Wall Street Transparency and Accountability Act 2010.*[97]

Swaps Enforcement Procedures

The *Dodd-Frank Act 2010* introduced amendments to deal with enforcement procedures under the *Commodity Exchange Act 1936*. The amendments provide that the CFTC shall have exclusive authority to enforce the provisions of the *Wall Street Transparency and Accountability Act* of 2010.[98]

Prudential regulators will also have exclusive authority to enforce provisions against swap dealers or major swap participants. Prudential regulators can refer any suspected breaches of non-prudential requirements by swap dealers or major swap participants under the *Commodity Exchange Act 1936* to the CFTC.[99] The CFTC has the authority to report to the prudential regulator any suspected breaches of prudential requirements by a swap dealer, including a major swap participant.[100]

---

96   See Section 22(a)(4) of the *Commodity Exchange Act 1936* (7 U.S.C) as amended by section 739 of the *Dodd-Frank Act 2010*, which introduced a new provision that "No hybrid instrument sold to any investor shall be void, voidable, or unenforceable, and no party to a hybrid instrument shall be entitled to rescind, or recover any payment made with respect to, the hybrid instrument under this section or any other provision of Federal or State law, based solely on the failure of the hybrid instrument to comply with the terms or conditions of section 29(f) or regulations of the Commission."

97   See Section 22(a)(5) of the *Commodity Exchange Act 1936* as amended by section 739 of the *Dodd-Frank Act 2010*, which provides that "Unless specifically reserved in the applicable swap, neither the enactment of the *Wall Street Transparency and Accountability Act* of 2010, nor any requirement under that Act or an amendment made by that Act, shall constitute a termination event, force majeure, illegality, increased costs, regulatory change, or similar event under a swap (including any related credit support arrangement) that would permit a party to terminate, renegotiate, modify, amend, or supplement 1 or more transactions under the swap."

98   See Section 4b-1 Enforcement Authority of *the Commodity Exchange Act 1936* (7 U.S.C 6b).

99   See Section 4b-1(c)(1) of the *Commodity Exchange Act 1936* as amended by section 741 of the *Dodd-Frank Act 2010*, which provides that "if the prudential regulator for a swap dealer or major swap participant may have engaged in conduct that constitutes a violation of the non-prudential requirements of this Act [...] the prudential regulator may promptly notify the Commission in a written report that includes – (A) a request that the Commission initiate an enforcement proceeding under this Act; and (B) an explanation of the facts and circumstances that led to the preparation of the written report."

100   See Section 4b-1(c)(2) of the *Commodity Exchange Act 1936* as amended by section 741 of the *Dodd-Frank Act 2010*, which provides that "If the Commission has cause to believe that a swap dealer or major swap participant that has a prudential regulator may have engaged in conduct that constitutes a violation of any prudential requirement of section 4s or rules adopted by the Commission under that section, the Commission may notify the prudential regulator of the conduct in a written report that includes – (A) a request that the

The enforcement procedures and referral process introduced by the *Dodd-Frank Act 2010* are designed to improve regulatory and prudential oversight of swap-related activity. Any suspected breach of prudential or non-prudential requirements by swap participants will be the subject of referral. Once referred to the prudential regulator, the alleged breach will be investigated and if found to have occurred will result in enforcement procedures against swap dealers and major swap participants.

Insider Trading

The *Dodd-Frank Act 2010* introduced amendments to the *Commodity Exchange Act 1936* to prohibit insider trading in relation to swap transactions, contracts of sale of a commodity for future delivery, and options executed or traded on a securities exchange.[101] Insider trading has been a perennial problem with exchange-traded transactions because of the difficulty of identifying and enforcing the dissemination of non-public information.

To aid with the enforcement of insider trading rules, the *Dodd-Frank Act 2010* introduced a new offence involving the imparting of non-public information with the intention to assist another person directly or indirectly in the use of that information. The use of the information must lead to the person entering into or offering to enter into a contract of sale of a commodity for future delivery.[102] Included in the new offence of insider trading for swaps is the offence of theft of non-public information.[103]

---

prudential regulator initiate an enforcement proceeding under this Act or any other Federal law (including regulations); and (B) an explanation of the concerns of the Commission, and a description of the facts and circumstances, that led to the preparation of the written report."

101   See Section 4c(a)(3) of the *Commodity Exchange Act 1936* (7 U.S.C) as amended by section 746 of *Dodd-Frank Act 2010*, which provides that "it shall be unlawful for any employee or agent of any department or agency of the Federal Government who, by virtue of the employment or position of the employee or agent, acquires information that may affect or tend to affect the price of any commodity in interstate commerce, or for future delivery, or any swap, and which information has not been disseminated by the department or agency of the Federal Government holding or creating the information in a manner which makes it generally available to the trading public, or disclosed in a criminal, civil, or administrative hearing, or in a congressional, administrative or Government Accountability Office report, hearing, audit, or investigation, to use the information in his personal capacity and for personal gain to enter into, or offer to enter into – (A) a contract of sale of a commodity for future delivery (or option on such a contract); (B) an option (other than an option executed or traded on a national securities exchange registered pursuant to section 6(a) of the Securities Exchange Act of 1934) [...] or (C) a swap."

102   See Section 4c(a)(4)(B) of the *Commodity Exchange Act 1936* as amended by section 746 of the *Dodd-Frank Act 2010*.

103   See Section 4c(a)(4)(C) of the *Commodity Exchange Act 1936* as amended by section 746 of the *Dodd-Frank Act 2010*, which provides: "It shall be unlawful for any

The insider trading provisions introduced by the *Dodd-Frank Act 2010* implicitly recognize that regulation of swap markets may in fact be prone to market manipulation. There has certainly been evidence that market manipulation, including insider trading, churning, runs and ramping, have been present in exchange-traded markets. However, with OTC derivatives markets, which are not exchange-traded but instead bilaterally negotiated between two or more sophisticated entities, there has been little evidence to suggest that insider trading is a problem.

This is likely to change once OTC derivatives markets become centrally cleared through a centralized derivatives organization, because swaps markets may then become prone to market manipulation. This is because price discovery is one of the by-products of centralized clearing.[104] With price discovery comes the potential problem of price or market manipulation as speculators move in to cash in on insider trading. Although public disclosure and centralized clearing can aid in overcoming the problems of opaqueness, centralized derivatives exchanges may also lead to problems of insider trading, as is currently found with other exchange-traded markets.

The new insider trading provisions introduced by the *Dodd-Frank Act 2010* represent a good starting point, but the provisions need to be broadened and enhanced to incorporate other types of market manipulation. If it is mandatory that swap dealers and large swap participants in the US clear their swap contracts through a centralized derivatives organization, there will need to be implementation of additional market manipulation provisions. Centralized exchanges such as securities and futures markets have detailed market manipulation provisions dealing with all types of market abuses including insider trading, churning and the spreading of false rumours.

---

person to steal, convert, or misappropriate, by any means whatsoever, information held or created by any department or agency of the Federal Government that may affect or tend to affect the price of any commodity in interstate commerce, or for future delivery, or any swap, where such person knows, or acts in reckless disregard of the fact, that such information has not been disseminated by the department or agency of the Federal Government holding or creating the information in a manner which makes it generally available to the trading public, or disclosed in a criminal, civil, or administrative hearing, or in a congressional, administrative, or Government Accountability Office report, hearing, audit, or investigation, and to use such information, or to impart such information with the intent to assist another person, directly or indirectly, to use such information to enter into, or offer to enter into – (i) a contract of sale of a commodity for future delivery (or option on such a contract); (ii) an option [...] or (iii) a swap, provided, however, that nothing in this subparagraph shall preclude a person that has provided information concerning, or generated by, the person, its operations or activities, to any employee or agent of any department or agency of the Federal Government, voluntarily or as required by law, from using such information to enter into, or offer to enter into, a contract of sale, option, or swap [...]."

104   See, for example, Section 2(a)(13) (B) of the *Commodity Exchange Act 1936* 7 U.S.C. 2(a) as amended by Section 727 of the *Dodd-Frank Act 2010*.

Regulation of Hedge Fund Advisers

In response to the call for greater transparency and regulation of Wall Street investment advisers, the *Dodd-Frank Act 2010* introduced amendments requiring hedge fund advisers to be registered with the Commission.[105] The registration and regulation of hedge fund advisers also extends to cover investment advisers of a private fund, as well as foreign private advisers undertaking transactions and providing advice to clients located in the United States.[106]

Investment advisers and hedge fund advisers will not only be required to register with the Commission but they may also need to maintain proper records and reports for members of the public. The reports should ordinarily include information which is relevant for the "protection of investors, or for the assessment of systemic risk by the Financial Stability Oversight Council."[107]

The maintenance of records for the purposes of providing relevant information regarding the financial stability of investment markets is consistent with the overall aim of the *Dodd-Frank Act 2010* to improve transparency of hedge fund activity. The records that are required to be maintained by hedge fund advisers are comprehensive and intended to provide a detailed picture of counterparty risk exposures and trading positions of clients.[108]

The records once developed and properly maintained will provide the Commission and other regulators with greater transparency regarding the trading activities and risk exposures of hedge fund counterparties. This is an important initiative since it provides additional information for regulators, including the CFTC and the SEC to make proper risk assessments of hedge funds and investment banks.

---

105   See for example Section 203(b) of the *Investment Advisers Act 1940* as amended by Section 403 of the *Dodd-Frank Act 2010*.

106   See the *Private Fund Investment Advisers Registration Act 2010*.

107   See Section 204 of the *Investment Advisers Act 1940* as amended by Section 404 of the *Dodd-Frank Act 2010*.

108   See Section 204(3) of the *Investment Advisers Act 1940* as amended by section 404 of the *Dodd-Frank Act 2010* which provides that "the records and reposts required to be maintained by an investment adviser and subject to inspection by the Commission under this subsection shall include, for each private fund advised by the investment adviser, a description of – (A) the amount of assets under management and use of leverage, including off-balance-sheet leverage; (B) counterparty credit risk exposure; (C) trading and investment positions; (D) valuation policies and practices of the fund; (E) types of assets held; (F) side arrangements or side letters, whereby certain investors in a fund obtain more favourable rights or entitlements than other investors; (G) trading practices; and (H) such other information as the Commission, in consultation with the Council, determines is necessary and appropriate in the public interest and for the protection of investors or for the assessment of systemic risk, which may include the establishment of different reporting requirements for different classes of fund advisers, based on the type or size of private fund being advised."

One of the major problems highlighted by the financial crisis was the lack of transparency with hedge fund and investment bank trading activity. The lack of adequate transparency with hedge fund reporting led to an inadequate understanding by regulators of the build-up of risk in the shadow banking sector. By requiring proper reporting and disclosure of counterparty credit risk exposure, off-balance sheet financing and trading and investment activity, market regulators will be in a better position to evaluate and assess any build-up of risk.

Importantly, the Commission can also make available to the FSOC,[109] "all reports, documents, records, and information filed with or provided to the Commission by an investment adviser [...] as the Council may consider necessary for the purpose of assessing the systemic risk posed by a private fund."[110] The ability of the Commission to collect and make available records from hedge fund and investment advisers to the FSOC for the purposes of assessing and evaluating systemic risk represents an important development in improving transparency with hedge funds and investment bank advisers.

The Financial Stability Oversight Council

The provision of records and relevant information to the FSOC for the assessment of systemic risk with financial markets and financial advisers in the United States represents an important major development. The FSOC was established by the *Dodd-Frank Act 2010* as part of significant reforms to the regulation and prudential oversight of financial markets and financial advisers, including investment bank advisers and hedge fund advisers, in the United States.[111]

The *Dodd-Frank Act 2010* provides that membership of the FSOC would comprise voting members, including the Secretary of the Treasury, who would serve as the Chairperson of the Council,[112] the Chairman of the Board of Governors,[113] the Comptroller of the Currency,[114] the Director of the Bureau,[115] the Chairman of the Commission,[116] the Chairperson of the Corporation,[117] the Chairperson of the Commodity Futures Trading Commission,[118] the Director of

---

109   The Financial Stability Oversight Council (FSOC) was established under the *Dodd-Frank Act 2010* following criticism by a number of regulators and enquiries that there was insufficient assessment and central coordination of systemic risk in the United States.

110   See Section 204(7) of the *Investment Advisers Act 1940* as amended by Section 404 of the *Dodd-Frank Act 2010*.

111   See Section 111 of the *Dodd-Frank Act 2010*, which provided that the FSOC would be established on the effective date of the enactment of the *Dodd-Frank Act 2010*.

112   Section 111(b)(1)(A).

113   Section 111(b)(1)(B).

114   Section 111(b)(1)(C).

115   Section 111(b)(1)(D).

116   Section 111(b)(1)(E).

117   Section 111(b)(1)(F).

118   Section 111(b)(1)(G).

the Federal Housing Finance Agency,[119] and the Chairman of the National Credit Union Administration Board;[120] and an independent member appointed by the President and acting with the advice and consent of the Senate.[121]

In addition to the formal voting members, the FSOC will also have non-voting members elected to the Council. In recognition of the valuable role research plays in providing relevant and reliable information for the purpose of assessment and evaluation of systemic risk, the non-voting members of the Council will include: the Director of the Office of Financial Research,[122] the Director of the Federal Insurance Office,[123] a State Insurance Commissioner,[124] a State banking supervisor,[125] and a State securities Commissioner.[126]

The purposes of the FSOC are multifaceted and include: "to identify risks to the financial stability of the United States that could arise from the material financial distress or failure, or ongoing activities, of large, interconnected bank holding companies or nonbank financial companies, or that could arise outside the financial services marketplace."[127] With the collapse of a large interconnected financial institution, stability of the financial system in the US could be adversely affected. The purpose of the FSOC is to identify these risks and to make a proper assessment of those risks in the event that a firm that is "too big to fail" is in danger of imminent collapse.

A repeat of the collapse of Lehman Brothers or similar large and interconnected financial firms would trigger wider ramifications in the US financial system and would now be placed under scrutiny by the FSOC. One of the main advantages of this new body is that the Council would be established to provide for effective risk assessment and crisis management. The Council would have the lead role in providing a coordinated response to any emerging issue that had systemic consequences.[128]

In addition to identifying relevant risks, the FSOC also has authority "to promote market discipline, by eliminating expectations on the part of shareholders, creditors, and counterparties of such companies" and "to respond to emerging threats to the stability of the United States financial system."[129] The need for proper assessment and identification of market-based risks has been highlighted by the financial crisis. Market regulators were blindsided by the build-up of risk

---

119   Section 111(b)(1)(H).
120   Section 111(b)(1)(I).
121   Section 111(b)(1)(J).
122   Section 111(b)(2)(A).
123   Section 111(b)(2)(B).
124   Section 111(b)(2)(C).
125   Section 111(b)(2)(D).
126   Section 111(b)(2)(E).
127   Section 112(a)(1)(A).
128   Section 112(a)(1)(C).
129   Section 112(a)(1)(B) and (C).

in the shadow banking sector, which, in turn, contaminated conventional markets and banks in the US.

In order to achieve the stated objectives, the FSOC has also a list of mandated statutory duties, which include:

1. To collect information from member agencies, other State and Federal Regulators, the Federal Insurance Office as well as the Office of Financial Research.[130]
2. To provide direction to and request data and analyses from the Office of Financial Research.[131]
3. To monitor the financial services marketplace in order to identify potential threats to the financial stability of the United States.[132]
4. To monitor domestic and international financial regulatory proposals and advise Congress and make recommendations in such areas that will enhance the integrity, efficiency, competitiveness, and stability of the US financial markets.[133]
5. To facilitate information sharing and coordination among member agencies.[134]
6. To make recommendations to member agencies regarding general supervisory priorities and principals.[135]
7. To identify gaps in regulation that could pose risks to the financial stability of the United States.[136]
8. To require supervision by the Board of Governors for nonbank financial companies that may pose risks to the financial stability of the United States in the event of a material financial collapse. [137]
9. To make recommendations to the Board of Governors regarding the establishment of heightened prudential standards for risk-based capital, leverage, liquidity, contingent capital, resolution plans and credit exposure reports, concentration limits, enhanced public disclosures and overall risk management for nonbank financial companies and large interconnected bank holdings.[138]
10. To identify systemically important financial market utilities and payment, clearing, and settlement activities.[139]

---

130   Section 112(a)(2)(A).
131   Section 112(a)(2)(B).
132   Section 112(a)(2)(C).
133   Section 112(a)(2)(D).
134   Section 112(a)(2)(E).
135   Section 112(a)(2)(F).
136   Section 112(a)(2)(G).
137   Section 112(a)(2)(H).
138   Section 112(a)(2)(I).
139   Section 112(a)(2)(J).

11. To make recommendations to primary financial regulatory agencies to apply new or heightened standards and safeguards for financial activities or practices that could create or increase risks of significant liquidity, credit or other problems spreading among bank holding companies, nonbank financial companies, and United States financial markets.[140]

The statutory duties contained under Section 112 of the *Dodd-Frank Act 2010* give a clear mandate for the FSOC to provide better coordination of any policy response to an emerging financial crisis. Importantly, the FSOC will provide better understanding of any build-up in risk that may have systemic consequences for financial markets in the United States. The lack of central coordination and preparation for the financial crisis represented a major structural weakness with regulatory and supervisory oversight of financial markets in the United States.

The large build-up of risk in the shadow banking sector represented a clear and present danger to both US and international financial markets. Regulators were simply not aware, nor did they appreciate fully, the systemic risks posed by the shadow banking sector to conventional credit markets and standard banks in the United States. The information-gathering mandate of the FSOC, along with the ongoing monitoring of market participants, will improve the level of understanding of systemic risks posed by large interconnected firms for market regulators.

Regulators such as the Securities and Exchange Commission, the Commodity Futures Trading Commission, the Board of Governors of the Federal Reserve, the US Department of the Treasury and the Office of Thrift Supervision will benefit from the ongoing monitoring and assessment of systemic risk in US financial markets by the FSOC. The FSOC will also be a valuable forum for discussion and analysis of emerging market developments and financial regulatory issues confronting US financial markets.[141]

The Council will also provide a central forum for the hearing and resolution of jurisdictional disputes among the members of the council.[142] This is an important development in minimizing regulatory "turf wars" involving the SEC and the CFTC over the regulation of hybrid financial instruments and OTC derivatives markets.

The Council will also report annually to Congress.[143] The report to Congress will provide information regarding significant developments in financial markets, both in the United States and internationally. Information concerning developments in the regulatory framework, including insurance and accounting regulations and standards, will also be reported.[144] The Council will provide information to Congress concerning developments in US financial markets and overall stability

---

140   Section 112(a)(2)(K).
141   Section 112(a)(2)(M)(i).
142   Section 112(a)(2)(M)(ii).
143   Section 112(a)(2)(N).
144   Section 112(a)(2)(N)(ii).

of the financial system.[145] Importantly, the Council will also give Congress detailed information and assessment of potential emerging threats to the overall financial stability of financial markets in the United States.[146]

In preparing the report to Congress, Council will be informed with up-to-date research provided to the Council by the Office of Research. The information will be timely and provide a comprehensive assessment of financial market trends, including sentiment, counterparty credit risk exposures, leverage and the use of off-balance sheet financing in US financial markets. The report will also allow the Council to advise and make recommendations to Congress in such areas as will enhance the integrity, efficiency, competitiveness and overall stability of financial markets.[147]

The Council can also make recommendations requiring supervision and regulation of non-bank financial entities by the US Federal Reserve.[148] In making this recommendation, the Council can require that non-bank financial entities be subject to prudential standards. In arriving at this recommendation, the Council may be influenced by factors including:

1. The extent of the use of leverage by the non-bank financial company.[149]
2. The extent and nature of off-balance sheet exposures.[150]
3. The relationship of the non-bank financial company with other significant non-bank financial companies and significant bank holding companies.[151]
4. The importance of the company as a source of credit for households, businesses and state and local governments and a source of liquidity for the United States financial system.[152]
5. The importance of the company as a source of credit for low-income minority or underserved communities and the impact such a failure would have on the community;[153]
6. The extent to which assets are owned rather than managed.[154]
7. The nature, scope, size, scale, concentration, interconnectedness, and mix of the activities of the company.[155]
8. The degree to which the non-bank financial company is subject to regulation by one or more primary financial regulatory agencies.[156]

---

145 Section 112(a)(2)(N)(ii).
146 Section 112(a)(2)(N)(iii).
147 Section 112(a)(2)(D).
148 Section 113(1).
149 Section 113(2)(A).
150 Section 113(2)(B).
151 Section 113(2)(C).
152 Section 113(2)(D).
153 Section 113(2)(E).
154 Section 113(2)(F).
155 Section 113(2)(G).
156 Section 113(2)(H).

9. The amount and nature of the financial assets of the company.[157]

10. The amount and types of the liabilities of the non-bank financial company, including the degree of reliance on short-term funding.[158]

11. Any other risk-related factors that the Council deems appropriate.[159]

The considerations that are taken into account by the Council are broad and comprehensive and require a thorough understanding of the role and nature of the non-bank financial company's operations. Requiring a non-bank financial company to be subject to the same regulatory and supervisory structure as conventional banks is, in effect, tantamount to a reclassification of a non-bank financial company to the status of a standard bank.[160] Not only will non-banks be subject to the same regulatory and supervisory framework as conventional banks but non-banks will also be subject to the prudential standards of standard US banks.[161]

The application of prudential standards to a non-bank financial corporation will provide regulators in the United States with greater scope to monitor trading activity. Regulators will no longer be left in the dark regarding the build-up of risk with non-bank financial corporations. The measures also provide scope for the rationalization of risky non-bank financial entities. Non-bank entities which fail to satisfy the prudential requirements will not be allowed to operate in the United States, and will instead be required either to recapitalize or be subject to further stringent capital requirements.[162]

---

157   Section 113(2)(I).

158   Section 113(2)(J).

159   Section 113(2)(K).

160   See Section 113(a)(1), which provides that "[T]he Council on a non-delegable basis and by a vote on not fewer than ⅔ of the voting members then serving, including an affirmative vote by the Chairperson, may determine that a US nonbank financial company shall be supervised by the Board of Governors and shall be subject to prudential standards, in accordance with this title, if the Council determines that material financial distress at the US nonbank financial company, or the nature, scope, size, scale, concentration, interconnectedness, or mix of the activities of the US nonbank financial company, could pose a threat to the financial stability of the United States."

161   The prudential standards for non-bank financial corporations will ordinarily be developed by the Council and may include: "(A) risk-based capital requirements; (B) leverage limits; (C) liquidity requirements; (D) resolution plan and credit exposure report requirements; (E) concentration limits; (F) a contingent capital requirement; (G) enhanced public disclosures; (H) short-term debt limits; and (I) overall risk management requirements" (Section 115(b)(1)).

162   See Section 115(c), which provides: "The Council shall conduct a study of the feasibility, benefits, costs, and structure of a contingent capital requirement for nonbank financial companies supervised by the Board of Governors and bank holding companies [...] which shall include – (A) an evaluation of the degree to which such requirement would enhance the safety and soundness of companies subject to the requirement,

Improving Investor Protection

The *Dodd-Frank Act 2010* also introduces a range of investor protection measures designed to address the concerns raised by investors during the financial crisis. One of the initiatives introduced by the *Dodd-Frank Act 2010* involves the establishment of an Investor Advisory Committee that will advise and report to the SEC.[163]

The Investor Advisory Committee will provide advice and will consult with the Securities and Exchange Commission on a number of investor-related issues including:

i.   regulatory priorities of the Commission;.
ii. issues relating to the regulation of securities products, trading strategies, and fee structures, and the effectiveness of disclosure;
iii. initiatives to protect investor interest; and
iv. initiatives to promote investor confidence and the integrity of the securities marketplace.[164]

In addition to the stated objectives, the SEC will also commission a study to evaluate:

1. the effectiveness of existing legal or regulatory standards of care for brokers, dealers, investment advisers, persons associated with brokers or dealers, and persons associated with investment advice including recommendations made to retail customers;[165] and
2. whether there exist legal or regulatory gaps, shortcomings, or overlaps in legal or regulatory standards in the protection of retail customers relating to the standards of care for brokers, dealers, investment advisers and advisers to retail customers.[166]

The study will better inform the SEC on what additional rules, procedures and processes will be required to assist investors who deal with investment advisers

---

promote the financial stability of the United States, and reduce the risks to United States taxpayers."

163   See Section 39 of the *Securities Exchange Act 1934* as amended by section 911 of the *Dodd-Frank Act 2010*.

164   See Section 39(a)(2) of the *Securities Exchange Act 1934* as amended by section 911 of the *Dodd-Frank Act 2010*.

165   See Section 913(b)(1). The term "retail customer" is defined in section 913 to mean "a natural person, or the legal representative of such natural person, who – (1) receives personalized investment advice about securities from a broker or dealer or investment adviser; and (2) uses such advice primarily for personal, family, or household purposes."

166   See Section 913(b)(2).

and broker dealers. The legal and regulatory gaps which currently exist with the protection of retail customers should be remedied to provide a much more robust legislative framework for investor protection. The concerns expressed by a number of investors, especially retail customers, during the financial crisis have demonstrated that gaps in US regulation have had an adverse effect on investor confidence and market sentiment.

To overcome some of the concerns, the *Dodd-Frank Act 2010* has also introduced amendments to securities regulation. The amendments are designed to provide retail customers with enhanced investor protection.[167] One such measure introduced by the recent regulatory reforms included establishing a fiduciary duty for brokers and dealers.[168]

The fiduciary duty between brokers and dealers and their investor client is to be extended to include a range of disclosures relating to the sale of products as well as the provision of investment advice. In relation to the sale of products to clients, the broker or dealer will be required to provide notice to each retail customer and obtain the customer's consent or acknowledgement to the sale.[169] The SEC will also seek additional disclosures regarding the terms of the investor's relationships with brokers, dealers, and investment advisers, including any material conflicts of interest.[170]

The disclosure of material conflicts of interest between brokers, dealers and investors represents an important regulatory development. During the global crisis, many investors felt they had become unwitting victims of financial abuse. A number of brokers and dealers had sold investment products to their clients without disclosing that they had taken opposing positions. This practice was particular prevalent with the sale of structured financial products such as residential mortgage-backed securities and CDOs at the height of the housing boom.

---

167   See Section 15 of the *Securities and Exchange Act 1934* as amended by Section 913 of the *Dodd-Frank Act 2010*.

168   See Section 15(1)(k) of the *Securities Exchange Act 1934* as amended by section 913(g) of the *Dodd-Frank Act 2010* which provides: "Standard of Conduct – (1) In General – Notwithstanding any other provision of this Act or the *Investment Advisers Act of 1940*, the Commission may promulgate rules to provide that, with respect to a broker or dealer, when providing personalized investment advice about securities to a retail customer (and such other customers as the Commission may by rule provide), the standard of conduct for such broker or dealer with respect to such customer shall be the same as the standard of conduct applicable to an investment adviser under section 211 of the *Investment Advisers Act of 1940*. The receipt of compensation based on commission or other standard compensation for the sale of securities shall not, in and of itself, be considered a violation of such standard applied to a broker or dealer. Nothing in this section shall require a broker or dealer or registered representative to have a continuing duty of care or loyalty to the customer after providing personalized investment advice about securities."

169   See Section 15(2) of the *Securities Exchange Act 1934* as amended by section 913(g) of the *Dodd-Frank Act 2010*.

170   See Section 15(1)(l) of the *Securities Exchange Act 1934* as amended by section 913(g) of the *Dodd-Frank Act 2010*.

The disclosure of material conflicts of interest is also extended to the role of investment advisers who provide advice about securities to retail investors.[171] Investment advisers will be required to act in the best interest of their client "without regard to the financial or other interest of the broker, dealer, or investment adviser providing the advice."[172] Consistent with the fiduciary duty of acting in the best interest of the client, investment advisers who disclose a material conflict of interest to the customer may be able to obtain the customer's consent, but only after full disclosure is made.[173]

The provisions relating to fiduciary duty and disclosure of material conflicts of interest are designed to provide enhanced protection to investors. Following the financial crisis, many investors felt that brokers, dealers and investment advisers who had acted not in the customer's best interests, had abused them. Instead of acting in the interests of the client, brokers, dealers and investment advisers involved with residential mortgage-backed securities acted to maximize profits and returns by selling the financial products to their customers without adequately disclosing conflicts of interest.

By requiring brokers, dealers and advisers to disclose material conflicts of interest, clients will have their interests protected. Conflicts of interest involving the broker–client relationship will be minimized, since there will be disclosure of any material benefit that the broker stands to gain. The recent regulatory reforms under the *Dodd-Frank Act 2010* are to be welcomed as they are designed to provide tangible improvements to investor protection.

Regulating Credit-rating Agencies in the United States

The role credit rating agencies played in the global financial crisis has been the subject of a number of public enquiries. The Inquiry Commission on Wall Street and the financial crisis recently established by the United States Senate concluded that credit rating agencies provided inaccurate and potentially misleading credit ratings on structured financial products.

As is discussed in Chapter 6, the residential-backed mortgage securities that were sold to institutional and retail customers on the basis of AAA ratings issued by the credit rating agencies were later downgraded to junk status. The downgrades triggered widespread panic among investors, which in turn led to a collapse in investor confidence and market sentiment.

Congress made similar findings on the role credit rating agencies played in the lead-up to the global financial crisis, concluding: "In the recent financial crisis, the ratings on structured financial products have proven to be inaccurate. This inaccuracy contributed significantly to the mismanagement of risks by financial

---

171   See Section 15(2)(g)(1) of the *Securities Exchange Act 1934* as amended by section 913(g) of the *Dodd-Frank Act 2010*.

172   Ibid.

173   Ibid.

institutions and investors, which in turn adversely impacted the health of the economy in the United States and around the world. Such inaccuracy necessitates increased accountability on the part of credit rating agencies."[174]

Congress proposed regulatory reforms designed to improve safeguards regarding the use of credit ratings by market participants. In justifying improvements to the regulation of credit rating agencies, Congress concluded that credit rating agencies were, in effect, "gatekeepers" and were required to be "carefully monitored," since credit rating agencies faced potential conflicts of interest.[175] Since credit rating agencies are fundamentally commercial in character, the agencies "should be subject to the same standards of liability and oversight as apply to auditors, securities analysts, and investment bankers."[176] Congress further concluded that the conflicts of interest should be "addressed explicitly in legislation in order to give clearer authority to the Securities and Exchange Commission."[177]

Designed to improve internal processes within credit rating agencies, the *Dodd-Frank Act 2010* introduced requirements that each credit rating agency "shall establish, maintain, enforce, and document an effective internal control structure governing the implementation of and adherence to policies, procedures, and methodologies for determining credit ratings, taking into consideration such factors as the Securities and Exchange Commission may prescribe, by rule."[178]

Credit rating agencies will be required to supply to the SEC an annual internal control report. The annual report should contain details concerning management processes and procedures in establishing and maintaining proper internal control structures.[179] An assessment of the effectiveness of internal control structures will also be required on an ongoing basis and be reported to the Commission annually.[180]

In addition to developing and maintaining internal control procedures and processes for credit rating agencies, the *Dodd-Frank Act 2010* also provides for the establishment of an Office of Credit Ratings to administer the rules of the Commission.[181] The Office of Credit Ratings will administer the rules with respect to the practices of credit rating agencies that are designed to protect users of credit ratings and members of the public.[182] The rules will also require credit rating

---

174   See Section 931(4) of the *Dodd-Frank Act 2010*.

175   See Section 931(3) of the *Dodd-Frank Act 2010*.

176   Ibid.

177   Section 931(4) of the *Dodd-Frank Act 2010*.

178   See Section 15E(3) of the *Securities Exchange Act 1934* as amended by section 932 of the *Dodd-Frank Act 2010*.

179   See Section 15E(3)(B)(i) of the *Securities Exchange Act 1934* as amended by section 932 of the *Dodd-Frank Act 2010*.

180   See Section 15E(3)(B)(ii) of the *Securities Exchange Act 1934* as amended by section 932 of the *Dodd-Frank Act 2010*.

181   See Section 15E of the *Securities Exchange Act 1934* as amended by Section 932 of the *Dodd-Frank Act 2010*.

182   Ibid.

agencies to promote accuracy in credit ratings which are issued by agencies and to ensure that such ratings are not unduly influenced by conflicts of interest.[183]

The recent reforms are important developments and represent an attempt by Congress to provide for more effective regulation of credit rating agencies. Possible conflicts of interest with credit rating agencies had become a concern for some regulators and some of the enquiries that had been established to investigate the causes of the financial crisis. There was a perception that some agencies may have acted with a conflict of interest when issuing credit ratings for structured financial products because compensation for the agencies was largely a function of providing a credit rating for financial products. The higher the number of financial products that were issued with a favourable credit rating, the higher level of compensation for credit rating agencies.

Indeed, the recent US Senate Report on the financial crisis concluded that conflicts of interest had "undermined the ratings process and the quality of the ratings themselves."[184] According to the Senate Inquiry, that conflict of interest was "inherent in an issuer–pay setup is clear: rating agencies are incentivized to offer the highest ratings, as opposed to offering the most accurate ratings, in order to attract business. It is much like a person trying to sell a home and hiring a third-party appraiser to make sure it is worth the price. Only with the credit ratings agencies, it is the seller who hires the appraiser on behalf of the buyer – the result is a misalignment of interests. This system, currently permitted by the SEC, underlies the 'issuers-pay' model."[185]

The desire of agency management in pursuing a growth strategy in market share also contributed to conflicts of interest. The relentless drive to pursue profit and to treat credit rating agencies as a commercial enterprise led to a cultural shift, which took place in early 2000. The US Senate Report describes the change in managerial expectations concerning the operations of rating agencies in its investigation of credit rating agencies in the lead-up to the global financial crisis.[186] Prior to pursuing the profit and growth strategy, rating agencies

---

183   Ibid.

184   Ibid., (n. 3), p. 273. US Government 2011 (United States Senate, Wall Street and the Financial Crisis: Anatomy of a Financial Collapse Majority and Minority Staff Report, April 13, 2011).

185   Ibid.

186   According to the US Senate Inquiry, the cultural shift within credit-rating agencies occurred with the desire to increase market share: "The credit rating agencies assured Congress and the investing public that they could 'manage' these conflicts, but the evidence indicates that the drive for market share and increasing revenues, ratings shopping, and investment bank pressures have undermined the ratings process and the quality of ratings themselves. Multiple former employees of Moody's and Standard & Poor's told the Subcommittee that in the years leading up to the financial crisis, gaining market share, increasing revenues, and pleasing investment bankers bringing business to the firm assumed a higher priority than issuing accurate RMBS and CDO credit ratings." Ibid., (n. 3), p. 273.

were academically oriented. The rating agencies largely exercised independent judgment, took pride in requesting information and provided higher accuracy with their ratings.[187]

Not only was there a cultural shift taking place with the management of credit rating agencies but the agencies were also placed under considerable pressure by investment banks to issue favourable ratings on their structured financial products. Investment bankers were keen to receive the highest possible rating for their financial products in the form of an AAA credit rating, and pressured analysts at credit rating agencies to ignore a host of factors that could increase credit risk.[188] Investment firms also engaged in the practice of "ratings shopping," whereby investment bankers "threatened to take their business to another credit rating agency if they did not get the favourable treatment they wanted."[189]

In a bid to improve transparency and mitigate the likelihood of inaccurate credit ratings, the *Dodd-Frank Act 2010* introduced new disclosure requirements for rating agencies. The SEC now has the legal mandate to require rating agencies to disclose information regarding the initial credit rating, including any changes that are subsequently made.[190]

The recently enacted disclosure requirements are designed to improve transparency for end- users of credit ratings. Credit rating agencies will now be required to disclose to users the precise statistical basis for providing ratings on

---

187   The US Senate Report found that "[p]rior to the explosive growth in revenues generated from the ratings of mortgage backed securities, the credit rating agencies had a reputation for exercising independent judgment and taking pride in requiring the information and performing the analysis needed to issue accurate credit ratings [...]. But a number of analysts who worked for Moody's during the 1990s and into the new decade told the Subcommittee that a major cultural shift took place at the company around 2000. They told the Subcommittee that, prior to 2000, Moody's was academically oriented and conservative in its issuance of ratings." Ibid., (n. 3), p. 273.

188   The US Senate Report concluded that "[a]t the same time Moody's and S&P were pressuring their RMBS and CDO analysts to increase market share and revenues, the investment banks responsible for bringing RMBS and CDO business to the firms were pressuring those same analysts to ease rating standards. Former Moody's and S&P analysts and managers interviewed by the Subcommittee described, for example, how investment bankers pressured them to get their deals done quickly, increase the size of the tranches that received AAA ratings, and reduce the credit enhancements protecting the AAA tranches from loss." Ibid., (n. 3), p. 278.

189   "The evidence collected by the Subcommittee indicates that the pressure exerted by investment banks frequently impacted the ratings process, enabling the banks to obtain more favourable treatment than they would otherwise have received." Ibid., (n. 3), p. 278.

190   Section 15E of the *Securities Exchange Act 1934* as amended by Section 932 of the *Dodd-Frank Act 2010*.

financial products. This is to give users clear information for "investors having a wide range of sophistication who use or might use credit ratings."[191]

The objectives of the recent amendments are clear and extend not only to current investors but also to future users, including sophisticated and retail end-users. The amendments to the regulation and disclosure requirements of credit rating agencies should minimize any actual or perceived concerns about conflicts of interest.

A major issue for investors in structured financial products during the GFC was the downgrading of residential mortgage-backed securities from AAA to junk status. The significant downgrades led to a collapse in the values of the underlying securities, with many investments now having little or no meaningful value. The recent amendments should improve rating accuracy and reliability, since end-users will have been provided with enhanced disclosure and transparency concerning the statistical basis and methodologies used in computing credit ratings.

The Volcker Rule

The *Dodd-Frank Act 2010* proposed introducing an amendment to the *Bank Holding Company Act 1956* to prohibit banking entities, including investment banks, from engaging in proprietary trading.[192] The proprietary trading ban is commonly called the "Volcker Rule," named after former US Federal Reserve Chairman Paul Volcker. The Volcker Rule prohibits banking entities, including investment banks from engaging in proprietary trading in securities and financial derivatives, as well as other financial instruments. The Volcker Rule also prohibits US banks from investing, sponsoring or having certain relationships with hedge funds or private equity funds.[193]

The Volcker Rule came into effect on 1 April 2011, following an announcement by the US Federal Reserve Board.[194] The Federal Reserve developed the rule in consultation with the Department of the Treasury, the Office of the Comptroller of the Currency, the Federal Deposit Insurance Corporation, the Securities and Exchange Commission and the Commodity Futures Trading Commission.[195] The Volcker Rule applies to banking entities

---

191   Ibid.

192   See Section 13 of the *Bank Holding Company Act 1956* as amended by Section 619 of the *Dodd-Frank Act 2010*.

193   Board of Governors of the Federal Reserve System 2010c. Press Release November 17, 2010. Washingon, DC.

194   Board of Governors of the Federal Reserve System. 2011. Press Release February 9, 2011. Washington, DC.

195   Ibid.

operating in the United States.[196] In relation to non-bank financial entities that are supervised by the Board of the Federal Reserve, the Volcker Rule does not prohibit non-bank entities from engaging in proprietary trading with hedge funds,[197] or private equity funds.[198]

The key objective of the Volcker Rule is to prohibit banking entities from trading in securities, derivatives or other financial instruments with their own money. The Volcker Rule does not prohibit a banking entity from allowing its clients to trade in securities, derivatives or other financial instruments. Hence, the Volcker Rule is designed to prohibit banking entities from engaging in speculative trading utilizing their own capital. The prohibition on proprietary trading was justified on the basis that a bank trading with its own capital might engage in highly risky and speculative investments.

The collapse of Lehman Brothers demonstrated that investment banks, which engage in proprietary trading in financial instruments and structured financial products, could find themselves speculating in excessively risky investments. This was the case with Lehman Brothers, which had absorbed a high level of financial risk with assets that proved to be illiquid and highly volatile. The build-up in risk in Lehman Brothers and its subsequent collapse led to an increase in systemic risk in financial markets and proved that some firms are "too big to fail."

The Volcker Rule will have an important impact on the risk profile of banking entities operating within the United States. The Rule will restrict a banking entity's ability to engage in risky speculative trading with the bank's own capital. Some have argued that if US banking entities cannot engage in proprietary trading, their subsequent lower risk profile will ultimately translate into lower returns for shareholders. Although this may well be true in the short term, by lowering investment risk US banks will prove to be more resilient and less volatile in the medium to longer term.

The Financial Services Act 2010 (UK)

In April 2010 the United Kingdom Parliament passed the *FSA 2010* (UK). The FSA amended the *Financial Services and Markets Act 2000* (UK) to include a new

---

196   The term "banking entity" is defined in section 13(h)(1) of the *Bank Holding Company Act 1956* to include "any insured depository institution, any company that controls an insured depository institution, any company that is treated as a bank holding company."

197   The term "hedge fund" is defined as an investment company pursuant to the *Investment Company Act 1940* as well as any similar fund as determined by the Securities and Exchange Commission or the Commodity Futures Trading Commission.

198   The term "private equity fund" is also defined as an investment company under the *Investment Company Act 1940*, or similar fund as determined by the Securities and Exchange Commission or the Commodity Futures Trading Commission.

financial stability objective. The existing regulatory and supervisory framework in the UK was considered to have inadequate protections to safeguard financial markets, financial institutions and investors in the UK.

The new objective was designed to address concerns that the regulatory framework failed to provide adequate protection to the financial stability of UK financial markets. The financial stability objective aimed to provide additional "protection and enhancement of the stability of the UK financial system."[199] To achieve the new objective of financial stability the Financial Services Authority would now take into account a number of factors including:

i.   the economic and fiscal consequences for the United Kingdom of instability of the UK financial system;[200]
ii. the effects on the growth of the economy of the United Kingdom of anything done for the purpose of meeting that objective;[201]
iii. the impact on the stability of the United Kingdom financial system of events or circumstances outside the United Kingdom.[202]

The new financial stability objective becomes one of four objectives that the Financial Services Authority (FSA) will now be responsible for under the *Financial Services and Markets Act 2000* (UK). These objectives include: maintaining confidence in the financial system; promoting public understanding of the financial system;[203] securing the appropriate degree of protection for consumers; and reducing financial crime.

The financial stability objective represents an important new direction for the FSA. The FSA will be required to consult with HM Treasury and the Bank of England to provide a structure to oversee the UK financial system. The governing framework will provide for distinct roles and responsibilities for all three agencies. Terms of Reference will also be established for a newly created Council for Financial Stability, which will replace the previous Memorandum of Understanding between the FSA, the Bank of England and the Chancellor of the Exchequer.

199   Section 3A of the *Financial Services and Markets Act* 2000 (UK) as amended by *FSA 2010* (UK).
200   Section 3A(2)(a) of the *Financial Services and Markets Act 2000* (UK) as amended by *FSA 2010* (UK).
201   Section 3A(2)(b) of the *Financial Services and Markets Act 2000* (UK) as amended by *FSA 2010* (UK).
202   Section 3A(2)(c) of the *Financial Services and Markets Act 2000* (UK) as amended by *FSA 2010* (UK).
203   The *Financial Services and Markets Act 2000* (UK) removes the objective of promoting public understanding of the financial system and replaces it with the requirement of the FSA of establishing a new consumer financial education body with the purpose of raising the understanding and knowledge of members of the public of financial matters and improving the ability of consumers to manage their financial affairs. See the Explanatory Notes to the Financial Services Act 2010 (UK), paragraph 9.

Council for Financial Stability (UK)

In July 2009, the Chancellor announced plans to create a new Council for Financial Stability to provide for greater oversight and transparency of financial markets in the United Kingdom.[204] The newly formed Council for Financial Stability would replace the previous Tripartite Standing Committee, which comprised the Chancellor of the Exchequer, the Governor of the Bank of England and the Chairman of the Financial Services Authority. The Chancellor of the Exchequer would chair the new Council for Financial Stability.[205]

The Tripartite Standing Committee was criticized for its handling of the collapse of the Northern Rock building society. One of the major criticisms involved the lack of clarity as to which agency was in charge and responsible for handling Northern Rock. HM Treasury in its White Paper, "Reforming Financial Markets in the United Kingdom," proposed establishing a new Council for Financial Stability, which would have clear statutory terms of reference outlining the responsibilities for each authority.[206]

The key objectives of the new Council for Financial Stability "will be to analyse and examine emerging risks to the financial stability of the UK's economy, and coordinate the appropriate response."[207] The Council for Financial Stability will also add regulatory focus and meaning to the new financial stability objective to be administered by the FSA under the amended *Financial Services and Markets Act 2000* (UK).

The intentions of the new regulatory reforms in the United Kingdom are clear. The objective of financial stability for financial markets will be the core responsibility for the FSA. The regulatory reforms will clarify the roles and responsibilities of each agency, including the Financial Services Authority, the Chancellor of the Exchequer and the Governor of the Bank of England. Importantly, the reforms will also provide a statutory basis for the new Council to replace the ad hoc arrangements which made up the Tripartite Standing Committee.

Improving Consumer Protection in the United Kingdom

The *FSA 2010* also introduced additional amendments to the *Financial Service and Markets Act 2000*, aimed at improving protection for consumers of financial

---

    204 HM Treasury 2009. White Paper on Reforming Financial Markets, July 2009 (London: HM Treasury).
    205 Ibid., paragraph 4.10.
    206 Ibid., paragraph 4.7–4.22.
    207 Ibid., paragraph 4.11.

products and financial services.[208] The *FSA 2010* allows the FSA to make rules requiring relevant firms[209] to establish a consumer redress scheme.[210]

If a financial entity does not have the ability to compensate customers for loss or damage and the firm is in default, the customer can access compensation under the Financial Services Compensation Scheme (FSCS). This compensation scheme was established by the *FSA 2010* (UK) under Part 15 of the *Financial Services and Markets Act 2000* (UK).

Both the statutory compensation scheme and the consumer redress scheme are designed to provide additional protection to consumers who suffer loss or damage as a result of a failure by a financial entity. The schemes are meant to complement existing common law rules regarding damages for breach of contract and tort and provide customers with a much easier compensation regime than would ordinarily be the case if an action were pursued through the courts.

The consumer redress scheme is also designed for the regulated financial entity to bear the costs of any loss or damage it has caused to its customers. In this sense, the redress scheme will also provide protection to UK taxpayers for any potential bailout or assistance that may be provided to customers of financial entities. The firm has the ultimate responsibility of making good any customer loss or damage. Hence, taxpayers are not obliged to offer redress at first instance; instead the firm would be responsible for the loss and have to bear the cost of compensating its customers. Only if the firm does not have the financial ability to compensate for loss or damage will the customer be able to access alternative compensation arrangements under the Compensation Scheme.

---

208   The term "consumer" is defined to mean persons who have services provided by – (a) authorized persons in carrying on regulated activities; (b) authorized persons in carrying on a consumer credit business in connection with the accepting of deposits; (c) authorized persons in communicating, or approving the communication by others of, invitations or inducements to engage in investment activity; (d) authorized persons who are investment firms, or credit institutions, in providing relevant ancillary services; (e) persons acting as appointed representatives; or (f) payment service providers in providing payment services See *Financial Services and Markets Act 2000* (UK), Section 404E(2).

209   The term "relevant firm" is defined in Section 404 of the *Financial Services and Markets Act 2000* (UK) as amended by Section 14 of the *Financial Services Act 2010* to mean (a) authorized persons; or (b) payment service providers.

210   A "consumer redress scheme" is defined in Section 404(4) of the *Financial Services and Markets Act 2000* (UK) to include "a scheme under which the firm is required to take one or more of the following steps in relation to the activity. [...]. The firm must first investigate whether, on or after the specified date, it has failed to comply with the requirements mentioned in subsection (1)(a) that are applicable to the carrying on by it of the activity. [...] The next step is for the firm to determine whether the failure has caused (or may cause) loss or damage to consumers. [...] If the firm determines that the failure has caused (or may cause) loss or damage to consumers, it must then – (a) determine what the redress should be in respect of the failure; and (b) make the redress to the consumes."

Short-selling Restrictions

The UK *FSA 2010* has recently introduced amendments to the Financial Services
Authority to make rules prohibiting investors from engaging in short-selling of
certain securities and financial derivatives.[211] The FSA now has the authority
to make rules requiring a person who has engaged in short-selling of financial
instruments, including brokers and dealers who have acted on behalf of their
clients, to disclose information about their short-selling activities.[212]

The short-selling amendments were designed to improve the market integrity
of securities markets in the UK. At the height of the GFC a number of listed
entities on the UK securities market faced significant selling pressure.[213] The
selling pressure was made worse by investors and traders engaging in the practice
of short-selling stock. As the equity price of the security decreased, the short-
seller's profit would increase, since the short-seller sold the security initially at a
higher price and would later purchase the stock at lower prices.

The short-selling practice was particularly prevalent for listed financial
companies and companies that had excessive leverage. Short-sellers often targeted
listed companies that had high levels of debt. As equity markets continued to lose
confidence following the collapse of Lehman Brothers, investors began to panic,
driving equity prices lower. Short-selling was highly correlated to share price
weakness, which caused further volatility and weakness in the overall market.
Many long-term investors suffered considerable paper losses as short-sellers
moved in to take advantage of volatile market conditions.

Securities regulators also expressed concern that short-selling could be used to
manipulate equity prices.[214] Shareholders, directors and boards of listed companies
also shared similar concerns. Some board members and shareholders were of the
view that short-sellers could be using the practice to cause long-term damage to
listed companies, affecting their ability to raise funds in short-term money markets.

211　See Section 131B(1) of the *Financial Services and Markets Act 2000* (UK) as
amended by Section 8 of the *Financial Services Act 2010* (UK).

212　See Section 131B(2) of the *Financial Services and Markets Act 2000* (UK) as
amended by Section 8 of the *Financial Services Act 2010* (UK).

213　Short-selling is defined to include cases in which a person "engages in short
selling in relation to a financial instrument (a shorted instrument) include any case where –
(a) S enters into a transaction which creates, or relates to, another financial instrument; and
(b) the effect (or one of the effects) of the transaction is to confer a financial advantage on
S in the event of a decrease in the price or value of the shorted instrument: Section 131C of
the *Financial Services and Markets Act 2000* (UK).

214　The FSA now has the authority to make short-selling rules without consultation
if it "considers that it is necessary to do so, in order to – (a) maintain confidence in the
UK financial system; or (b) protect the stability of the UK financial system." See Section
131D of the *Financial Services and Markets Act 2000* (UK) as amended by section 8 of the
Financial Services Act 2010 (UK).

This is because a number of listed entities that had borrowed money from lenders had market-linked banking covenants included in their loan documentation.

The banking covenants were usually tied to underlying share prices of the listed security. As the share price continued to fall, short-sellers would move in to take advantage by increasing the sale of the company's stock. The large share price falls would then trigger covenant breaches as the market capitalization of the listed entity fell below the covenant requirement contained in the firm's loan documentation.

To minimize the potential for market manipulation, the new amendments introduced by the *FSA 2010* would either ban the practice of short-selling or require the short-seller to disclose the transaction to the market. By improving disclosure standards it is anticipated that investors will not react so negatively to a company's declining share price if the price falls are due to short-selling activity instead of fundamentals. The mere act of a speculator engaging in the act of short-selling will be insufficient to drive larger declines in a company's listed price unless the decline is due to some other fundamental issue.

Conclusion

The recently enacted financial markets regulation in the US and the UK represents a serious attempt at improving the stability and integrity of financial markets. The new regulatory framework in the US provides enhanced protection for investors and consumers of financial instruments, including structured financial products, financial derivatives and mortgages. New regulation aimed at swap markets is an improvement to the previous regulatory framework and attempts to overcome many of the deficiencies, loopholes and inherent risks that existed with OTC derivatives markets.

Rules introduced to regulate hedge fund advisers and credit rating agencies are also designed to improve transparency and market integrity, and promote investor protection. Credit-rating agencies played a prominent role in the global crisis and were responsible for issuing inaccurate credit ratings on residential mortgage-backed securities and structured financial products. Subsequent downgrades to these financial instruments led to significant losses for investors and catastrophic consequences for international financial markets.

The creation of the Council for Financial Stability in the US and the UK also represents an important development in financial markets regulation and supervisory oversight. Both countries now have financial stability as a core objective in their respective regulatory frameworks. The financial stability councils will be responsible for monitoring, assessing and advising market regulators, including central banks and the Treasury. In response to the Lehman Brothers collapse, the Council will also have the responsibility of coordinating an effective response to emerging systemic risk concerns posed by large interconnected firms that are "too big to fail." The newly enacted Volcker Rule for proprietary trading in the US, along with other market integrity measures that include new disclosure rules for short-selling, are aimed at enhancing investor protection and minimizing the build-up of risk in financial markets.

Chapter 8
The Way Forward

Introduction

The global financial crisis has been a truly an international crisis. The crisis had its genesis in the US sub-prime mortgage market and quickly spread to other financial markets, leading to dislocation in international credit, debt and equity markets. The market volatility that emerged in the summer of 2007 continued to undermine investor confidence well into 2011.

Following Lehman's collapse in late 2008, the financial crisis transformed itself into a crisis in the real economy. Credit markets froze, banks stopped lending and some financial institutions collapsed as investor panic set in. All of the ingredients were now in place for a full-blown economic catastrophe not witnessed since the Great Depression of the 1930s. The GFC led to significant declines in industrial production, described by the International Monetary Fund as the "Great Recession," with millions of workers losing their jobs worldwide.[1]

Although the international economy staged a recovery at the end of 2010, by the beginning of 2011 cracks began to emerge in Europe. The sovereign debt crisis, which initially started in Greece and Ireland, soon spread to other debt-laden countries, including Portugal, Spain and Italy. This euro debt crisis sparked fresh fears that the recovery would stall and a new crisis would emerge to engulf international currency and financial markets.

International Council for Financial Stability

The United States and the United Kingdom have led the way towards reform and enhanced regulatory oversight with the creation of a Council for Financial Stability which has its primary focus on examining, analysing and making recommendations for addressing systemic risk concerns. Systemic risk is now a core objective in financial markets regulation in the US and the UK. The

---

1 According to the International Labour Organization (ILO), during the global financial crisis the United States saw 780,000 jobs lost in the construction industry, 500,000 workers lost their jobs in Spain, 100,000 workers lost their jobs in the United Kingdom and an estimated 4 million construction workers lost their jobs in China. The ILO estimated that 5 million workers lost their jobs in the construction industry in 2008 alone: International Labour Organization 2008, The Crisis in the Construction Industry. Available at: <http://www.ilo.org/wow/Articles/lang--en/WCMS_115508/index.htm>.

European Union has also expressed a desire to achieve greater cooperation and coordination among national supervisors, central banks and governments in its member states.[2] With the sovereign debt crisis in Greece continuing to undermine investor and market confidence, the EU has pledged to develop more robust crisis prevention and management procedures in order to promote financial stability throughout Europe.[3]

With this objective in mind, it is appropriate and timely to propose that a new Council for Financial Stability be established at the international level. The proposed International Council for Financial Stability (ICFS) will have financial stability of international financial markets as its core objective. The ICFS will have a similar regulatory objective to the Council for Financial Stability in the US and the UK, but will be international in its regulatory focus.

Membership

The need to develop an international council has been established by recent events, which revealed structural shortcomings in the ability of national regulators and governments to coordinate a rapid response to the onset of the crisis. The ICFS would be an association of financial stability councils, central banks and national treasuries, whose aim would be to promote financial stability and to provide an integrated approach to crisis prevention and the resolution of bank and large entity collapses. Further, the IFCS should not only provide a forum to discuss significant economic events but it would also include policy development and provide up-to-date risk assessments that accurately quantify the probability of systemic risk confronting the global economy.

The ICFS would be tasked with developing a comprehensive and international framework for the purposes of formulating clear policy guidelines to achieve the global policy objective of financial stability. Unlike current arrangements of the G8[4] and the G20[5] finance and leaders' summits, the ICFS would be expanded

---

2   See T. Ciro and M. Longo (2010). The Global Financial Crisis Part II: Causes and Implications for Regulation, *Journal of International Banking Law and Regulation*, 25(1), pp. 9–18 at pp. 14–15.

3   European Union Council 2009. Council conclusions on strengthening EU financial stability arrangements. Council Meeting Economic and Financial Affairs. Press release 2967, 20 October 2009, Luxembourg: Council of the European Union.

4   The G8 is made up of the eight wealthiest nations: The United States of America, Japan, Germany, France, Italy, The United Kingdom, Canada and Russia. However, the G8 does not include China, which instead is a member of the Group of 20 Nations (G20).

5   The G20 Finance Ministers and Central Bank Governors, established in 1999, is a forum which brings together the 20 wealthiest nations to discuss economic events confronting the global economy. The G20 members are: Argentina, Australia, Brazil, Canada, China, France, Germany, India, Indonesia, Italy, Japan, Mexico, Russia, Saudi Arabia, South Africa, The Republic of Korea, Turkey, The United Kingdom, The United States of America and the European Union.

beyond the richest nations of the world to include developing and emerging nations, in order to be a truly international organization.

The ICFS should have representation from all countries, as developed and emerging nations are interconnected through the phenomenon of globalization. As is discussed in Chapter 1, serious ramifications can flow even from relatively small economies, as the world witnessed in the Asian currency crisis of the 1990s, which was sparked by Thailand. As the more recent example of Greece has shown, in a global and interconnected world, problems with small nations can lead to more significant reverberations across the international economy.

Core Objectives

The ICFS should also develop a set of core objectives to achieve the overall stated aim of promoting financial stability in the international economy. These core principles should ordinarily include the following:

1. To monitor, assess and anlayse the probability of systemic risk confronting the global economy.
2. To provide up-to-date risk assessments and risk mapping of significant economic events, including the collapse or imminent collapse of large interconnected entities.
3. To provide leadership in the coordination of government, central bank and treasury responses.
4. To manage and resolve economically significant events, including bank runs, collapses of large interconnected entities and excessive market volatility on international securities exchanges.
5. To exchange information with member state organizations, including central banks, treasuries and governments, with the aim of promoting financial stability and market integrity.
6. To make recommendations for policy reform designed to improve market transparency and overcome deficiencies in the regulatory and supervisory framework of the financial markets of the member states.
7. To collaborate with other international agencies, including the International Monetary Fund, the International Organization of Securities Commissions and The Council for Financial Stability in the United States, the Council for Financial Stability in the United Kingdom, the European Commission, the World Bank and the Bank for International Settlements.

Core Principles

Consistent with the overall aim of promoting financial stability in the international economy, the ICFS should also take a leadership role in developing a set of core principles that will minimize systemic risk in international financial markets. The

core principles will provide guidelines for member states to choose to adopt as part
of their legislative agenda, and could include:

1. To develop a set of core principles for central banks, treasuries and
    governments to adopt to promote financial stability and minimize systemic
    risk within their nations' financial markets and domestic economies.
2. To develop a set of principles to ensure that market transparency and
    corporate, banking and financial disclosures are promoted in financial
    markets regulation.
3. To develop a set of regulatory principles that are designed to minimize
    systemic, regulatory and legal risk and to provide for a robust regulatory
    regime.
4. To develop core principles designed to provide effective prudential
    oversight of banking activities consistent with Basel III guidelines and
    pronouncements.[6]
5. To design appropriate regulatory principles to minimize excessive risk-
    taking and speculation capable of causing damage to financial markets and
    the real economy.
6. To develop a set of regulatory principles for the use of credit ratings within
    the banking sector and financial products with special emphasis on product
    issuers, promoters and underwriters of securities, derivatives and structured
    financial products.
7. To design a set of principles in conjunction with the International
    Organization of Securities Commissions for good practice for derivatives
    clearing organizations;[7]
8. To develop a common set of standards for financial reporting requirements
    which will aid comparability and the understanding of financial reports,
    and allow meaningful analysis of potential weaknesses and structural
    vulnerabilities in the international banking and financial system.[8]
9. To develop a common set of principles for good banking practices which
    emphasizes consumer protection and minimizes the instances of abusive or
    misleading practices.

---

6   See the Basel III guidelines at <http://www.bis.org/bcbs/basel3.htm>. These replace
the Basel II guidelines for banks and deposit-taking institutions. See also Chapter 6.

7   Derivatives Clearing Organizations (DCOs) were established under the *Dodd-
Frank Act 2010* and were designed to improve market transparency for standardized OTC
Derivatives.

8   See also the Office of Financial Research in the United States, which was created
under the *Dodd-Frank Act 2010* with the purpose of providing relevant and reliable data and
research to the Financial Stability Oversight Council. One of the stated aims of the Office of
Financial Research in the United States is to provide for a set of common standards for data
and information that is obtained for financial reporting requirements.

10. To design a set of common standards on due diligence regulating the use of credit ratings by users and investors so as to avoid over-reliance on ratings.[9]

Policy and Research Development

The ICFS would also be responsible for making recommendations for regulatory reform designed to promote financial stability and minimize systemic risk with international financial markets. The recommendations for reform would be made to member states that can adopt the recommendations as part of their legislative agenda. The ICFS could coordinate policy development and provide an effective international forum to debate proposals for regulatory and supervisory reform of financial markets with the aim of promoting financial stability at the international level.

To aid the proper and effective assessment of systemic risk, the ICFS should also establish an international systemic research office capable of providing timely research and up-to-date data. Like the Office of Financial Research, which was created under the *Dodd-Frank Act 2010* and serves the Financial Stability Oversight Council in the United States, an International Stability Research Office should be created for the ICFS.[10] The International Stability Research Office would provide for the ICFS up-to-date and timely data and analysis which would be focused on promoting financial stability and minimizing the incidence of systemic risk in global financial markets.

Providing timely, relevant and up-to-date data and analysis to the ICFS would also support the Council in anticipating and responding to future crises. The assessment of systemic risk concerns and risk mapping of structural vulnerabilities can be supported with the provision and use of timely data and information. The provision of reliable data will, in turn, allow the ICFS to better anlayse, examine and monitor structural weaknesses with international banks and global financial markets.

Ongoing Monitoring and Reporting Requirements

Like the Financial Stability Oversight Council in the United States, the ICFS would also provide ongoing monitoring and reporting to its member state representatives. The reports by the ICFS would provide relevant and reliable information to central banks, treasuries and governments regarding any potential systemic threats to financial markets, banks and non-bank financial institutions.

---

9   The issue of over-reliance on the use of credit ratings had been raised before by the Financial Stability Forum, which undertook an analysis of the causes and weaknesses of the current crisis following a request by the G7 Ministers and Central Bank Governors. See Financial Stability Forum. 2008. Report of the Financial Stability Forum on Enhancing Market and Institutional Resilience (Washington, DC: Financial Stability Forum, 7 April), pp. 37–39.

10   See Section 112(a)(2) of the *Dodd-Frank Act 2010*. See also Chapter 7 in this volume.

The reports prepared by the ICFS would also contain information regarding risk analysis and structural weaknesses in regulatory and supervisory frameworks of member states. In the lead-up to the GFC, many national and international regulators were caught unaware of the build-up in risk in the shadow banking system that later spilled over and contaminated the conventional banking sector.

The continuous monitoring of risk is important, since financial innovation has demonstrated that changes in systemic risk can happen quite suddenly and unexpectedly. Liquidity strains and changes in market or investment sentiment can also trigger a chain reaction to an otherwise isolated event. It is, therefore, imperative that changes in market conditions in equity and wholesale debt markets are monitored carefully to avoid sudden or unexpected adverse ramifications flowing to the international economy.

Stress-testing of Banks

Bank stress tests should also be conducted on an ongoing basis to assess whether any weaknesses or vulnerabilities exist in the banking sector. This is particularly important since a strong and robust banking sector is vital to providing an effective defence against any cross-border systemic risk that may arise from the collapse of a large, interconnected firm. Regular stress-testing of a nation's banks and financial institutions can also provide valuable information as to the overall preparedness of the financial sector to cope with a large-scale collapse.

Stress-testing of banks and financial institutions also allows sufficient planning and time to ensure that banks that fail to meet appropriate liquidity standards can be recapitalized to avoid funding constraints. Proper planning can also allow central banks to provide additional liquidity to banks and financial institutions where liquidity is considered to be inadequate.

As is discussed in Chapter 1, panic runs on banks by depositors have the potential to cause a major disruption to the banking and financial sector. There is evidence to suggest that at the height of the current crisis some depositors and investors had begun to panic, withdrawing funds from a number of banks, credit institutions and financial institutions. Bank runs had been evident with Northern Rock in the UK, where it had been widely reported that depositors had been withdrawing funds from the bank at an alarming rate, causing the building society to collapse.[11] Similar bank runs occurred in the United States

---

11   A Parliamentary enquiry that was established to investigate the collapse of Northern Rock found that "[a]t 8.30 pm on the evening of Thursday 13 September 2007 the BBC reported that Northern Rock plc had asked for and received emergency financial support from the Bank of England […]. The terms of the funding facility were finalised in the early hours of Friday 14 September and announced at 7am that day. That day, long queues began to form outside some of Northern Rock's branches; later, its website collapsed and its phone lines were reported to be jammed. The first bank run in the United Kingdom since Victorian times was under way." See UK Parliament 2008. House of Commons Select Committee

with Washington Mutual and Wachovia Bank, requiring those entities to be bailed out by the US Federal Reserve and the US Department of the Treasury.

Enhanced International Cooperation and Coordination

The proposed ICFS would play a key role in providing a clear set of principles for member nations to undertake regular stress tests of their banks and financial institutions. The ICFS would develop the core principles, working together with central banks, treasuries and governments to implement regular stress-testing and reporting requirements. Stress-testing of banks and financial institutions should be coordinated with central banks, whilst the proposed ICFS would act as the central facilitator.

In facilitating stress-testing of banks and reporting requirements with central banks, the ICFS would assume a leadership role in coordination. The ICFS would replace the previous ad hoc actions that had been initiated by a number of central banks during 2007 and 2008. As is discussed in Chapter 5, central banks established swap lines to facilitate additional funding and liquidity for mainstream banks during the credit freeze on international wholesale markets. The central banks that participated in the emergency funding measures included the US Federal Reserve, the European Central Bank, the Bank of Canada, the Bank of Japan and the Swiss National Bank.

The Financial Stability Forum noted:

> differences in collateral frameworks across central banks may stem from differences in the structure of national financial systems. However, in some cases, less differentiated collateral frameworks could make it easier for banks, especially multinational banks, to mobilize collateral at different central banks.[12]

The Financial Stability Forum's analysis has revealed a need for greater international and centralized cooperation and coordination of collateral structures and emergency funding measures in times of crisis.

At the height of the GFC, a number of central banks were forced to intervene to establish emergency swap lines, provide collateral and funding and facilitate additional liquidity measures. The emergency funding measures were designed to overcome funding constraints in wholesale credit markets which had become dislocated. The ensuing liquidity crisis was made worse with the collapse of Lehman Brothers, when central banks were again forced to intervene to supplement additional liquidity to overcome market dislocation.

The proposed ICFS can provide assistance to facilitate and coordinate emergency liquidity measures which are implemented by central banks to alleviate any funding

---

on the Treasury, Fifth Report (London: TSO). Available at: <http://www.publications. parliament.uk/pa/cm200708/cmselect/cmtreasy/56/5604.htm>.

12   Financial Stability Forum (Ibid., (n. 8)), pp. 48–49.

constraints confronting national banks and financial institutions. The ICFS role as the central facilitator would ensure that cooperation and coordination is maximized and emergency funding measures are implemented in a timely manner.

Importantly, the ICFS would strengthen crisis management and policy responses at the international level. The proposal here builds on the work of the Financial Stability Forum, which arranged for the signing of a Memorandum of Understanding on cross-border financial stability cooperation involving regulatory and supervisory authorities, central banks and finance ministers from the European Union.[13]

The GFC, together with previous crises, have demonstrated the need to take this one step further and implement a Memorandum of Understanding (MOU) on cross-border financial stability at the international level. The International MOU on cross-border financial stability would include not only the European Union but also the United States, South and Central America, Asia, Australia and New Zealand, the Middle East and Africa. The Asian Currency Crisis in the 1990s and the sovereign debt problems now being experienced by Greece, Portugal and Ireland have shown that even relatively small economies can produce serious cross-border ramifications, particularly at a time of heightened sensitivity. The Financial Stability Forum called for a strengthening in cross-border crisis management as well as improvements in the legal and regulatory arrangements for resolving problem institutions.[14]

Legal and regulatory arrangements will need to be standardized at an international level to facilitate cross-border management of large interconnected firms that are in imminent danger of collapse. Legal and regulatory frameworks can hamper the efficient resolution of problem institutions that are required to file for bankruptcy. It is often the case that large interconnected and international firms have obligations and creditors all over the world.

This was indeed the case with the collapse of Lehman Brothers, which had international operations and counterparty creditors in Europe, Asia and the Middle East. At the time of Lehman's collapse, thousands of counterparties were exposed to Lehman's default. The derivatives contracts that were in place were terminated and reset with new counterparties at a considerable discount to their original cost. Most of the derivatives contracts utilized standardized Master Agreements that had been customized to take into account the counterparty's credit needs and exposures.

Despite the use of Master Agreements, considerable uncertainty remained in international financial markets following Lehman's collapse. The regulatory

---

13   Ibid., (n. 8), pp. 51–2. A Memorandum of Understanding on cross-border financial stability was signed on 1 June 2008, see European Union 2008. Memorandum of Understanding on Cooperation between the Financial Supervisory Authorities, Central Banks and Finance Ministries of the European Union on Cross-Border Financial Stability ECFIN/CEFCPE (2008) REP/53106 REV (Brussels: EU: 1 June 2008).

14   Ibid. p. 52.

framework in the United States failed to make adequate provision for an orderly and timely resolution of Lehman Brothers. The collapse of Lehman Brothers revealed that resolution regimes were in need of significant improvement.[15]

The International Monetary Fund also noted the need for compatible bank resolution regimes and information-sharing legislation to be implemented by "home and host countries of the financial firms along a number of fronts."[16] Cross-border resolution arrangements and schemes should be harmonized and synchronized to allow regulatory authorities to implement in a timely manner wind-up procedures, so that a failing institution's value is preserved and maximized for an orderly liquidation.[17] The ICFS would establish a common set of principles for a cross-border resolution regime in conjunction with other international bodies that would provide for an orderly wind-up of financial firms with cross-border operations.

Harmonization of Financial Markets Regulation

The improvements to financial markets regulation in the United States and the United Kingdom are discussed in Chapter 7. Improvements have been made to the regulation of swap markets, hedge fund advisers and credit-rating agencies, all of which had prominent roles in the GFC. Despite these reforms, there still remains a need to provide for greater harmonization and strengthening of cross-border financial markets regulation, particularly with OTC financial derivatives, investor and customer protection and the use of credit ratings by investors.

The regulatory reforms recently introduced in the United States have made improvements in the way financial markets are now regulated. Swaps, which had been largely unregulated and not subject to supervisory oversight, will now be regulated along similar lines to exchange-traded securities and futures markets. Despite these regulatory reforms, there is an ongoing need to harmonize the regulation of financial derivatives at the international level.

Jurisdictions all over the world regulate financial derivatives, particularly OTC derivatives, differently. The disparity in rules and financial markets regulation that currently exists with domestic regulatory frameworks creates the almost perfect condition for product issuers to engage in regulatory arbitrage. Product issuers have

---

15 This was also the conclusion of the United States Congress when enacting the *Dodd-Frank Act 2010*, which introduced a new resolution regime for the orderly wind-up of a financial institution. The amendments introduced by the *Dodd-Frank Act 2010* broadened the types of financial institutions which would be covered by the Federal Deposit Insurance Corporation. In addition to the FDIC, the US Department of the Treasury can make use of the Orderly Liquidation Fund to provide for the recapitalization of the defaulting financial institution.

16 International Monetary Fund, 2009a. Lessons of the Financial Crisis for Future Regulation of Financial Institutions and Markets and for Liquidity Management (New York: IMF, 4 February 2009), paragraph 38.

17 Ibid.

an incentive to "shop around" and choose the least-regulated jurisdiction to issue new products and undertake trading activities. The problem of regulatory arbitrage at the international level has been confirmed by the International Monetary Fund in its recent enquiry into the causes of the financial crisis:

> improving cross-border cooperation has been a perennial issue at international fora [...]. However, further significant improvement is still needed for better cooperation and effective supervision of global and regionally important financial firms.[18]

International harmonization of financial markets regulation, including the regulation of securities and derivatives markets, is now long overdue. The current crisis has demonstrated the need for greater cooperation and harmonization of rules, laws and regulation with financial markets, financial products and services and large interconnected firms. Without international harmonization of regulatory and supervisory frameworks, structural weaknesses and vulnerabilities will continue to exist and pose a threat to the financial stability of international financial markets. The recent GFC has demonstrated vividly how problems in one jurisdiction can spill over to adversely affect other jurisdictions.[19]

The International Organization of Securities Commissions (IOSCO) is the most appropriate agency to coordinate the harmonization of financial markets regulation at an international level. The proposed new ICFS could collaborate with IOSCO to ensure that securities and derivatives regulation is harmonized in an orderly and timely manner. The proposed ICFS could also put forward principles for the regulation of OTC derivatives in overseas jurisdictions. There is a need for comprehensive and harmonized regulation of all financial markets and financial products, which will help to minimize systemic risk and disruptions from one jurisdiction spilling over to contaminate other jurisdictions.

Harmonized regulation of securities and derivatives markets would help promote the overall goal of financial stability at the international level for all financial markets and financial products. Different jurisdictions with have similar financial markets regulation in place would remove the incentive for

---

18   Ibid., paragraphs 34–35.

19   The International Monetary Fund confirmed the threat of spillover in its recent analysis of the causes and lessons to be learnt from the financial crisis, noting: "Ahead of the crisis, supervisory authorities do not appear to have been effective in sharing information and identifying a buildup of vulnerabilities in globally active and systemically important financial institutions. The problems which hit AIG and the potential impact on the CDS market (and, consequently, the banking system in the United States and Europe) are a clear example of insufficient cross-functional cooperation and understanding. The need for further cooperation between home and host authorities in handling problem cases is most starkly illustrated by the recent crisis response to deal with the bankruptcy of Lehman Brothers and the three Icelandic banks." Ibid., paragraphs 34–35.

product issuers to engage in regulatory arbitrage. Harmonized legal rules and regulations would also minimize the risk and incidence of regulatory gaps being exploited by opportunistic market intermediaries, and help mitigate systemic risk concerns for market regulators and central banks.

Future Crises

The GFC was not a novel phenomenon that adversely affected the operation of the world's financial markets. As is discussed in Chapter 1, the world has witnessed previous financial crises, of which the 1930s Great Depression remains one of the most severe economic and financial catastrophes of the modern era. The current crisis has also produced harsh outcomes, both in its initial impact on financial markets and in its immediate aftermath in the slowdown in the global economy.

Although the international economy has staged a recovery from the depths of the financial crisis, the recovery remains fragile with considerable headwinds remaining. The recent euro debt crisis, the bailouts of Greece, Ireland and Portugal, the mounting public debt in the United States, and geopolitical tensions in the Middle East continue to threaten the sustainability of the international recovery. Tensions between the United States and China, including China's slow transition to a market-based economy, its persistent undervalued currency and massive trade surpluses have resulted in large and unsustainable global imbalances. All of these concerns continue to pose threats to the overall financial stability of the international economy.[20]

Speculators in international markets continue to engage in potential excessive risk-taking activities. The recent sharp rises and subsequent falls in commodity prices, including base metals such as gold, silver, copper, zinc, coal and aluminum, continue to cause much volatility in financial and commodity markets. Concern has also been expressed as to inflated house prices in parts of Asia, including China, India, Australia and New Zealand, as potential headwinds that could threaten recovery and the pace of economic growth in the Asia–Pacific region.

---

20 See, for example, the *China Currency Manipulation Act 2008*, which was passed by the US Government House of Representatives in 2010 but did not become law. Lawmakers in the United States have reinstated their intention of reintroducing the Bill into the House of Representatives in 2011. The Bill provides Treasury with the authority to "(1) make an affirmative determination that the People's Republic of China is manipulating the rate of exchange between its currency and the US dollar; (2) establish and report to Congress on a plan of action to remedy such currency manipulation; (3) initiate expeditiously bilateral negotiations with the PRC to ensure that it regularly adjusts the rate of exchange between its currency and the US dollar in order to permit effective balance of payment adjustments and eliminate unfair competitive advantage in trade; and (4) instruct the Executive Director to the International Monetary Fund (IMF) to use the US vote to ensure that the PRC takes such action to achieve such goals."

Continued environmental concerns also pose challenges for economic stability and the sustainability of economic growth over the medium to longer term. Ongoing debate over climate change and carbon dioxide emissions and the role of the United States, China and India in global emissions has cast considerable doubt over the sustainability of high growth rates in the longer term.

Conclusion

The GFC involved dislocation in the world's financial markets. The proposals put forward in this chapter, along with the significant regulatory reforms announced in the US, the UK and Europe, have paved the way for stronger and more robust financial markets. However, there remain substantial headwinds on the international horizon. These challenges have the potential to derail the fragile economic recovery currently under way, or worse, lead to a future crisis.

Despite these concerns, there is much to be optimistic about, given the progress and policy responses that allowed the world to be shielded from the more adverse consequences of a global economic downturn. Even with much uncertainty, the world continues to demonstrate resilience in the face of much adversity. Governments have been quick to respond to the crisis and have demonstrated flexibility in turning their attention to finding solutions both short and long-term to the financial and economic malaise inflicting much of the developed world.

Resilience, flexibility and innovation in crisis management and crisis prevention, along with new structures that focus regulatory and supervisory attention on achieving global financial stability, will provide strong and robust defences against any future financial crisis. Continued cooperation and collaboration at an international level will also aid in minimizing systemic risk and promoting financial stability at the international level. This, in turn, will aid the economic recovery and provide a more secure pathway for achieving sustainable and secure international financial markets and a global economy.

Bibliography

American Insurance Group. 2008a. AIG signs definitive agreement with Federal Reserve Bank of New York for $85 billion credit facility. Press release, Business Wire, 23 September. Available at: <http://www.businesswire.com/news/home/20080923006681/en/AIG-Signs-Definitive-Agreement-Federal-Reserve-Bank> (accessed 1 October 2010).

— 2008b. AIG statement on announcement by Federal Reserve Board of $85 billion secured revolving credit facility addresses liquidity issues and policyholder concerns. Press release, 16 September, 2008. Available at: <http://ir.aigcorporate.com/phoenix.zhtml?c=76115&p=irol-newsArticle&ID=1197918> (accessed 9 October 2011).

— 2008c. US Treasury, Federal Reserve and AIG Establish Comprehensive Solution for AIG. Press release, 10 November, 2008. Available at: <http://ir.aigcorporate.com/phoenix.zhtml?c=76115&p=irol-newsArticle&ID=1224188&highlight> (accessed 9 October 2011).

Australian Government. 2010. Nation building economic stimulus plan: Commonwealth Coordinator-General's Progress Report to 31 December, 2009. Canberra: Commonwealth of Australia. Available at: <http://www.economicstimulusplan.gov.au/documents/pdf/YearinfocusWEB4.pdf>.

Bagehot, W. 1873. *Lombard Street: A Description of the Money Market*. London: Henry S. King.

Bair, S.C. 2010. Chairman, Federal Deposit Insurance Corporation on Systemically Important Institution and the Issue of Too Big to Fail, before the Financial Crisis Inquiry Commission, 2 September, 2010. Available at: <http://www.c-spanvideo.org/program/Shei> (accessed 1 October 2010).

Bank for International Settlements. 2011. International regulatory framework for banks (Basel III). Bank for International Settlements. Available at: <http://www.bis.org/bcbs/basel3.htm?ql=1> (accessed 1 June 2011).

Bank of Canada. 2008a. Bank of Canada keeps overnight rate target at 3 percent. Press release, 3 September 2008. Ottawa: Bank of Canada. Available at: <http://www.bankofcanada.ca/2008/09/press-releases/bank-canada-keeps-overnight-rate-at-3-per-cent/> (accessed 1 October 2010).

— 2008b. Bank of Canada lowers overnight rate target by ¼ percentage point to 2¼ per cent. Press release, 21 October 2008. Ottawa: Bank of Canada. Available at: <http://www.bankofcanada.ca/2008/10/press-releases/bank-of-canada-lowers-overnight-rate-target/> (accessed 1 October 2010).

— 2008c. Bank of Canada lowers overnight rate target by ¾ percentage point to 1½ percent. Press release, 9 December 2008. Ottawa: Bank of Canada.

Available   at: <http://www.bankofcanada.ca/2008/12/press-releases/bank-canada-lowers-overnight-rate-2/> (accessed 1 October 2010).

— 2008d. Central banks announce coordinated interest rate reductions. Press release, 8 October, 2008. Ottawa: Bank of Canada. Available at: <http://www.bankofcanada.ca/2008/10/press-releases/central-banks-announce-coordinated-interest-rate-reductions/> (accessed 1 October 2010).

— 2009a. Bank of Canada lowers overnight rate target by ½ percentage point to 1 percent. Press release, 20 January, 2009. Ottawa: Bank of Canada. Available at: <http://www.bankofcanada.ca/2009/01/press-releases/fad-press-release-2009-01-20/> (accessed 1 October 2010).

— 2009b. Bank of Canada lowers overnight rate target by ½ percentage point to ½ percent. Press release, 3 March 2009. Ottawa: Bank of Canada. Available at: <http://www.bankofcanada.ca/2009/03/press-releases/fad-press-release-2009-03-03/> (accessed 1 October 2010).

— 2009c. Bank of Canada lowers overnight rate target by ¼ percentage point to ¼ percent and, conditional on the inflation outlook, commits to hold current policy rate until the end of the second quarter of 2010. Press release, 21 April, 2009. Ottawa: Bank of Canada. Available at: <http://www.bankofcanada.ca/2009/04/press-releases/fad-press-release-2009-04-21/> (accessed 1 October 2010).

— 2009d. Bank of Canada maintains overnight rate target at ¼ percent and reiterates conditional commitment to hold current policy rate until the end of the second quarter of 2010. Press release, 20 October 2009 (Ottawa: Bank of Canada. Available at: <http://www.bankofcanada.ca/2009/10/press-releases/fad-press-release-2009-10-20/ (accessed 1 October 2010).

— 2010a. Bank of Canada increases overnight rate target to ½ percent and re-establishes normal functioning of the overnight market. Press release, 1 June 2010. Ottawa: Bank of Canada. Available at: <http://www.bankofcanada.ca/2010/06/press-releases/fad-press-release-2010-06-01/> (accessed 1 October 2010).

— 2010b. Bank of Canada increases overnight rate target to 1 percent. Press release, 8 September 2010. Ottawa: Bank of Canada. Available at: <http://www.bankofcanada.ca/2010/09/press-releases/fad-press-release-2010-09-08/> (accessed 1 October 2010).

Bank of England. (n.d.). Official bank rate. Available at: <http://www.bankofengland.co.uk/mfsd/iadb/Repo.asp (accessed at 1 October 2010).

— 2008a. Bank of England reduces bank rate by 0.5 percentage points to 4.5%. News release, 8 October 2008. London: Bank of England. Available at: <http://www.bankofengland.co.uk/publications/news/2008/067.htm> (accessed 1 October 2010).

—. 2008b. Bank of England reduces bank rate by 0.5 percentage points to 3%. News release, 6 November 2008. London: Bank of England. Available at: <http://www.bankofengland.co.uk/publications/news/2008/index.htm> (accessed 13 October 2011).

— 2008c. Bank of England reduces bank rate by 1.0 percentage points to 2.0%. News release, 4 December 2008. London: Bank of England. Available at: <http://www.bankofengland.co.uk/publications/news/2008/121.htm> (accessed 1 October 2010).

— 2009a. Bank of England maintains bank rate at 0.5% and increases size of Asset Purchase Programme by £50 billion to £125 billion. News release, 7 May 2009. London: Bank of England. Available at: <http://www.bankofengland.co.uk/publications/news/2009/037.htm> (accessed 1 October 2010).

— 2009b. Bank of England maintains bank rate at 0.5% and increases size of Asset Purchase Programme by £25 billion to £200 billion. News release, 5 November 2009. London: Bank of England. Available at: <http://www.bankofengland.co.uk/publications/news/2009/081.htm> (accessed 1 October 2010).

— 2009c. Bank of England reduces bank rate by 0.5 percentage points to 1.5%. News release, 8 January 2009. London: Bank of England. Available at: <http://www.bankofengland.co.uk/publications/news/2009/001.htm> (accessed 1 October 2010).

— 2009d. Bank of England reduces bank rate by 0.5 percentage points to 1.0%. News release, 5 February 2009. London: Bank of England. Available at: <http://www.bankofengland.co.uk/publications/news/2009/008.htm> (accessed 1 October 2010).

— 2009e. Bank of England reduces bank rate by 0.5 percentage points to 0.5% and announces £75 billion Asset Purchase Programme. News release, 5 March 2009. London: Bank of England. Available at: <http://www.bankofengland.co.uk/publications/news/2009/019.htm> (accessed 1 October 2010).

Bank of Japan. 2008a. Further measures to improve liquidity in short-term U.S. dollar funding markets. Press release, 13 October 2008. Tokyo: Bank of Japan. Available at: <http://www.boj.or.jp/en/announcements/release_2008/un0810b.pdf (accessed 1 October 2010).

— 2008b. Introduction of money market operation measures to facilitate corporate financing. Press release, 2 December 2008. Tokyo: Bank of Japan. Available at: <http://www.boj.or.jp/en/announcements/release_2008/un0812b.pdf> (accessed 1 October 2010).

— 2008c. On monetary policy decisions. Press release, 31 October 2008, Tokyo: Bank of Japan. Available at: <http://www.boj.or.jp/en/announcements/release_2008/k081031.pdf> (accessed 1 October 2010).

— 2009a. Statement on monetary policy. Press release, 19 February 2009. Tokyo: Bank of Japan. Available at: <http://www.boj.or.jp/en/announcements/release_2009/k/090219.pdf> (accessed 1 October 2010).

— 2009b. Statement on monetary policy. Press release, 18 March 2009. Tokyo: Bank of Japan. Available at: <http://www.boj.or.jp/en/announcements/release_2009/k090318.pdf> (accessed 1 October 2010).

— 2009c. Statement on monetary policy. Press release, 16 June 2009. Tokyo: Bank of Japan. Available at: <http://www.boj.or.jp/en/announcements/release_2009/k090616.pdf> (accessed 1 October 2010).

— 2009d. Statement on monetary policy. Press release, 11 August 2009. Tokyo: Bank of Japan. Available at: <http://www.boj.or.jp/en/announcements/release_2009/k090811.pdf> (accessed 1 October 2010).

— 2009e. Statement on monetary policy. Press release, 14 October 2009. Tokyo: Bank of Japan. Available at: <http://www.boj.or.jp/en/announcements/release_2009/k091014.pdf> (accessed 1 October 2010).

— 2010a. Statement on monetary policy. Press release, 26 January 2010. Tokyo: Bank of Japan. Available at: <http://www.boj.or.jp/en/announcements/release_2010/k100126.pdf> (accessed 1 October 2010).

— 2010b. Statement on monetary policy. Press release, 30 April 2010. Tokyo: Bank of Japan. Available at: <http://www.boj.or.jp/en/announcements/release_2010/k100430.pdf (accessed 1 October 2010).

— 2010c. Statement on monetary policy. Press release, 21 May 2010. Tokyo: Bank of Japan. Available at: <http://www.boj.or.jp/en/announcements/release_2010/k100521.pdf (accessed 1 October 2010).

— 2010d. Statement on monetary policy. Press release, 28 October 2010. Tokyo: Bank of Japan. Available at: <http://www.boj.or.jp/en/announcements/release_2010/k101028.pdf (accessed 31 October 2010).

— 2011. Statement on monetary policy. Press release, 25 January 2011. Tokyo: Bank of Japan. Available at: <http://www.boj.or.jp/en/announcements/release_2011/k110125a.pdf> (accessed 31 January 2011).

Bank of Russia. 2010. Financial Stability Review 2009. Moscow: Research and Information Department of the Bank of Russia. Available at: <http://www.cbr.ru/eng/today/publications_reports/F-ST_2009.pdf> (accessed 1 October 2010).

Barsky, R.B. and Kilian, L. 2001. Do we really know that oil caused the Great Stagflation? A monetary alternative. In *NBER Macroeconomics Annual*, ed. Bernanke, B.S. and Rogoff, K. Cambridge, MA: MIT Press.

— and — 2004. Oil and the macroeconomy since the 1970s. *Journal of Economic Perspectives*, Vol. 18, Fall.

Basel Committee on Banking Supervision 2010. The Basel Committee's response to the financial crisis: Report to the G20, October 2010. Basel: Bank for International Settlements. Available at: <http://www.bis.org/publ/bcbs179.pdf> (accessed 31 October 2010).

— 2010. Strengthening the resilience of the banking sector. Consultative Document. Basel: Bank for International Settlements. Available at: <http://www.bis.org/publ/bcbs164.pdf> (accessed 1 October 2010).

Baxter Jr, T. C. 2010. Statement by Thomas C. Baxter, Executive Vice President and General Counsel Federal Reserve Bank of New York, before the Financial Crisis Inquiry Commission, 1 September 2010. New York: US Government Financial Crisis Inquiry Commission.

BBC Today. 2009. Small business loan plan unveiled. BBC News, 14 January 2009. Available at: <http://news.bbc.co.uk/today/hi/today/newsid_7827000/7827793.stm (accessed 1 October 2010).

Bernanke, B.S. 1983. Nonmonetary effects of the financial crisis in the propagation of the Great Depression. *American Economic Review*, Vol. 73, June.

— 2000. *Essays on the Great Depression*. Princeton, NJ: Princeton University Press.

— 2005. The global savings glut and the US current account deficit. Remarks by Governor Ben S. Bernanke at the Sandridge Lecture, Virginia Association of Economics, Richmond, Virginia, 10 March 2005. Available at: <http://www.federalreserve.gov/boarddocs/speeches/2005/200503102/> (accessed 1 October 2010).

— 2009a. Asia and the global financial crisis. Speech by B.S. Bernanke, Chairman of the Board of Governors of the US Federal Reserve System, presented at the Federal Reserve Bank of San Francisco's Conference on Asia and the Global Financial Crisis, Santa Barbara, California, 19 October 2009. Available at: <http://www.federalreserve.gov/newsevents/speech/bernanke20091019a.htm> (accessed 1 October 2010).

— 2009b. Financial regulation and supervision after the crisis – the role of the Federal Reserve. Speech by Chairman Ben S. Bernanke at the Federal Reserve Bank of Boston 54th Economic Conference, Chatham, Massachusetts, 23 October 2009. New York: Board of Governors of the Federal Reserve System. Available at: <http://www.bis.org/review/r091027a.pdf> (accessed 1 October 2010).

— 2009c. On the outlook for the economy and policy. Speech delivered at The Economic Club of New York, 16 September, 2009. New York: The Federal Reserve Board. Available at: <http://www.federalreserve.gov/newsevents/speech/bernanke20091116a.htm> (accessed 1 October 2010).

— 2009d. Reflections on a year in crisis. Speech delivered at the Federal Reserve Bank of Kansas City's Annual Economic Symposium, Jackson Hole, Wyoming. New York: The Federal Reserve Board. Available at: <http://www.federalreserve.gov/newsevents/speech/bernanke20090821a.htm> (accessed 1 October 2010).

— 2010a. Fiscal sustainability and fiscal rules. Speech by Ben S. Bernanke, Chairman of the Board of Governors of the Federal Reserve System, delivered at the Annual Meeting of the Rhode Island Public Expenditure Council, Providence, Rhode Island, 4 October 2010. Available at: <http://www.federalreserve.gov/newsevents/speech/bernanke20101004a.htm> (accessed 31 October 2010).

— 2010b. Monetary policy and the housing bubble. Speech at the Annual Meeting of the American Economic Association, Atlanta, Georgia, 3 January 2010. Bank for International Settlements. Available at: <http://www.bis.org/review/r100113a.pdf> (accessed 1 October 2010).

— 2010c. Statement by Ben S. Bernanke, Chairman of the Board of Governors of the Federal Reserve System before the Financial Crisis Inquiry Commission, Washington, DC, 2 September 2010. Stanford, CT: Stanford Law School. Available at: <http://fcic-static.law.stanford.edu/cdn_media/

fcic-docs/2010-09-02%20Ben%20Bernanke%20Written%20Testimony.pdf> (accessed 1 October 2010).

Board of Governors of the Federal Reserve System. 2007a. Press release, 17 August 2007. Available at: <http://www.federalreserve.gov/newsevents/press/monetary/20070817b.htm> (accessed 1 October 2010).

— 2007b. Press release, 18 September 2007. Available at: <http://www.federalreserve.gov/newsevents/press/monetary/20070918a.htm (accessed 1 October 2010).

— 2007c. Press release, 31 October 2007. Available at: <http://www.federalreserve.gov/newsevents/press/monetary/20071031a.htm> (accessed 1 October 2010).

— 2008a. Press release, 22 January 2008. Available at: <http://www.federalreserve.gov/newsevents/press/monetary/20080122b.htm> (accessed 1 October 2010).

— 2008b. Press release, 30 January 2008. Available at: <http://www.federalreserve.gov/newsevents/press/monetary/20080130a.htm> (accessed 1 October 2010).

— 2008c. Press release, 11 March 2008. Board of Governors of the Federal Reserve System. Available at: <http://www.federalreserve.gov/newsevents/press/monetary/20080311a.htm> (accessed 1 October 2010).

— 2008d. Press release, 18 March 2008. Available at: <http://www.federalreserve.gov/newsevents/press/monetary/20080318a.htm> (accessed 1 October 2010).

— 2008e. Press release, 16 September 2008. Available at: <http://www.federalreserve.gov/newevents/press/other/20080916a.html> (accessed 9 October 2011).

— 2008f. Press release, 8 October 2008. Available at: <http://www.federalreserve.gov/newsevents/press/other/20081008a.htm> (accessed 1 October 2010).

— 2008g. Press release, 10 November 2008. Board of Governors of the Federal Reserve System. Available at: <http://www.federalreserve.gov/newsevents/press/other/20081110a.htm> (accessed 1 October 2010).

— 2009. Press release, 23 September 2009. Available at: <http://www.federalreserve.gov/newsevents/press/monetary/20090923a.htm> (accessed 1 October 2010).

— 2010a. Press release, 9 May 2010. Available at: <http://www.federalreserve.gov/newsevents/press/monetary/20100509a.htm> (accessed 1 October 2010).

— 2010b. Press release, 3 November 2010. Available at: <http://www.federalreserve.gov/newsevents/press/monetary/20101103a.htm> (accessed 1 October 2010).

— 2010c. Press release, 17 November 2010. Washington, DC. Available at: <http://www.federalreserve.gov/newsevents/press/bcreg/20101117a.htm> (accessed 1 November 2010).

— 2011. Press release, 9 February 2011. Washington, DC. Available at: <http://www.federalreserve.gov/newsevents/press/bcreg/20110209a.htm> (accessed 28 February 2011).

Borensztein, E. and Panizza, U. 2008. The costs of sovereign default. Working Paper No. 08-238. Washington, DC: International Monetary Fund. Available at: <http://www.imf.org/external/pubs/ft/wp/2008/wp08238.pdf> (accessed 1 October 2010).

Center for Financial Studies. 2009. White Paper No. I and White Paper No. II. New financial order recommendations by the Issing Committee, Part I (October 2008) and Part II (March 2009). CFS, White Paper Series, February 2009.

Central Intelligence Agency. 2010. *The CIA World Factbook*. Online. Available at: <https://www.cia.gov/library/publications/the-world-factbook/fields/2186. html> (accessed 1 October 2010).

Ciro, T. 1999. Gaming law and derivatives. *Company and Securities Law Journal*, 17(3), pp. 171–86.

— 2004. Derivatives regulation and legal risk: Managing uncertainty in derivatives transactions. London: Euromoney Books.

— Trading in financial derivatives: Does it increase market volatility and systemic risk? *Company and Securities Law Journal*, 22(1), 23, pp. 43–45.

— 2005. Game theory in financial markets litigation. *Journal of International Banking Law and Regulation*, 20(7), p. 315.

— and Longo, M. 2009. The global financial crisis Part 1: Causes and implications for future regulation. *Journal of International Banking Law and Regulation*, 24(12), p. 599 and p. 602.

— and — 2010. The Global financial crisis Part 2: Causes and implications for future regulation. *Journal of International Banking Law and Regulation*, Vol. 13.

Collins, M. and Baker, M. 2003. *Commercial Banks and Industrial Finance in England and Wales, 1860–1913*. London: Oxford University Press.

Corsetti, G., Presenti, P. and Roubini, N. 1999. What caused the Asian currency and financial crisis? *Japan and the World Economy*, 11.

Cox, C. 2008. Turmoil in US credit markets: Recent actions regarding government sponsored entities, investment banks and other financial institutions. Statement of SEC Chairman Christopher Cox before the US Senate Committee on Banking, Housing and Urban Affairs, Senate Hearing, Washington, DC, 23 September 2008. Available at: <http://www.sec.gov/news/testimony/2008/ts092308cc.htm> (accessed 1 October 2010).

— 2010. Testimony by Christopher Cox, Former Chairman, US Securities and Exchange Commission before the Financial Crisis Inquiry Commission, 5 May 2010. Available at: <http://fcic-static.law.stanford.edu/cdn_media/fcic-testimony/2010-0505-Cox.pdf> (accessed 1 October 2011).

de Larosière, J. 2009. The High-Level Group on Financial Supervision in the European Union. Report, 25 February 2009. Brussels: European Union Commission. Available at: <http://ec.europa.eu/internal_market/finances/docs/de_larosiere_report_en.pdf (accessed 1 October 2010).

Del Negro, Marco and Otrok, Christopher. 2007. 99 Luftballons: Monetary policy and house price boom across US states. *Journal of Monetary Economics*, 54(7), October, pp. 1962–85.

Elliott, G. 2006. *The Mystery of Overend and Gurney: A Financial Scandal in Victorian London*. London: Methuen.

European Central Bank. 2008a. European Central Bank again offering US dollar liquidity. Press release, 10 January 2008. Available at: <http://www.ecb.europa.eu/press/pr/date/2008/html/pr080110_2.en.html> (accessed 1 October 2010).

— 2008b. Measures to enhance the US dollar term auction facility. Press release, 30 July 2008. Available at: <http://www.ecb.europa.eu/press/pr/date/2008/html/pr080730.en.html (accessed 1 October 2010).

— 2008c. Press release, 26 September 2008. Measures designed to address elevated pressures in the short-term US dollar funding markets. Available at: <http://www.ecb.europa.eu/press/pr/date/2008/html/pr080926.en.html   (accessed 1 October 2010).

— 2008d. Measures designed to address elevated pressures in the short-term US dollar funding markets. Press release, 29 September 2008. Available at: <http://www.ecb.europa.eu/press/pr/date/2008/html/pr080926.en.html>.

— 2008e. Measures designed to address elevated pressures in the short-term US dollar funding markets. Press release, 13 October 2008. Available at: <http://www.ecb.europa.eu/press/pr/date/2008/html/pr081013.en.html>. (accessed 1 October 2010).

— 2008f. Financial Stability Review December 2008: Risks and vulnerabilities in financial system persist. Press release, 15 December 2008. Available at: <http://www.ecb.europa.eu/press/pr/date/2008/html/pr081215.en.html> (accessed 1 October 2010).

— 2009. Financial Stability Review December 2009. Press release, 18 December 2009. Available at: <http://www.ecb.europa.eu/press/pr/date/2009/html/pr091218.en.html> (accessed 1 October 2010).

— 2010. Financial Stability Review June 2010. Press release, 31 May 2010. Available at: <http://www.ecb.europa.eu/press/pr/date/2010/html/pr100531.en.html> (accessed 1 October 2010).

— 2011. Key ECB interest rates. European Central Bank Monetary Rate Policy. Available at: <http://www.ecb.int/stats/monetary/rates/html/index.en.html> (accessed 1 October 2010).

European Union. 2008. Memorandum of Understanding on Cooperation between the Financial Supervisory Authorities, Central Banks and Finance Ministries of the European Union on Cross-Border Financial Stability ECFIN/CEFCPE(2008)REP/53106 REV. Brussels, 1 June 2008). Available at: <http://www.ecb.int/pub/pdf/other/mou-financialstability2008en.pdf> (accessed 12 October 2011).

European Union Commission. 2008a. The application of state aid rules to measures taken in relation to financial institutions in the context of the current global financial crisis. *Official Journal of the European Union* (2008/C 270/02), 13 October 2008, paragraph 1. Available at: <http://eurlex.europa.eu/LexUriServ/LexUriServ.do?uri=OJ:C:2008:270:0008:0014:EN:PDF> (accessed 1 October 2010).

— 2008b. Commission sets out proposal to increase minimum protection for bank deposits to €100,000. Press release, 15 October 2008 (IP/08/1508). Available at: <http://europa.eu/rapid/pressReleasesAction.do?reference=IP/08/1508&fo rmat=HTML&aged=0&language=EN> (accessed 1 October 2010).

— 2008c. State aid: Commission approves Cypriot scheme to support credit institutions. Press release, 22 October 2008 (IP/09/1569). Available at: <http:// europa.eu/rapid/pressReleasesAction.do?reference=IP/09/1569&format=HT ML&aged=1&language=EN&guiLanguage=en> (accessed 1 October 2010).

— 2008d. State aid: Commission approves Danish state support scheme for banks. Press release, 10 October 2008 (IP/08/1483). Available at: <http://europa.eu/ rapid/pressReleasesAction.do?reference=IP/08/1483&format=HTML&aged= 1&language=EN&guiLanguage=en> (accessed 1 October 2010).

— 2008e. State aid: Commission approves Dutch guarantee scheme for financial institutions. Press release, 31 October 2008 (IP/08/1610). Available at: <http:// europa.eu/rapid/pressReleasesAction.do?reference=IP/08/1610&format=HT ML&aged=1&language=EN&guiLanguage=en> (accessed 1 October 2010).

— 2008f. State aid: Commission approves Finnish support scheme for financial institutions. Press release, 14 November 2008 (IP/08/1705). Available at: <http://europa.eu/rapid/pressReleasesAction.do?reference=IP/08/1705&form at=HTML&aged=1&language=EN&guiLanguage=en> (accessed 1 October 2010).

— 2008g. State aid: Commission approves revised Irish support scheme for financial institutions. Press release, 13 October 2008. Available at: <http:// europa.eu/rapid/pressReleasesAction.do?reference=IP/08/1497&format=HT ML&aged=1&language=EN&guiLanguage=en> (accessed 1 October 2010).

— 2008h. State aid: Commission approves Slovenian support scheme for credit institutions. Press release, 12 December 2008 (IP/08/1964). Available at: <http://europa.eu/rapid/pressReleasesAction.do?reference=IP/08/1964&form at=HTML&aged=1&language=EN&guiLanguage=en> (accessed 1 October 2010).

— 2008i. State aid: Commission approves Spanish fund for acquisition of financial assets from financial institutions. Press release, 4 November 2008 (IP/08/1630). Available at: <http://europa.eu/rapid/pressReleasesAction.do?re ference=IP/08/1630&format=HTML&aged=1&language=EN&guiLanguage =en> (accessed 1 October 2010).

— 2008j. State aid: Commission approves Swedish support schemes for financial institutions. Press release, 30 October 2008 (IP/08/1600). Available at: <http:// europa.eu/rapid/pressReleasesAction.do?reference=IP/08/1600&format=HT ML&aged=1&language=EN&guiLanguage=en> (accessed 1 October 2010).

— 2008k. State aid: Commission approves UK support scheme for financial institutions. Press release, 13 October 2008 (IP/08/1496). Available at: <http:// europa.eu/rapid/pressReleasesAction.do?reference=IP/08/1496&format=HT ML&aged=1&language=EN&guiLanguage=en> (accessed 1 October 2010).

— State aid: Commission authorises support package for Greek credit institutions. Press release, 13 October 2008 (IP/08/1497). Available at: <http://europa.eu/

rapid/pressReleasesAction.do?reference=IP/08/1742&format=HTML&aged=
1&language=EN&guiLanguage=en> (accessed 1 October 2010).
— 2008m. State aid: Commission authorises Italian scheme for refinancing credit
institutions. Press release, 14 November 2008 (IP/08/1706). Available at:
<http://europa.eu/rapid/pressReleasesAction.do?reference=IP/08/1706&form
at=HTML&aged=1&language=EN&guiLanguage=en> (accessed 1 October
2010).
— 2008n. State aid: Commission authorises French scheme for refinancing credit
institutions. Press release, 31 October 2008 (IP/08/1609). Available at: <http://
europa.eu/rapid/pressReleasesAction.do?reference=IP/08/1609&format=HT
ML&aged=1&language=EN&guiLanguage=en> (accessed 1 October 2010).
— 2008o. State aid: Commission authorises support package for Lithuanian
financial institutions. Press release, 5 August 2010 (IP/10/1032). Available at:
<http://europa.eu/rapid/pressReleasesAction.do?reference=IP/10/1032&form
at=HTML&aged=1&language=EN&guiLanguage=en> (accessed 1 October
2010).
— 2009a. Communication from the Commission – The recapitalisation of financial
institutions in the current financial crisis: limitation of aid to the minimum
necessary and safeguards against undue distortions of competition. *Official
Journal of the European Union*, 15 January 2009 (2009/C 10/03). Available at:
<http://eur-lex.europa.eu/LexUriServ/LexUriServ.do?uri=OJ:C:2009:010:000
2:0010:EN:PDF> (accessed 12 October 2011).
— 2009b. State aid: Commission approves impaired asset relief measure and
restructuring plan of Royal Bank of Scotland. Press release, 14 November
2009 (IP/09/1915). Available at: <http://europa.eu/rapid/pressReleasesAction.
do?reference=IP/09/1915&format=HTML&aged=1&language=EN&guiLang
uage=en> (accessed 1 October 2010).
— 2009c. State aid: Commission approves Polish support scheme for financial
institutions. Press release, 25 September 2009 (IP/09/1360). Available at:
<http://europa.eu/rapid/pressReleasesAction.do?reference=IP/09/1360&form
at=HTML&aged=1&language=EN&guiLanguage=en> (accessed 1 October
2010).
— 2009d. State aid: Commission approves Portuguese support scheme for financial
institutions. Press release, 30 October 2008 (IP/08/1601). Available at: <http://
europa.eu/rapid/pressReleasesAction.do?reference=IP/08/1601&format=HT
ML&aged=1&language=EN&guiLanguage=en> (accessed 1 October 2010).
— 2009e. State aid: Commission approves recapitalisation of Anglo Irish Bank.
Press release, 14 January 2009 (IP/09/50). Available at: <http://europa.eu/
rapid/pressReleasesAction.do?reference=IP/09/50&format=HTML&aged=1
&language=EN&guiLanguage=en> (accessed 1 October 2010).
— 2009f. State aid: Commission approves recapitalisation of Bank of Ireland.
Press release, 26 March 2009 (IP/09/483). Available at: <http://europa.eu/
rapid/pressReleasesAction.do?reference=IP/09/483&format=HTML&aged=1
&language=EN&guiLanguage=en> (accessed 1 October 2010).

— 2009g. State aid: Commission approves restructuring package for Northern Rock. Press release, 28 October 2009 (IP/09/1600). Available at: <http:// europa.eu/rapid/pressReleasesAction.do?reference=IP/09/1600&format=HT ML&aged=1&language=EN&guiLanguage=en> (accessed 1 October 2010).

— 2009h. State aid: Commission approves restructuring plan of Lloyds Banking Group. Press release, 18 November 2009 (IP/09/1728). Available at: <http:// europa.eu/rapid/pressReleasesAction.do?reference=IP/09/1728&format=HT ML&aged=1&language=EN&guiLanguage=en> (accessed 1 October 2010).

— State aid: Commission approves Slovak bank support scheme. Press release, 8 December 2009 (IP/09/1889). Available at: <http://europa.eu/rapid/ pressReleasesAction.do?reference=IP/09/1889&format=HTML&aged=1&la nguage=EN&guiLanguage=en> (accessed 1 October 2010).

— 2009j. State aid: Commission authorises support package for Hungarian financial institutions. Press release, 12 February 2009 (IP/09/253). Available at: <http://europa.eu/rapid/pressReleasesAction.do?reference=IP/09/253&for mat=HTML&aged=1&language=EN&guiLanguage=en> (accessed 1 October 2010).

— 2009k. State aid: Commission provides guidance for the treatment of impaired assets in the EU banking sector. Press release, 25 February 2009 (IP/09/322). Brussels. Available at: <http://europa.eu/rapid/pressReleasesAction.do?refere nce=IP/09/322&format=HTML&aged=0&language=EN&guiLanguage=en> (accessed 1 October 2010).

— 2010a. Commission proposes package to boost consumer protection and confidence in financial services. Press release, 12 July 2010. The EU in Cyprus (IP/10/918). Brussels. Available at: <http://ec.europa.eu/cyprus/ news/20100712_financial_system_en.htm> (accessed 1 October 2010).

— 2010b. DG Competition Staff Working Document. The application of state aid rules to government guarantee schemes covering bank debt to be issued After 30 June 2010. European Union Commission Competition, Brussels, 30 April 2010. Available at: <http://ec.europa.eu/competition/state_aid/studies_reports/ phase_out_bank_guarantees.pdf> (accessed 1 October 2010).

— 2010c. Europe in Figures – Eurostat Yearbook 2010. Available at: <http:// epp.eurostat.ec.europa.eu/portal/page/portal/product_details/publication?p_ product_code=KS-CD-10-220> (accessed 1 October 2010).

— 2010d. State aid: Commission approves liquidation of Bradford & Bingley. Press release, 25 January 2010 (IP/10/47). Brussels. Available at: <http:// europa.eu/rapid/pressReleasesAction.do?reference=IP/10/47&format=HTML &aged=1&language=EN&guiLanguage=en> (accessed 1 October 2010).

— 2010e. State aid: Commission approves restructuring plan of Bank of Ireland. Press release, 15 July 2010 (IP/10/954). Available at: <http://europa.eu/rapid/ pressReleasesAction.do?reference=IP/10/954&format=HTML&aged=1&lan guage=EN&guiLanguage=en> (accessed 1 October 2010).

— 2011. European economy. The Economic Adjustment Programme for Greece. Third Review – Winter 2011. Directorate-General for Economic and Financial

Affairs: Occasional Papers 77, February 2011. Available at: <http://ec.europa.
  eu/economy_finance/publications/occasional_paper/2011/pdf/ocp77_en.pdf>
  (accessed 28 February 2011).
European Union Council. 2009. Council conclusions on strengthening EU financial
  stability arrangements. Council Meeting Economic and Financial Affairs.
  Press release 2967, 20 October 2009. Luxembourg: Council of the European
  Union. Available at: <http://www.consilium.europa.eu/uedocs/cms_data/docs/
  pressdata/en/ecofin/110622.pdf> (accessed 1 October 2010).
— 2010. Extraordinary Council Meeting on Economic and Financial Affairs. Press
  release 108 (9596/10), 9/10 May 2010. Brussels: Council of the European
  Union. Available at: <http://www.consilium.europa.eu/uedocs/cms_data/docs/
  pressdata/en/ecofin/114324.pdf> (accessed 1 October 2010).
Federal Reserve Bank of New York. 2005. Statement regarding meeting on credit
  derivatives. Press release. Federal Reserve Bank of New York. Press release,
  15 September. Available at: <http://www.newyorkfed.org/newsevents/news_
  archive/markets/2005/an050915.html> (accessed 1 October 2010).
— 2008a. Federal Reserve announces establishment of primary dealer credit
  facility. Press release, 16 March 2008. Available at: <http://www.newyorkfed.
  org/newsevents/news/markets/2008/rp080316.html> (accessed 1 October
  2010).
— 2008b. Statement by the Federal Reserve Bank of New York regarding AIG
  transaction. Press release, 29 September 2008. Available at: <http://www.
  newyorkfed.org/newsevents/news/markets/2008/an080929.html> (accessed 1
  October 2010).
— 2008c. Primary dealer monitoring: liquidity stress analysis, 25 June 2008.
  Available at: <http://www.newyorkfed.org/> (accessed 1 October 2010).
— 2008d. Statement on financing arrangement of J.P. Morgan Chase's acquisition
  of Bear Stearns. Press release, 24 March. Available at: <http://www.
  newyorkfed.org/newsevents/news/markets/2008/rp080324.html> (accessed
  1 October 2010).
Federal Reserve System, Board of Governors, see Board of Governors of the
  Federal Reserve System.
Federal Reserve System. 2011. Rules and regulations. Federal Register, Vol. 76, No.
  30, pp. 8265–78. Available at: <http://www.federalreserve.gov/reportforms/
  formsreview/RegY1_20110214_ffr.pdf> (accessed 28 February 2011).
Financial Crisis Inquiry Commission of the United States. 2010a. Opening remarks
  of Phil Angelides, Chairman of the Financial Crisis Inquiry Commission, at
  the hearing on the role of derivatives in the financial crisis, 30 June 2010,
  Washington, DC. Available at: <http://fcic-static.law.stanford.edu/cdn_media/
  fcic-testimony/2010-0630-Angelides.pdf> (accessed 1 October 2010).
— 2010b. Preliminary staff report: Credit ratings and the financial crisis,
  2 June 2010. Available at: <http://fcic-static.law.stanford.edu/cdn_media/fcic-
  reports/2010-0602-Credit-Ratings.pdf> (accessed 1 October 2010).

— 2010c. Preliminary staff report: Shadow banking and the financial crisis, 4 May 2010. Available at: <http://fcic-static.law.stanford.edu/cdn_media/fcic-reports/2010-0505-Shadow-Banking.pdf> (accessed 1 October 2010).

— 2011. *Final Report of the National Commission on the Causes of the Financial and Economic Crisis in the United States.* Washington, DC: G.P.O.

Financial Services Authority. 2008. Strengthening liquidity standards. Consultation Paper 8/22 December 2008. London: FSA. Available at: <http://www.fsa.gov.uk/pubs/cp/cp08_22.pdf> (accessed 1 October 2010).

— 2009. The Turner Review: A regulatory response to the global financial crisis, March 2009. London: FSA. Available at: <http://www.fsa.gov.uk/pubs/other/turner_review.pdf> (accessed 1 October 2010).

Financial Stability Forum. 2008. Report of the Financial Stability Forum on enhancing market and institutional resilience. G7 Ministers and Central Bank Governors. Basel: Financial Stability Board, Bank of International Settlements, 7 April, pp. 37–39.

Foster, J.B. and Magdoff, F. 2009. The great financial crisis: Causes and consequences. *Monthly Review Press.* New York.

Friedman, J. 2011. *What Caused The Financial Crisis?* Philadelphia, PA: University of Pennsylvania Press.

Friedman, M. and Schwartz, A. 1963. *A Monetary History of the United States, 1867–1960.* Princeton, NJ: Princeton University Press.

G8 Summit. 2009. The Summit, at L'Aquila, Italy, 8–10 July 2009. Available at: <http://www.g8summit.it/G8/Home/G8-G8_Layout_locale-1199882116809_Summit.htm> (accessed 1 October 2010).

G30 Working Group on Financial Stability. 2009. Financial reform: A framework for financial stability. Washington, DC: Group of Thirty, January 15.

Geithner, T.F. 2010. Testimony before the Financial Crisis Inquiry Commission, Causes of the financial crisis and the case for reform, 6 May 2010. Press Centre, US Department of the Treasury. Available at: <http://www.treasury.gov/press-center/press-releases/Pages/tg690.aspx> (accessed 1 October 2010).

Gensler, G. 2010. Testimony of Gary Gensler, Chairman of the Commodity Futures Trading Commission, before the Financial Crisis Inquiry Commission, 1 July 2010. Commodity Futures Trading Commission. Available at: <http://www.cftc.gov/pressroom/speechestestimony/opagensler-48.html> (accessed 9 October 2011).

Greenspan, A. 1999. Financial derivatives. Remarks by Chairman Alan Greenspan before the Futures Industry Association, Boca Raton, Florida, March 19, 1999. The Federal Reserve Board. Available at: <http://www.federalreserve.gov/boarddocs/speeches/1999/19990319.htm> (accessed 1 October 2010).

— 2004. Risk and uncertainty in monetary policy. Remarks by Alan Greenspan at the Meeting of the American Economic Association, San Diego, California, 3 January 2004. The Federal Reserve Board. Available at: <http://www.federalreserve.gov/boarddocs/speeches/2004/20040103/default.html> (accessed 1 October 2010).

— 2008. Testimony of Dr Alan Greenspan to the Senate Committee of Government Oversight and Reform, US House of Representatives, 23 October 2008. Available at: <http://oversight-archive.waxman.house.gov/documents/20081023100438.pdf> (accessed 1 October 2010).

— 2010a. The crisis. Greenspan Associates LLC. Available at: <http://www.brookings.edu/~/media/Files/Programs/ES/BPEA/2010_spring_bpea_papers/spring2010_greenspan.pdf> (accessed 1 October 2010).

— 2010b. Testimony of Chairman Alan Greenspan before the Financial Crisis Inquiry Commission, 7 April 2010. Stanford, CT: Stanford Law School. Available at: <http://fcic-static.law.stanford.edu/cdn_media/fcic-docs/2010-04-07%20Alan%20Greenspan%20Written%20Testimony.pdf> (accessed 1 October 2010).

HM Treasury. 2009. White Paper on reforming financial markets. London: HM Treasury.

International Labour Organisation 2008. The crisis in the construction industry. ILO. Available at: <http://www.ilo.org/wow/Articles/lang--en/WCMS_1155 08/index.htm> (accessed 1 October 2010).

International Monetary Fund. 1998. Economic crisis in Asia. Address by Shigemitsu Sugisaki, Deputy Managing Director of the International Monetary Fund, at the Harvard Business School, 30 January 1998.

— 2008. World economic outlook. Financial stress, downturns, and recoveries. World Economic and Financial Surveys. Available at: <http://www.imf.org/external/pubs/ft/weo/2008/02/index.htm> (accessed 1 October 2010).

— 2009a. Lessons of the financial crisis for future regulation of financial institutions and markets and for liquidity management, IMF, Monetary and Capital Markets Department, 4 February 2009. Available at: <http://www.imf.org/external/np/pp/eng/2009/020409.pdf> (accessed 1 October 2010).

— 2009b. World economic outlook crisis and recovery. Washington, DC: IMF World Economic and Financial Surveys, April 2009. Available at: <http://www.imf.org/external/pubs/ft/weo/2009/01/index.htm> (accessed 1 October 2010).

— 2010a. IMF Executive Board approves €22.5 billion extended arrangement for Ireland, International Monetary Fund. Press release, 16 December 2010. Available at: <http://www.imf.org/external/np/sec/pr/2010/pr10496.htm> (accessed 31 December 2010).

— 2010b. IMF signs US$10 billion note purchase agreement with Brazil. Press release 10/14, 22 January 2010. Washington, DC: IMF. Available at: <http://www.imf.org/external/np/sec/pr/2010/pr1014.htm> (accessed 1 October 2010).

— 2010c. Latin America helps shape global economic recovery. *IMF Survey Magazine*, 24 May 2010: In the News. Washington, DC: IMF. Available at: <http://www.imf.org/external/pubs/ft/survey/so/2010/NEW052410A.htm> (accessed 1 October 2010).

— 2010d. People's Republic of China: 2010 Article IV Consultation – Staff Report; Staff Statement; Public Information Notice on the Executive Board

Discussion. IMF Country Report 10/238, July 2010. Washington, DC: IMF. Available at: <http://www.imf.org/external/pubs/ft/scr/2010/cr10238.pdf (accessed 1 October 2010).

— 2010e. Statement by IMF Managing Director Dominique Strauss-Kahn on Ireland. Press release 10/452, 21 November 2010. Washington, DC: IMF. Available at: <http://www.imf.org/external/np/sec/pr/2010/pr10452.htm> (accessed 30 November 2010).

— 2011. Ireland: extended arrangement – Interim Review under the Emergency Financing Mechanism. IMF Country Report 11/47, February 2011. Washington, DC: IMF. Available at: <http://www.imf.org/external/pubs/ft/scr/2011/cr1147. pdf> (accessed 28 February 2011).

Issing, O. et al. New financial order recommendations by the Issing Committee, Part I (October 2008), Part II (March 2009) see Center for Financial Studies 2009.

Jarocinski, Marek and Smets, F. 2008. House prices and the stance of monetary policy. *Federal Reserve Bank of St. Louis Review*, 90(4), July/August 2008, pp. 339–65.

Keen, S. 2010. Analysing the global debt bubble, Steve Keen's Debtwatch. Available at: <http://www.debtdeflation.com/blogs/> (accessed 1 October 2010).

Keynes, J.M. 1936. *The General Theory of Employment, Interest and Money*. Cambridge: Palgrave Macmillan.

Kroszner, R.S. and Shiller, R.J. 2009. *Reforming US Financial Markets: Reflections Before and Beyond Dodd-Frank*. Cambridge, MA: The MIT Press.

Krugman, P. 2009. *The Return of Depression Economics and the Crisis of 2008*. New York: W.W. Norton.

Lehman Brothers Holdings. 2008. Lehman Brothers reports second quarter results. Lehman Brothers Holdings. Press release, 16 June 2008. Available at: <http:// www.lehman.com/press/qe/past/2_08qe.htm> (accessed 1 October 2010).

— 2008. Lehman Brothers Holdings Inc. Announces it intends to file Chapter 11 Bankruptcy Petition. Press release, 15 September 2008. New York: LBHI.

Northern Rock Annual Report. 2006. Available at: <http://companyinfo.northern rock.co.uk/downloads/results/res2006PR_AnnualReportAndAccounts.pdf> (accessed 9 October 2011).

Northern Rock Community Report. 2006. Available at: <http://www.onrec.com/ news/news-archive/northern-rock-has-published-its-fifth-community-report-this-week> (accessed 1 October 2010).

Nowotny, E. 2009. The euro – A stability anchor in turbulent times. Speech by E. Nowotny, Governor of the Austrian National Bank, delivered at the John Hopkins University, Bologna, 10 September 2009. Bank for International Settlements. Available at: <http://www.bis.org/review/r091008b.pdf> (accessed 1 October 2010).

Office of Federal Housing Enterprise Oversight. 2006. Report of the special examination of Fannie Mae, Federal Housing Finance Agency. Available at:

<http://www.fhfa.gov/webfiles/747/FNMSPECIALEXAM.pdf> (accessed 1 October 2010).

OPEC 1973. Communiqué from the Secretary General, Dr Abderrahman Khene, 25 December 1973. Kuwait: Organisation of Petroleum Exporting Countries.

Organization for Economic Cooperation and Development (OECD). 2009. Economic survey of Ireland 2009. OECD Economics Department, November 2009. Paris: OECD. Available at: <http://www.oecd.org/document/35/0,3343 ,en_2649_34569_43948003_1_1_1_1,00.html> (accessed 1 October 2010).

Ortiz, G. 2009. The global financial crisis – a Latin American perspective. Speech by G. Ortiz, Governor of the Bank of Mexico and Chairman of the Board of Directors of the Bank for International Settlements, delivered at the conference, Financial Globalization: Culprit, Survivor or Casualty of the Great Crisis? at Yale University, New Haven, Connecticut, 13 November. Bank for International Settlements. Available at: <http://www.bis.org/review/r091207a. pdf> (accessed 1 October 2010).

Paulson, H.M. 2010a. *On the Brink: Inside the Race to Stop the Collapse of the Global Financial System.* New York: Business Plus, Hachette Book Group.

Paulson, H.M. 2010b. Testimony by Henry M. Paulson Jr before the Financial Crisis Inquiry Commission, 6 May 2010. Available at: <http://fcic-static.law. stanford.edu/cdn_media/fcic-testimony/2010-0506-Paulson.pdf> (accessed 10 October 2010).

President's Working Group on Financial Markets. 2009. Report on over-the-counter derivatives markets and the Commodity Exchange Act. President's Working Group, Washington, DC: G.P.O., November 2009.

— 2010. Report on money market fund reform options. President's Working Group, October 2010. Washington, DC: G.P.O.

Prime Minister of Australia. 2008. Global financial crisis: Statement by P. M. Kevin Rudd. Press release, 12 October 2008. Australian Government. Available at: <http://pmrudd.archive.dpmc.gov.au/node/5533> (accessed 1 October 2010).

Provopoulos, G. 2009. Key challenges for South East Europe in light of the Crisis. Opening address by G. Provopoulos, Governor of the Bank of Greece, delivered at the Conference of Bank of Greece and Oxford University: Challenges and prospects of South East European economies in the wake of the financial crisis, held at Athens, 16 October 2009. Bank for International Settlements. Available at: <http://www.sant.ox.ac.uk/seesox/pdf/Challengesreport.pdf> (accessed 1 October 2010).

Real Estate Institute of Victoria (RIV). 2011. Latest REIV quarterly median prices. Victoria: REIV. Available at: <http://www.reiv.com.au/home/inside. asp?ID=1048&nav1=652&nav2=165> (accessed 1 October 2010).

Reserve Bank of Australia. (n.d.). Official cash rate. Available at: <http://www. rba.gov.au/statistics/cash-rate.html> (accessed 1 October 2010).

— 2008a. Statement by Glenn Stevens, Governor: Monetary Policy. Press release, 2 September 2008. Sydney: RBA. Available at: <http://www.rba.gov.au/ media-releases/2008/mr-08-14.html> (accessed 13 October 2011).

— 2008b. Statement by Glenn Stevens, Governor: Monetary Policy. Press release, 7 October 2008. Sydney: RBA. Available at: <http://www.rba.gov.au/media-releases/2008/mr-08-20.html> (accessed 1 October 2010).

— 2008c. Statement by Glenn Stevens, Governor: Monetary Policy. Press release, 4 November 2008. Sydney: RBA. Available at: <http://www.rba.gov.au/media-releases/2008/mr-08-25.html> (accessed 1 October 2010).

— 2008d. Statement by Glenn Stevens, Governor: Monetary Policy, Press release, 2 December 2008. Sydney: RBA. Available at: <http://www.rba.gov.au/media-releases/2008/mr-08027.html> (accessed 1 October 2010).

— 2009. Statement by Glenn Stevens, Governor: Monetary Policy. Press release, 3 February 2009. Sydney: RBA. Available at: <http://www.rba.gov.au/media-releases/2009/mr-09-01.html> (accessed 1 October 2010).

— 2010a. Statement by Glenn Stevens, Governor: Monetary Policy. Press release, 2 March 2010. Sydney: RBA. Available at: <http://www.rba.gov.au/media-releases/2010/mr-10-04.html> (accessed 1 October 2010).

— 2010b. Statement by Glenn Stevens, Governor: Monetary Policy. Press release, 6 April 2010. Sydney: RBA. Available at: <http://www.rba.gov.au/media-releases/2010/mr-10-06.html> (accessed 1 October 2010).

— 2010c. Statement by Glenn Stevens, Governor: Monetary Policy. Press release, 4 May 2010. Sydney: RBA. Available at: <http://www.rba.gov.au/media-releases/2010/mr-10-07.html> (accessed 1 October 2010).

— 2010d. Statement by Glenn Stevens, Governor: Monetary Policy. Press release, 2 November 2010. Sydney: RBA. Available at: <http://www.rba.gov.au/media-releases/2010/mr-10-26.html> (accessed 30 November 2010).

Reserve Bank of India. 2008. RBI measures for improving domestic and foreign currency liquidity. *Monetary and Credit Information Review*, Vol. V, Issue 6, December 2008, pp. 1–4. Available at: <http://rbidocs.rbi.org.in/rdocs/Publications/PDFs/899476.pdf> (accessed 1 October 2010).

— 2009a. Policy. *Monetary and Credit Information Review*, Vol. V, Issue 7, January 2009, pp. 1–4. Available at: <http://rbidocs.rbi.org.in/rdocs/Publications/PDFs/EMCIR09JAN.pdf> (accessed 1 October 2010).

— 2009b. Policy. *Monetary and Credit Information Review*, Vol. V, Issue 9, March 2009, pp. 1–4. Available at: <http://rbidocs.rbi.org.in/rdocs/Publications/PDFs/MCIREMar09F.pdf> (accessed 1 October 2010).

— 2009c. Annual policy statement for 2009–10. *Monetary and Credit Information Review*, Vol. V, Issue 10, April 2009, pp. 1–4. Available at: <http://rbidocs.rbi.org.in/rdocs/Publications/PDFs/MCIREApr09F.pdf> (accessed 1 October 2010).

— 2009d. Second quarter review of monetary policy 2009–10. *Monetary and Credit Information Review*, Vol. VI, Issue 5, November 2009, pp. 1–4. Available at: <http://rbidocs.rbi.org.in/rdocs/Publications/PDFs/MCIRENov09.pdf> (accessed 1 October 2010).

— 2010e. 'Policy', *Monetary and Credit Information Review*. Vol. VI, Issue 9, March 2010, pp. 1–4. Available at: <http://rbidocs.rbi.org.in/rdocs/Publications/PDFs/MCIRMR0310F.pdf> (accessed 1 October 2010).

—2010f. 'Policy', *Monetary and Credit Information Review*. Vol. VII, Issue 1, July 2010, pp. 1–4. Available at: <http://rbidocs.rbi.org.in/rdocs/Publications/PDFs/MCIR290710.pdf (accessed 1 October 2010).

— 2010g. First quarter review of monetary policy for the year 2010–11. *Monetary and Credit Information Review*. Vol. VII, Issue 2, August 2010, pp. 1–4. Available at: <http://rbidocs.rbi.org.in/rdocs/Publications/PDFs>.

Reserve Bank of New Zealand. 2008a. Deposit guarantee scheme introduced. Press release, 12 October 2008. Wellington: RBNZ. Available at: <http://rbnz.govt.nz/news/2008/3462912.html> (accessed 1 October 2010).

Reserve Bank of New Zealand. 2008b. Domestic markets operations. Wellington: RBNZ. Available at: <http://rbnz.govt.nz/finmarkets/domesticmarkets/index.html> (accessed 1 October 2010).

— 2008c. OCR reduced to 8.0 percent. Press release, 24 July 2008. Wellington: RBNZ. Available at: <http://rbnz.govt.nz/news/2008/3376920.html> (accessed 1 October 2010).

— 2008d. OCR reduced to 7.5 percent. Press release, 11 September 2008. Wellington: RBNZ. Available at: <http://rbnz.govt.nz/news/2008/3416797.html> (accessed 1 October 2010).

— 2008e. OCR reduced to 6.5 percent. Press release, 23 October 2008. Wellington: RBNZ. Available at: <http://rbnz.govt.nz/news/2008/3470882.html> (accessed 1 October 2010).

— 2008f. OCR reduced to 5.0 percent. Press release, 4 December 2008, Wellington: RBNZ. Available at: <http://rbnz.govt.nz/news/2008/3504509.html> (accessed 1 October 2010).

— 2008g. Reserve Bank announces new facilities. Press release, 7 November 2008, Wellington: RBNZ. Available at: <http://rbnz.govt.nz/news/2008/3483444.html> (accessed 1 October 2010).

— 2009a. OCR reduced to 3.5 percent. Press release, 29 January 2009, Wellington: RBNZ. Available at: <http://rbnz.govt.nz/news/2009/3544313.html> (accessed 1 October 2010).

— 2009b. OCR reduced to 3 percent. Press release, 12 March 2009, Wellington: RBNZ. Available at: <http://rbnz.govt.nz/news/2009/3581433.html> (accessed 1 October 2010).

— 2009c. OCR reduced to 2.5 percent. Press release, 30 April 2009. Wellington: RBNZ. Available at: <http://rbnz.govt.nz/news/2009/3621204.html> (accessed 1 October 2010).

— 2010a. Financial system outlook improved but fragile. Press release, 19 May 2010. Reserve Bank of New Zealand. Available at: <http://rbnz.govt.nz/news/2010/3989153.html> (accessed 1 October 2010).

— 2010b. Reserve Bank raises OCR to 2.75 percent. Press release, 10 June 2010. Wellington: RBNZ. Available at: <http://rbnz.govt.nz/news/2010/4014913. html> (accessed 1 October 2010).

— 2010c. Reserve Bank raises OCR to 3.0 percent. Press release, 29 July 2010. Wellington: RBNZ. Available at: <http://rbnz.govt.nz/news/2010/4127034. html> (accessed 1 October 2010).

Rotemberg, J.J. and Woodford, M. 1996. Imperfect competition and the effects of energy price increases on economic activity. *Journal of Money, Credit and Banking*, Part 1, 28(4), November.

Roubini, N. and Mihm, S. 2010. *Crisis Economics: A Crash Course in The Future of Finance*. New York: The Penguin Press.

Sorkin A.R. 2009. *Too Big To Fail: The Inside Story of how Wall Street and Washington Fought to Save the Financial System – and Themselves*. London: Viking Penguin.

Stein, S. 2008. Alan Greenspan: This is the worst economy I've ever seen. Huffpost Politics. Available at: <http://www.huffingtonpost.com/2008/09/14/ greenspan-this-is-the-wor_n_126274.html> (accessed 1 October 2010).

UK Parliament. 2008. House of Commons Select Committee of the Treasury Fifth Report. Available at: <http://www.publications.parliament.uk/pa/cm200708/ cmselect/cmtreasy/56/5604.htm> (accessed 1 October 2010).

UK Parliamentary Enquiry into Northern Rock. 2007. Select Committee of the Treasury Fifth Report. London: House of Commons. Available at: <http:// www.publications.parliament.uk/pa/cm200708/cmselect/cmtreasy/56/5604. htm#a4> (accessed 1 October 2010).

United States Senate Permanent Subcommittee on Investigations see US Government 2011.

Upham, C.B. and Lamke, E. 1934. *Closed and Distressed Banks: A Study in Public Administration*. Washington, DC: The Brookings Institution.

US Department of the Treasury. 1988. Report of the Presidential Task Force on market mechanisms. Washington, DC: G.P.O.

— 2009. Financial regulatory reform: A new foundation, rebuilding financial supervision and regulation. Washington, DC, 17 June 2009. Available at: <http://www.treasury.gov/initiatives/Documents/FinalReport_web.pdf>.

— 2010. Comptroller of the Currency Administrator of National Banks. The importance of preserving a system of national standards for national banks, OCC White Paper. Washington, DC: OCC, Department of the Treasury, Attachment 1.

US Government. 1973. National Energy Policy. The President's address to the nation announcing additional actions to deal with the energy emergency. Weekly Compilation of Presidential Documents, 1 December, No. 48, Vol. 9. Washington, DC: G.P.O.

— 2008. *Emergency Economic Stabilisation Act 2008*. Pub.L. 110-343 HR1424 (USA). Washington, DC: G.P.O. Available at: <http://frwebgate.access.gpo.

gov/cgibin/getdoc.cgi?dbname=110_cong_public_laws&docid=f:
publ343.110.pdf> (accessed 1 October 2010).

—2009a. The White House, Office of the Press Secretary, Obama administration
auto restructuring initiative Chrysler–Fiat alliance, April 30, 2009. Available
at: <http://www.whitehouse.gov/the_press_office/Obama-Administration-Auto-
Restructuring-Initiative/ (accessed 1 October 2010).

— 2009b. The White House, Office of the Press Secretary, joint press release by
President Obama and Prime Minster Harper, United States–Canada support
for Chrysler LLC, 30 April 2009. Available at: <http://www.whitehouse.gov/
the-press-office/joint-statement-president-obama-and-prime-minister-harper-
united-states-canada-supp> (accessed 1 October 2010).

— 2010. The Congress of the United States. Federal debt and the risk of a fiscal
crisis. Washington, DC: Congressional Budget Office, July 27, 2010. Available
at: <http://www.cbo.gov/doc.cfm?index=11659&zzz=41052> (accessed 1
October 2010).

— 2011. The Congress of the United States. Reducing the deficit: Spending and
revenue options. Washington, DC: Congressional Budget Office, March 2011.
Available at: <http://www.cbo.gov/doc.cfm?index=12085 (accessed 31 March
2011).

— 2011. US Senate Permanent Subcommittee on Investigations, Committee on
Homeland Security and Governmental Affairs. Wall Street and the financial
crisis: anatomy of a financial collapse, Majority and Minority Staff Report,
April 13, 2011. Washington, DC. Available at: <http://hsgac.senate.gov/
public/_files/Financial_Crisis/FinancialCrisisReport.pdf> (accessed 1 October
2010).

US Securities and Exchange Commission. 2003. Report on the role and function
of credit rating agencies in the operation of the securities markets. Washington,
DC: SEC. Available at: <http://www.sec.gov/index.htm> (accessed 1 October
2010).

— 2007. Freddie Mac, four former executives settle SEC action relating to multi-
billion dollar accounting fraud. Press release, 27 September 2007. Available at:
<http://www.sec.gov/news/press/2007/2007-205.htm>.

Wall Street Transparency and Accountability Act. 2010. US Senate. Washington,
DC: G.P.O. Available at: <http://ag.senate.gov/site/legislation.html>.

Yellen, J.L. 2010. Fiscal responsibility and global rebalancing. Speech delivered
at the Committee for Economic Development. International Counterparts
Conference, New York, 1 December 2010. Board of Governors of the Federal
Reserve System. Available at: <http://www.federalreserve.gov/newsevents/
speech/yellen20101201a.htm> (accessed 31 December 2010).

Index

For Product Safety Concerns and Information please contact our
EU representative GPSR@taylorandfrancis.com Taylor & Francis
Verlag GmbH, Kaufingerstraße 24, 80331 München, Germany